MW00830445

MIGRATIONAL RELIGION

MIGRATIONAL RELIGION

Context and Creativity in the Latinx Diaspora

João B. Chaves

BAYLOR UNIVERSITY PRESS

Cover and book design by Kasey McBeath
Cover images: Photo of Christ the Reedemer by Joshua Gresham/Unsplash
Photo of Statue of Liberty by Parshva Shah/Unsplash
Photo of clouds by Kumiko SHIMIZU/Unsplash

The Library of Congress has cataloged this book under ISBN 978-1-4813-1594-4.
Library of Congress Control Number: 2021939849

Printed in the United States of America on acid-free paper with a minimum of thirty percent recycled content.

Em memória de Ophir Barros, o "Bispo" dos Batistas Brasileiros na América do Norte. E para todos os imigrantes de fé, que todos os dias cruzam várias fronteiras.

CONTENTS

PREFACE

This book began when I crossed the US border by plane. In this general sense, it has been in progress for over twenty years. When I arrived in Tampa, Florida, in January 2000—as a teenager who spoke less English than he thought he did—it was a Pentecostal church made up of immigrants, mostly from Brazil, mostly undocumented, that helped me deal with many of the difficulties of living in this strange new land. The church helped me navigate issues of housing, documentation, and work and even provided a social network from which I built friendships that I cherish to this day. It was also through my involvement in this immigrant church's activities that I participated in my first community service events, feeding local homeless people, most of whom were born in the United States. The pastor of the church—a successful business owner who, though now a US citizen, initially worked without papers for several years—often summarized his vision for his church thus: "If the city of Tampa doesn't miss this church when we are gone, we have no reason to exist." The pastor also often encouraged people to visit the Without Walls International Church, then pastored by Randy and Paula White. Paula White would later become a spiritual advisor to and strong supporter of Donald Trump, going so far as to call for transnational angelic intervention in Trump's ex post facto reelection efforts.[1] My sense is that although Paula White's political

---

[1]   Paula White's (now Paula White-Cain's) prayer was performed in early November 2020. Her words in reference to transnational angels were: "For angels have even been dispatched from Africa right now, Africa right now, Africa right now, from Africa right now. They are coming here; they are coming here. In the name of Jesus, from South America, they are coming here. They are coming here, they are coming here, they are coming here. From Africa, from South America, angelic forces, angelic reinforcement, angelic reinforcement, angelic reinforcement." See Joe Sommerlad, "'The Lord Says It Is Done': White House Spiritual Adviser Paula White Prays for 'Angels

dispositions became pronounced later in her career, they were not necessarily disharmonious with her theology; nor would they stop the aforementioned pastor from recommending her religious services.

I was soon fascinated by the complexities and contradictions of that church—and of other immigrant churches I visited in Tampa. In these faith communities, explicit theological sensibilities were often in tension with (and sometimes in contradiction to) implicit social and political dispositions. As time passed, I had the opportunity to hold leadership positions in several immigrant churches with different denominational and nondenominational affiliations: as worship leader, deacon, Sunday school teacher, church planter, interim pastor, translator, etc. Serving in these capacities, I began to notice that, over time, the US context changes immigrant churches, and how parishioners frequent these institutions for reasons that go far beyond theological convictions, civic sensibilities, and denominational affiliations. The immigrant church, above all else, is a place of ethnic belonging and a mediating structure that facilitates parishioners' transitions into life as migrants. Very often, especially in small towns, these churches are the most effective forms of community organization for immigrants, the place where they go to feel closer to home, insofar as immigrants have a home at all. The churches are also locations from which immigrants serve their broader communities, providing a wide range of social services in their immediate geographical area as well as supporting transnational religious and social causes.

As I dove into the literature on immigrant and World Christianity during my seminary and graduate training, I realized that this is not only my story. Nor is it only the story of immigrant churches in Florida or Texas, the states with which I was most familiar at the time. Rather, this is the story of millions of immigrants today, one that moreover has deep, long-standing connections to the history of the United States. Since this nation's beginnings, churches filled with immigrants have helped foreign-born Christians negotiate different spaces, languages, and imagined communities. Immigrants from Germany, Ireland, Italy, China, South Korea, Mexico, Brazil, India, Russia, Syria, Greece, England, Argentina, Haiti, Vietnam, El Salvador, Ghana, Senegal, Nigeria, Guatemala, and other countries have worshiped, and continue to worship, in their native tongues in the United States. If migration has always been central to the history of this country, immigrant churches have been a central element in the lives of people who have migrated here from the world over.

---

from Africa' to Cement Trump's Re-election," *Independent*, November 5, 2020, https://www.independent.co.uk/news/world/americas/us-election-2020/us-election-trump-paula-white-house-prayer-b1616014.html.

Today, the role of immigrant Christians in the United States is multifaceted. It can be seen in the significant presence of Nigerian Catholic priests pastoring predominantly white parishes across the country, the prominence of Asian leaders in religious and theological education, theological seminaries in which the primary language of instruction is not English, growing churches of the African diaspora, Spanish-language church services offered for US- and foreign-born populations, a Baptist vice president who is a daughter of immigrants, and more. The American religious market continues to be informed thoroughly by migration patterns. The importance of immigrant churches' role in the building of the America of the future cannot be overstated, because they participate in the process of forming new immigrants and their children—that is, they help shape the worldview of future citizens in a context characterized by increasing diversification. Given current demographic trends, Latinx churches have an especially important role in this dynamic. Paying attention to how immigrant churches have changed the landscape of the US religious market, therefore, has not only religious but also broad social, cultural, and political implications.

This book recognizes that a fuller understanding of US history and society requires documentation of how the country's religious market continues to change as a result of migration patterns. As such, it contributes to the growing body of literature that aims to catch up to our rapidly evolving context. At the same time, this manuscript illuminates the ways in which the American context itself affects immigrant religious communities, commitments, and imaginations. An appropriate understanding of this dialectic demands the production of more studies focusing on both sides of this coin. On the one hand, this is a deeply human condition; on the other, it manifests itself in peculiar ways in communities formed by immigrants whose lives have been upended by radical dislocations. Part of the challenge with this approach is that it must be done from within the entanglements of particularity. That is, it must analyze religious networks based on an outlook that takes seriously archival history, oral history, ethnography, and the social sciences and that dwells in worlds only available to scholars proficient in languages often not valued by the US academy as "scholarly languages," whatever those are. While this book takes these particularities into account and values them independently, it also hopes to contribute to a better understanding of the diversification of the United States as exemplified by the churches of diaspora peoples.

João Chaves
San Antonio, 2020

ACKNOWLEDGMENTS

A multitude of people made this book possible. Although all limitations present in this work are fully mine, its strengths are the result of a communal effort. Numerous immigrants, living in several places, participated in the data-collection process that culminated in this manuscript. Dozens of immigrant faith leaders provided formal interviews and informal conversations that informed my analysis; several administrative assistants took the time to sit with me as I pored over the archives of immigrant churches—sometimes for days; people opened their houses to help me better understand how their churches affected their daily lives—often over coffee and *pão de queijo*; dozens of pastors welcomed me into their official meetings and let me peruse documents normally only available to them. They knew I would write their story, and I am indebted to them for opening the doors of their homes and offices to me.

Among the many names of immigrant faith leaders that could be mentioned here, I want to single out that of Pr. Ophir de Barros, who was taken from this world by COVID-19 while in Brazil. This work is dedicated to his memory. Many Brazilian Baptist pastors in the Unites States referred jokingly to Ophir as the "Bishop" of Brazilian Baptist pastors in North America. He opened many doors that made this project possible. Pastors Josias Bezerra and Aloísio Campanha agreed to read the historical portions of this manuscript and provided indispensable support along the way. In addition, a great many other immigrant pastors and leaders were crucial to this research. They are too many to list, but the following stand out as especially helpful: Silair Almeida, Paulo Capelozza, Lécio Dornas, Antônio Ferreira, Gessuy Freitas, Sérgio Freitas, Francisco Izidoro, Hélio Martins, Carlos Mendes, Ribamar Monteiro,

Geriel de Oliveira, Daniel Paixão, Levy Penido, Alcione Silva, Girlan Silva, Mariluce Soma, and Fausto Vasconcelos—the last of whom, as I write this section, serves as the president of the Brazilian Baptist Convention. To them, I say: obrigado pelo apoio e encorajamento.

Several academics were also part of this journey in significant ways. My conversations with Brazilian scholars Kenner Terra, Wanderley Rosa, Marconi Monteiro, Maria Monteiro, Ivan Dias, Flávio Conrado, and Ronislo Pacheco helped me work through some of the aspects of this project as they relate to the manifestation of Brazilian religiosity in Brazil itself. Several Brazilian scholars rooted in the United States also provided invaluable assistance. Raimundo Barreto and Matt Reis—scholars of World Christianity—read a version of the full manuscript and provided crucial comments. Sociologists Rodrigo Serrão and H. B. (Keo) Cavalcanti also provided important insights. Rodrigo read parts of the work through the lens of a sociologist of religion and helped sharpen some of my comments—particularly those related to the ethnic identities of Brazilian immigrants in the United States. Keo's help was of a different nature—our friendship, which often took the path of cross-generational conversations about religion and politics in the United States and Latin America, pushed me to look further into the importance of a Brazilian Protestant disposition and its connection to US evangelicalism.

The feedback and encouragement I received from scholars who work primarily in English also informed this project at various stages. My mentor and friend C. Douglas Weaver read different versions of the manuscript and challenged me to sharpen as well as to expand some sections. When the project was still only a section of a doctoral dissertation, Doug Weaver, Philip Jenkins, William L. Pitts, Bill J. Leonard, Raimundo Barreto, David Whitford, and Beverly Gaventa provided important comments. During these early stages, I also benefited from the feedback of sociologists Jerry Park, Paul Froese, and James Davison Hunter, whose works and university courses influenced some of my thinking. Brandon Morgan's close reading of specific chapters and his insights regarding my claims that deal with the development of incipient immigrant theologies were extremely helpful—he allowed me to benefit from a theologian's perspective. I am thankful for these scholars' roles in shaping this project and, more importantly, in my formation as a scholar of religion.

Participants of the 2016 CEHILA meeting–US chapter (Comisión para el Estudio de la Historia de la Iglesia en América Latina y Caribe), such as Sergio González, Deborah Kanter, Tim Matovina, Daniel Ramírez, and Robert Wright, shared important insights about my research that worked their way into the introductory section of this manuscript. Afe Adogame read an early version of chapter 5, providing insights for which I am thankful. A Political Theology Network dissertation workshop grant allowed me to discuss a section of my work that developed into a chapter in this book, with scholars such as Vincent Lloyd, Martin Kavka, Inese Radzins, and Cathleen Kaveny, as well as with other grantees—their feedback was crucial to the chapter's development. The feedback and support I received from members of the National Association of Baptist Professors of Religion—which included a dissertation fellowship—was also indispensable.

The Hispanic Theological Initiative (HTI) provided me with crucial financial, emotional, and logistical backing. An HTI fellowship assisted in the initial phase of this work. After I joined the HTI staff, Rev. Joanne Rodríguez, HTI's executive director, encouraged me to write and provided vital support for me to continue to further my research agenda. I appreciate the care and love that HTI shows its scholars and constituents; indeed, many of the scholarly interlocutors I engaged with throughout my journey were connected to this institution. The HTI scholars who shared with me their kind and nurturing spirit, as well as their sharp criticisms and challenges, include Leo Guardado, Ángel Gallardo, Yvette Garcia, Andrés Albertsen, Tony Alonso, Jen Owens-Jofré, Néstor Morales, Erica Ramírez, Rafael Reyes III, among many others. Tito Madrazo, whose ethnographic research on Hispanic preachers has also been published by Baylor University Press, read an early version of this manuscript and challenged me to revisit significant elements of my approach. Conversations I had for HTI's Open Plaza podcast with Tony Lin and Jonathan Calvillo, both sociologists whose recent books deal with different aspects of immigrant Christianity, helped me understand better how different expression of Latinx Christianities in the United States manifest themselves. I am thankful for these scholars' giftedness and insights. They, together with the many mentors, faculty, editors, and staff members at HTI, made this and several other books possible. Uli Guthrie, my editor during my time as an HTI scholar and beyond, has helped me tremendously in my path toward writing intelligibly in English. I am thankful for her guidance and giftedness.

I am deeply indebted to the editorial team at Baylor University Press for believing in this project and helping nurture it to completion. Cade Jarrell's demeanor in the process of acquiring, editing, and guiding the review process of this book has been nothing but gracious and encouraging. I am thankful for Cade, David Aycock, and the entire team at BUP.

Finally, I want to thank my family members for their enduring support. Beijanete, Carla, Josias, Julia, Lucas, Michael, Jo Ann, Andrew, Joelle, Sarah,

Ed, Eloise, and Maisie have not always been enthusiastic about or even aware of the joys of the academic study of immigrant religion but continued to be supportive, patient, and kind the whole way. I love you all. My kids, Jonathan and Rebecca, accompanied this research for more than half of their lives—they keep me going for many reasons. My wife, Clare Duffy, critiqued a number of sections with unmatched patience—sometimes taking a break from her own work in order to listen to or read paragraphs. Thank you, pretty! I wouldn't have finished this installment of my writing journey without you.

ABBREVIATIONS

AIBBAN	Association of the Brazilian Baptist Churches in North America
BBC	Brazilian Baptist Convention
Brazuca	Brazilian immigrants and Brazilian Americans living in the US
BWA	Baptist World Alliance
CONJUBBRAN	Congress of the Brazilian Baptist Youth in North America
FMB	Foreign Mission Board
FPLBC	First Portuguese-Language Baptist Church
IMB	International Mission Board
NBC	National Baptist Convention (Brazil)
OBBPNA	Order of Brazilian Baptist Pastors in North America
OBPB	Order of Baptist Pastors of Brazil
SBC	Southern Baptist Convention
WMB	World Mission Board

1
FRAMING

Diasporic Networks and Immigrant Christianity

In short, borders fuel many of the fears of our time, and they are invoked ever more frequently without any consideration for their real effectiveness. They multiply at the same rate as disorder. Some of them, even if they have no legal existence, nonetheless determine the course of existence of millions of people.

Manlio Graziano[1]

Within the context of globalization and transnational movements, simply stated the peoples called Hispanics, Latinos, and Latinas in the United States are those who have roots in Latin America. But as is the case for much of life, what seems simple may be quite complex.

Edwin Aponte[2]

I t is 2016, and during an apparently unpretentious summer afternoon in San Francisco, California, a group of prominent transnational religious leaders are meeting to advance the cooperative work of their religious network. Although several participants in the meeting speak at least two languages, English is not spoken among them during sessions. One of the keynote speakers for the group of approximately forty pastors is one of the most successful authors of the past decade, with fifteen million books sold in over seventy countries and

---

[1] Manlio Graziano, *What Is a Border?* (Stanford, Calif.: Stanford University Press, 2018), 53.
[2] Edwin Aponte, *Santo: Varieties of Latino/a Spirituality* (Maryknoll, N.Y.: Orbis, 2012), 9.

a blockbuster movie based on one of his books. Another speaker is a pastor of a church with over fourteen thousand members and the founder of a network with considerable social, economic, and political influence in one of the most prosperous Latin American states. The attendees and event organizers include a pastor of a multisite church in the Bay Area, the pastor of a megachurch in Florida whose thousands of members speak English mostly as a second language, a church leader whose social media accounts reveal relationships with prominent politicians in his country of origin, and a number of pastors who would later attend an event with the president of their country, Jair Bolsonaro, when he visited the United States on official business. This was the 2016 annual meeting of the Ordem dos Pastores Batistas Brasileiros na América do Norte (Order of Brazilian Baptist Pastors in North America [OBBPNA])—a group formed mostly of Brazilian Baptists whose churches are affiliated to the Southern Baptist Convention (SBC) but whose denominational life and transnational influence are marked by ethnic and linguistic boundaries that transcend official institutional affiliations.[3]

The attendees and organizers of this meeting comprised some of the immigrant leaders on whose communities this manuscript focuses; communities whose complexities and value may escape the gaze of those not familiar with their languages, cultural codes, and transnational movements. In these communities, the transnational prestige and social capital of their leaders—clearly illustrated by their access to political, cultural, and religious elites in their countries of origin—coexist with the fact that the majority of their members are undocumented immigrants from the Global South. Many of these latter start businesses that earn them much higher wages than those earned by the average US citizen.[4] Their financial contributions and voluntary work help support foreign missions, social initiatives, salaries of church workers, and the purchase of church buildings. Undocumented Christians also worship in their immigrant communities, together with compatriots who include university professors, nurses, high-school teachers, government officials, police officers, professional soccer players, mixed martial arts fighters, and international students. The story that unites immigrant religious leaders with considerable transnational access, undocumented Christians who populate immigrant churches, and foreign-born students and workers who prefer to worship in their native tongue is one of migration. This story is multifaceted, but it is marked by an

---

[3]   All translations of primary written sources, secondary sources, and interviews for this manuscript were done by the author.

[4]   For a thick description of undocumented immigrant Christians who are successful entrepreneurs and leaders in their immigrant churches, see Tony Tian-Ren Lin, *Prosperity Gospel: Latinos and Their American Dream* (Chapel Hill: University of North Carolina Press, 2020).

overarching sentiment of unbelonging that, in conjunction with complex migration patterns, informs central elements in the trajectories of religious communities. It is this multifaceted and complex story that this book tells.[5]

Migration and Theologies

This book offers a particular narrative that advances a broad thesis. In other words, although the following pages focus mostly on the story of a circumscribed network of faith communities of the Latinx diaspora in the United States, my overarching argument engages the fields of World Christianity, Latinx Studies, American Religious History, Theology, and Migration Studies. While *Migrational Religion* tells of how immigrants from Latin America are changing the religious landscape of the United States broadly speaking, it also describes how their experiences of migration and adaptation affect the role and identity of particular immigrant faith communities. The particularity and historical contributions of my argument become clear in the narrative of the specific group on which I focus—a network of denominationally connected churches formed primarily of undocumented immigrants, which are sometimes led by individuals with considerable transnational prestige. Yet the particularities of this narrative contain lessons that can be applied toward a broader conceptual understanding of immigrant faith communities.

One of the ways in which the US context affects immigrant faith communities is by upsetting the theological imagination of Global South Christians who migrate to this country.[6] Although immigrants often remain within the general

---

[5] The role of communities of faith in providing a sense of belonging to immigrants is well documented. In 2020, for example, Jonathan Calvillo provided examples of how this dynamic can function among Roman Catholic and evangelical parishioners in Santa Ana, California (in Calvillo, *The Saints of Santa Ana: Faith and Ethnicity in a Mexican Majority City* [New York: Oxford University Press, 2020]); similarly, Tito Madrazo has provided examples of how Hispanic evangelical preachers' reading of the Bible is an important element in their sense of belonging (in Madrazo, *Predicadores: Hispanic Preaching and Immigrant Identity* [Waco, Tex.: Baylor University Press, 2021]). In part because this is well documented, my argument here takes the role of immigrant communities in creating spaces for ethnic belonging largely for granted. Although I name this dynamic in several places, my primary focus is on how a sense of unbelonging is not fully transcended and has theological and ecclesiological implications in a particular religious network.

[6] I agree with Edwin Aponte's observation that "there are many groups under the single umbrella rubric of 'Hispanic' or 'Latino/a' in the United States. Part of the challenge for a basic understanding of Hispanics of Latino/as is to be descriptive of empirical realities while not reducing such a description to essentialist stereotypes." See Aponte, *Santo*, 9. Although I name dynamics within Latinx churches, I recognize that there is tremendous diversity within Latinx Christian expressions.

contours of the theological frameworks provided by their particular traditions, the struggles of immigrant living create space for incipient immigrant theologies, which are born out of contextual challenges that shape faith communities forced to search for their own theological self-understanding vis-à-vis historical allegiances and external demands. Put simply, the contextual effects of migration push immigrant religious networks to both reconfigure aspects of the theological arrangements imagined in their constituents' home countries and uncover the theological limitations of the specific traditions to which they become affiliated in their host country. I recognize that faith communities—immigrant or not—often engage in practices that may differ from the official theologies of their particular traditions for contextual purposes. These incipient immigrant theologies, however, are situated in a particular liminal space between pragmatic forms of community survival and new theological articulations.

Paying attention to this dynamic is important because, for a great many immigrants from Latin America, their theological imagination is an indispensable part of their worldview. As such, theological convictions are central to a number of social, civic, and behavioral commitments that help shape immigrant identity. Attending to this helps us transcend reductionist notions of immigrant identity, which can otherwise insulate the religious lives of immigrants from other meaningful activities, imply that immigrant identities are configured solely in the immigrants' countries of origin, or even suggest that immigrant religious life does not posit creative challenges to the role of churches as vehicles of adaptation.[7]

In immigrant communities of faith, the struggles of daily life connected to migration dynamics affect how parishioners imagine the function, meaning,

---

[7] The complexity of identity construction within diasporic faith communities in the United States has been documented in a number of contexts. Margarita Mooney, for example, studied the adaptation of Haitian immigrants affiliated to the Roman Catholic Church in Miami (see Mooney, *Faith Makes Us Live: Surviving and Thriving in the Haitian Diaspora* [Berkeley: University of California Press, 2009]). More recently, Tony Lin and Jonathan Calvillo provided excellent ethnographically grounded studies that also document the role of diaspora churches in helping shape immigrant identity (see Lin, *Prosperity Gospel*; and Calvillo, *Saints of Santa Ana*). Despite differences in approach and methodology, this book joins forces with a growing body of literature that considers not only how immigrant faith communities change the United States but also how the country changes these communities. To quote Afe Adogame's seminal work on the African Christian diaspora, this book tries to follow in the trajectory of the "increasing tendency to think of the longue durée of the migration process, migration (non-) settlement as a transient, lifelong process encapsulating crucial life stages." See Afeosemime U. Adogame, *The African Christian Diaspora: New Currents and Emerging Trends in World Christianity* (London: Bloomsbury, 2013), 2.

and identity of their churches. More specifically, in the churches of the Lat-inx diaspora, the quotidian social and existential unbelonging of immigrant living is in dialectical relationship with ecclesiological and theological convic-tions. Immigrant life in the United States often creates a sense of not belong-ing to society; in diasporic faith communities, this unbelonging often sheds light on the limitations of traditional theological systems and ecclesiological arrangements. That is not to say that immigrant communities of faith nec-essarily create formal theological treatises. The communities considered here do not compose official theological statements explicitly calling into question available formal theologies. The immigrant theological unbelonging created by sociological factors, however, interrogates traditional commitments in ways that reveal the insufficiency of available formal theologies in dealing with issues faced by immigrant communities. This book narrates a particular his-tory of an immigrant religious network and reveals some general implications of this history for a broader understanding of American religious life, thereby uncovering understudied aspects in the literature on World Christianity and speaking to ways in which incipient theologies develop.

Imagine theologies as maps of an always-changing land drawn by itiner-ant cartographers or inhabitants, perhaps immigrants. Changes in landscape, geopolitics, and in the cartographers themselves make old maps obsolete and require the production of new ones that better represent the new realities. Intellectual elites with specific agendas, who are often tempted to be more particular to the cartographers themselves than descriptive of groups they claim to represent, construct new maps and new cartographies in response to the perceived inadequacies of old theological maps. The varieties of Anglo-European theologies, Latin American Liberation theologies, Latinx theologies, Black theologies, and Feminist theologies, to name a few, are a testament to the fact that theological maps are tentative, limited, and temporary. Theologies are in constant dialogue with contexts. Contextual changes, such as the ones faced by migrants trying to adapt to a new land, are often pregnant with theo-logical possibilities.[8] Theological constructions that address perceived needs in minoritized communities have great value in the sense that the theologians who produce them are often indeed invested in their conceptualization of the community's best interest. Such theologians also have the training, social capital, resources, and networking abilities to facilitate the dissemination of

---

[8]   Daniel Ramírez's *Migrating Faith* provides a powerful historical account of how theological sensibilities have been affected by migration in a particular Latinx group. See Ramírez, *Migrating Faith: Pentecostalism in the United States and Mexico in the Twentieth Century* (Chapel Hill: University of North Carolina Press, 2015).

their ideas. The precariousness of theological interventions that are not developed in community, however, shows itself in the potential gaps present in the nuanced distinction between the use of a community's struggle for the theologizing of traditional academic theologians and the way in which theological convictions develop in actual faith communities. It is the latter concern that this project attempts to engage. *Migrational Religion* presents a historically grounded account of how an incipient immigrant theology has developed in a particular network of religious communities. Ethnographic work and interviews, even when not presented in traditional format, are also central to this story. As such, this book functions primarily as a narrative of particular historical developments as they happened on the ground, rather than constructing an ideal theological reality. Although this manuscript considers the theological implications of this history, it is descriptive, not prescriptive.

Brazilian Baptists in the United States

The particular religious network that is the focus of *Migrational Religion* is one formed of communities of Brazilian Baptist immigrants that participated in the Associação de Igrejas Batistas Brasileiras na America do Norte (Association of Brazilian Baptist Churches in North America [AIBBAN]). These churches started to appear consistently on the US religious landscape in the 1980s after the Brazilian Baptist Convention (BBC)—influenced by the SBC—sent a missionary to reach the Iberian Portuguese population on the American East Coast. Migration to the United States from Portugal and the Azores was initially driven by the needs of the whaling industry, which shaped immigration to New England and California from the 1870s until the 1920s. From the 1960s to the 1980s, another wave of migration increased the numbers of immigrants from Portugal and the Azores in these regions.[9] Initially, it was this Iberian Portuguese population that the BBC had in mind when it sent a missionary to the United States.

Brazilian migration to the United States, however, grew in the last decades of the twentieth century, and as thousands of Brazilian evangelicals migrated to the United States, hundreds of Brazilian evangelical churches were created to cater to these immigrants. These Baptist communities were under constant pressure to adapt to their rapidly changing context as immigrant churches. Initially their leaders—male pastors who wanted to replicate the communities of the BBC from which they came—conceived of these churches as extensions

---

[9] João Leal, "Migrant Cosmopolitanism: Ritual and Cultural Innovation among Azorean Immigrants in the USA," in *Cosmopolitanism in the Portuguese-Speaking World*, ed. Francisco Bethencourt (Leiden: Brill, 2017), 233–34.

of their denomination in Brazil. The challenges of immigrant living, however, pushed these church communities in a direction that moved them beyond their usual role in Brazil.

Brazilian Baptists in the United States are part of what historian of missions Andrew Walls has called "the new Christian diaspora." In this project, the SBC and its Brazilian Baptist associates name the transnational network whose story I am telling. Limiting this story to a primary, well-defined religious network allows for a meso-level analysis that does two things: it avoids the broad generalizations of macrolevel approaches that are often present in works that deal with World Christianity across large geographical regions, and it skirts the tendency of microlevel studies of individual transnational religious communities to show little evidence of or connection to a broader context of transnational religious networks. This meso-level analysis enables me to introduce major individuals and institutions in more detailed fashion than would be typical of macrolevel studies, without precluding me from tracing general implications for broader religious landscapes, as many microlevel analyses unfortunately do.[10]

The close historical connection between Brazilian Baptists and the SBC provides an additional benefit for the study of World Christianity. For though concepts such as "reverse mission" and "multidirectional mission" are widely accepted across an array of fields that deal with transnational religious networks, more studies that trace how these phenomena develop within a particular network of immigrants from Latin America are needed. The historical and ideological Southern Baptist/Brazilian Baptist relationships represent an ideal case study for illustrating how these concepts develop across chronological and geographical boundaries. Under Southern Baptist control, the BBC already had missionaries in other Latin American countries and in Europe by 1911, and missionaries who received training in

[10] Here, I depart from David Cook's types of transnational religious networks. For Cook, microlevel transnational networks include individual and married couples; meso-level networks include churches, temples, and seminaries; and macrolevel networks include international religious bodies, such as denominations with transnational components. Given that works on individuals and married couples are not prominent in the literature of Latinx religious networks, in terms of scholarly units of analysis, it is more appropriate to treat individual religious communities as microlevel networks, international religious bodies as meso-level networks, and broad geographical regions as macrolevel networks. This categorization better reflects the scholarly production on World Christianity and on transnational religious movements. See David A. Cook, "The Variety of Transnational Religious Networks," in *Religion across Borders: Transnational Immigrant Networks*, ed. Helen Ebaugh and Janet Chafetz (Walnut Creek, Calif.: AltaMira, 2002), 166–67.

Brazil worked among Mexican and Italian immigrants in the United States in the first decades of the twentieth century. The multidirectional nature of missions was an assumption in the global network of Baptists, not a novel reality. A brief commentary on this connection, therefore, is important in order to place my analysis of Brazilian Baptist immigrant communities in the United States within a broader historical context. This latter will help illustrate how denominationally informed transnational networks, like immigrant networks in general, "depend on multiple and constant interconnections across international borders and their public identities are configured in relationship to more than one nation-state."[11]

The SBC and Their Brazilian Baptists

Generally speaking, Southern Baptists shaped the theological imagination of Brazilian Baptists strongly.[12] The SBC, which is now the largest Protestant denomination in the United States, began in 1845 because of a controversy about slavery.[13] The racialized form in which the SBC developed in the United States is well documented.[14] The ways in which the denomination exported its racialized gospel to many countries around the world, however, are less widely known.[15] For example, Brazil was one of the most successful fields for Southern Baptist missions. The development of this mission, which has been important to the success of Brazilian Protestantism in general, began with groups of disgruntled Confederates.

Despite the fact that the official missionary agency of the SBC, namely, the Foreign Mission Board (FMB), showed interest in Brazil as early as 1859, the sustained phase of Southern Baptist missions in that country would come much later. In 1860 SBC missionary Thomas Bowen went to

[11] Adogame, *African Christian Diaspora*, 161.

[12] My book *The Global Mission of the Jim Crow South* (Macon, Ga.: Mercer University Press, forthcoming) shows in detail some of the historical reasons why the relationship between the BBC and the SBC was shaped such that Brazilian Baptists in Brazil are still ideologically close to the SBC. Primary sources and additional commentary supporting the claims made in this section can be found in this forthcoming manuscript.

[13] Leon McBeth, *The Baptist Heritage: Four Centuries of Baptist Witness* (Nashville: Broadman, 1987), 382.

[14] Robert P. Jones, *White Too Long: The Legacy of White Supremacy in American Christianity* (New York: Simon & Schuster, 2020); Paul Harvey, *Redeeming the South: Religious Cultures and Racial Identities among Southern Baptists, 1865–1925* (Chapel Hill: University of North Carolina Press, 1997); C. Douglas Weaver, *In Search of the New Testament Church: The Baptist Story* (Macon, Ga.: Mercer University Press, 2008).

[15] See João B. Chaves, *O Racismo na História Batista Brasileira: Uma Memória Inconveniente do Legado Missionário* (Brasília: Novos Dialogos, 2020).

Brazil but had returned to the United States in 1861. Given the depletion of the SBC's financial resources because of the American Civil War, Brazil would not become a sustainable mission field for the convention until 1881. After the war ended in 1865, however, Southerners migrated in large numbers to Brazil and formed Confederate colonies with the intention of reconstructing the antebellum South in Brazil. Brazil remained a slave-holding country until 1888, and it was in such a Confederate colony that the first Baptist church in Brazil was formed in 1871 to cater to Confederate immigrants living in the country.[16]

Southern Baptist missionaries began arriving in Brazil consistently in 1881, and churches that formed with the objective of converting Brazilians to the Baptist faith started to appear in 1882. As expected, Baptists in Brazil grew and organized according to the Southern Baptist model. First, missionaries organized churches, then regional and state conventions, and in 1907 a national convention. They also established theological seminaries and denominational publications, controlling these denominational institutions of cultural production for most of the history of Baptists in Brazil.

Timeline of the Baptists in Brazil (1845-1982)

By 1936, after more than a decade of public controversy, Brazilians controlled important denominational institutions, such as schools, denominational boards, and theological seminaries. This institutional autonomy, however, was short lived. By 1945 missionaries were back in the control. As the denomination grew and the number of missionaries diminished in proportion to the number of locals, missionaries became more sophisticated in how they influenced the BBC. Thus, publishing houses, denominational periodicals, and seminaries became the centers of missionary power

---

[16] For more on the Confederate exiles, see Eugene Harter, *The Lost Colony of the Confederacy* (College Station: Texas A&M University Press, 2006); Judith Mac Knight Jones, *Soldado Descansa! Uma Epopéia Norte-Americana sob os Céus do Brasil* (São Paulo: Jarde, 1967); Frank Goldman, *Os Pioneiros Americanos no Brasil: Educadores, Sacerdotes, Covos e Reis* (São Paulo: Pioneira, 1972); and Ana Maria Costa de Oliveira, *O Destino (Não) Manifesto: Os Imigrantes Norte-Americanos no Brasil* (São Paulo: União Cultural Brasil-Estados Unidos, 1995). More recent research indicates that a major factor in the Southern migration to Brazil was the possibility of perpetuating the Southern lifestyle through slavery or, in the case of poor white Southerners, the possibility of acquiring slaves in Brazil. See Gerald Horne, *The Deepest South: The United States, Brazil, and the African Slave Trade* (New York: New York University Press, 2007); Célio Antônio Alcantara Silva, "Capitalismo e Escravidão: A Imigração Confederada para o Brasil" (Ph.D. diss., Universidade Estadual de Campinas, 2011); and "Confederate and Yankees under the Southern Cross," *Bulletin of Latin American Research* 34, no. 3 (2015): 270–304.

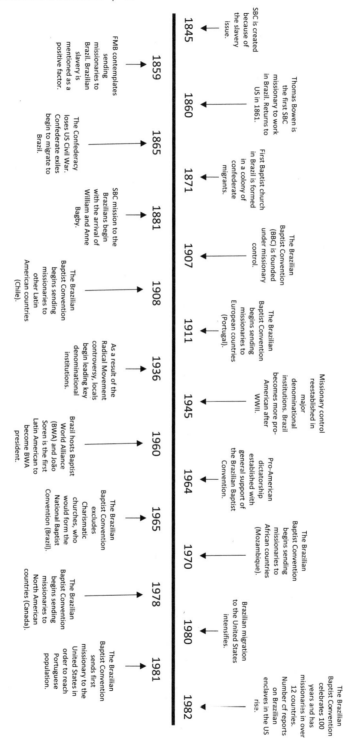

1845 — SBC is created because of the slavery issue.

1859 — FMB contemplates sending missionaries to Brazil. Brazilian slavery is mentioned as a positive factor.

1860 — Thomas Bowen is the first SBC missionary to work in Brazil. Returns to US in 1861.

1865 — The Confederacy loses US Civil War. Confederate exiles begin to migrate to Brazil.

1871 — First Baptist church in Brazil is formed in a colony of confederate migrants.

1881 — SBC mission to the Brazilians begin with the arrival of William and Anne Bagby.

1907 — The Brazilian Baptist Convention (BBC) is founded under missionary control.

1908 — The Brazilian Baptist Convention begins sending missionaries to other Latin American countries (Chile).

1911 — The Brazilian Baptist Convention begins sending missionaries to European countries (Portugal).

1936 — As a result of the Radical Movement controversy, locals begin leading key denominational institutions.

1945 — Missionary control reestablished in major denominational institutions. Brazil becomes more pro-American after WWII.

1960 — Brazil hosts Baptist World Alliance (BWA) and João Soren is the first Latin American to become BWA president.

1964 — Pro-American dictatorship established with general support of the Brazilian Baptist Convention.

1965 — The Brazilian Baptist Convention excludes Charismatic churches, who would form the National Baptist Convention (Brazil).

1970 — The Brazilian Baptist Convention begins sending missionaries to African countries (Mozambique).

1978 — The Brazilian Baptist Convention begins sending missionaries to North American countries (Canada).

1980 — Brazilian migration to the United States intensifies.

1981 — The Brazilian Baptist Convention sends first missionary to the United States in order to reach Portuguese population.

1982 — The Brazilian Baptist Convention celebrates 100 years and has missionaries in over 12 countries. Number of reports enclaves in the US rise.

in Brazil after World War II. When the BBC sent its first missionary to the United States in 1981, a Southern Baptist missionary was still president of one of the two most important denominational seminaries, and missionaries had been successful in their explicit plan of recruiting and equipping locals who would advance the Southern Baptist vision in Brazil. Raimundo Barreto summarizes the broader elements of this history well: "Whereas North American Protestant missions that arrived in the nineteenth century helped to break the monopoly of European colonial Catholicism, they offered their own version of colonial Christianity, functioning as the religious legitimizers of a neocolonial order."[17] Through the instrumentality of the BBC's World Mission Board (WMB), Brazilians would also further the SBC vision around the world. As a result, despite notable exceptions, by the time the Brazilian Baptist mission arrived in the United States, the Brazilian Baptist mind had been largely colonized by the SBC.

I am fully aware that Baptists have always been a diverse bunch, and I recognize and honor this diversity in a number of places in this project. Cognizant of the largely colonizing denominational spirit into which the leaders of the churches of the Brazilian diaspora were instructed, however, I focus on the official positions and administrative structures of the BBC. When I mention the position of the Baptists in Brazil, it is on these documents and positions that I rely. In the case of the churches of the Brazilian diaspora, diversity is also present. I will focus, however, on elements that characterize the general dispositions of Brazilian Baptist religious communities.

That Brazilian Baptists, unlike their SBC forebears, have recently been more open to the ordination of women does not mean that the participation of women is uncontroversial in denominational politics. Partially because of the male-dominated way in which the denomination operates, however, there is an insufficient focus on sources provided by women leaders in this project. At the same time, women have been crucial in the history of Brazilian Baptists—despite the fact that they have not been particularly visible in key denominational institutions. A structural example of women leadership is the powerful Women's Missionary Union of Brazil, which is yet to receive appropriate historical attention. In Brazilian Baptist churches in the United States, women's leadership is more evident, but women still do not share the visibility and influence of male leaders, which prevented me from investing more space

---

[17] Raimundo Barreto, "Beyond Contextualization: Gospel, Culture, and the Rise of Latin American Christianity," in *World Christianity as Public Religion*, ed. Raimundo Barreto, Ronaldo Cavalcanti, and Wanderley Rosa (Minneapolis: Fortress, 2017), 111.

in discussing their indispensable history. I recognize and lament this particular limitation that I hope will be remedied by future scholarly narratives.

Brazilian Baptist Churches in the United States

Because Brazilian Baptist churches in the United States are often pastored by ministers who were part of the BBC and trained in seminaries that espouse forms of Southern Baptist theology, they have a historical and ideological link to the SBC. However, this relationship is complicated by the fact that immigrant churches have to deal with a number of issues peculiar to their nature as diasporic communities. These include the struggles of undocumented parishioners, the pressures of membership fluctuation caused by national and international migration patterns, the stronger presence of women in leadership roles, the increasing number of Pentecostal migrants joining these mostly non-Pentecostal churches, the pressures to incorporate English and Spanish into social and worship services, and the experience of an anti-immigrant disposition within the SBC. These challenges have pushed Brazilian Baptist immigrant churches to adapt to a context in which ministering successfully to parishioners has meant rethinking traditional ways of addressing spiritual, existential, logistic, and social needs.

Based on six years of ethnographic work conducted in eleven congregations across the United States, dozens of interviews with Brazilian Baptist pastors, and extensive archival research carried out in English and Portuguese, *Migrational Religion* traces the history of Brazilian Baptist immigrant churches in the United States (referred to throughout the manuscript as Brazuca Baptist churches), describes some of the practices of these immigrant communities, and documents how the peculiarities of immigrant living affect the theological imagination of immigrant churches.

While I will deal with these tensions in greater detail in what follows, it suffices to mention for now that the Brazilian Baptist case shows that Global South Christians undergo changes in the US context that are at times driven by factors peculiar to labor migrations and cannot be properly explained in terms of a priori theological innovations. That is, although such changes have, for religious agents, clear theological implications that are in dialectic relationship with their immigrant social location, new theological sensibilities are mostly due to migration dynamics, not to root causes of theological difference. In the case of immigrant groups affiliated with denominations based in the United States, these changes generate tensions that reveal the difficulties evangelical denominations have in dealing with the specific experiences of such groups. The paradox of the

Brazilian Baptists is that, generally speaking, the closer they get to the SBC geographically, the further they get from them ideologically, in significant and demonstrable ways.[18]

Literature on an Invisible Minority

There are few published manuscripts that focus on Brazilian Baptists in the United States.[19] The monolingual limitations manifested in the English-speaking histories of the denomination's presence in England and/or the United States is also apparent, and more English-language works that look at the religious identity of immigrants from Latin America as it develops across national borders are needed. The few works that do look into Latinx Baptist groups fail to explore the effect of migration on religious identity and denominational practice.[20] As a matter of fact, although Brazilians in the United States

---

[18] Writing on African-initiated churches in Europe, Jenkins noted that diaspora churches, which freely move across national boundaries, tend to found groups apart from established national churches. This observation is generally true of Brazilian Baptists in the United States. The difference is that Brazilian ethnic denominationalism does not necessarily preclude churches of the Brazilian diaspora from being affiliated with national churches. See Philip Jenkins, *God's Continent: Christianity, Islam, and Europe's Religious Crisis* (Oxford: Oxford University Press, 2010), 96.

[19] It is also noteworthy that a look at the major works on Baptist history in Brazil reveals either a neglect of the changes in Brazilian Baptist identity, a hagiographical tendency that obscures any critical assessment, or both. For examples, see Betty Antunes de Oliveira, *Antônio Teixeira de Albuquerque: O Primeiro Pastor Batista Brasileiro* (Rio de Janeiro: Edição de Autora, 1982); Zaqueu Moreira de Oliveira, *Perseguidos, Mas Não Desamparados: 90 Anos de Perseguição Religiosa contra os Batistas Brasileiros (1880–1970)* (Rio de Janeiro: JUERP, 1999); Zaqueu Moreira de Oliveira, *Panorama Batista em Pernambuco* (Recife: Junta Evangelizadora Batista de Pernambuco, 1964); J. Reis Pereira, *História dos Batistas no Brasil (1882–1982)* (Rio de Janeiro: JUERP, 1982); Marcelo Santos, *O Marco Inicial Batista* (São Paulo: Convicção, 2003); Elizete da Silva, *William Buck Bagby: Um Pioneiro Batista nas Terras do Cruzeiro do Sul* (Brasilia: Editora Novos Diálogos, 2011); and Enéas Tognini, *História dos Batistas Nacionais: Documentário* (Brasília: Convanção Batista Nacional, 1993).

[20] See Paul Barton, *Hispanic Methodists, Presbyterians, and Baptists in Texas* (Austin: University of Texas Press, 2006); Richard Carrera, "Mexican American Baptists' Dependency on Anglo Baptist Institutions in South Texas: A Case Study in Bee County" (master's thesis, University of Texas Pan American, 2000); João Chaves, "Where Should We Go Next? A Call for the Critical Investigation of Possible Racial Encounters between Anglo-American and Mexican-American Baptists in Texas during the Pioneer Period," *Baptist History and Heritage* 49, no. 3 (2004): 23–38; Becky Elliott, *Crossing at San Vicente: A History of First Baptist Church, Midland, Texas, and Their Commitment to the Mexican People across the Rio Grande River* (Austin: Nortex, 1998); Joshua Grijalva, "The Story of Hispanic Southern Baptists," *Baptist History and Heritage* 18, no. 3 (1983); idem, *A History of Mexican Baptists in Texas 1881–1981: Comprising an Account of the Genesis, the Progress, and the Accomplishments of the*

are usually categorized pan-ethnically as Hispanics or Latinxs, works on the history of Hispanic and Latinx Christianity in the United States tend to exclude an analysis of Brazilians partially because of differences in language, the comparatively small number of Brazilian scholars researching Latinx Christianity, and the unique history of the country's colonization (in which Portugal, not Spain, played the major role).[21] Much more attention has been given to Protestantism in Brazil than to Brazilian Protestantism abroad.[22]

People Called "Los Bautistas de Texas" (Dallas: Baptist General Convention of Texas, 1982); Moises Rodriguez, "The Cultural Context of Southern Baptist Work among Mexican-Americans in Texas" (Ph.D. diss., Baylor University, 1997).

[21] Most historical works on Hispanic and Latinx Christianity in the United States do not consider the Brazilian experience deeply and are understandably marked by a greater representation of Mexican/Mexican American and Puerto Rican examples. For examples, see Victor De Leon, *The Silent Pentecostals: A Biographical History of the Pentecostal Movement among the Hispanics in the Twentieth Century* (La Habra: De Leon, 1979); David Maldonado, *Protestantes/Protestants: Hispanic Christianity within Mainline Traditions* (Nashville: Abingdon, 1999); Daisy L. Machado, *Of Borders and Margins: Hispanic Disciples in Texas, 1888–1945* (Oxford: Oxford University Press, 2003); Barton, *Hispanic Methodists*; Gastón Espinosa, "Third Class Soldiers: A History of Hispanic Pentecostal Clergywomen in the Assemblies of God," in *Philip's Daughters: Women in Pentecostal-Charismatic Leadership*, ed. Estrelda Alexander and Amos Yong (Eugene, Ore.: Pickwick, 2009), 95–111; Arlene Walsh, "Jesus in the Hispanic Community: Images of Christ from Theology to Popular Religion," in *Jesus in the Hispanic Community: Images of Christ from Theology to Popular Religion*, ed. Harold J. Recinos and Hugo Magallanes (Louisville: Westminster John Knox, 2010), 92–104; Moises Sandoval, ed., *Fronteras: A History of the Latin American Church in the USA since 1513* (San Antonio, Tex.: Mexican American Cultural Center, 1983); Arlene M. Sanchez-Walsh, *Latino Pentecostal Identity: Evangelical Faith, Self, and Society* (New York: Columbia University Press, 2003); Lara Medina, *Las Hermanas: Chicana/Latina Religious-Political Activism in the U.S. Catholic Church* (Philadelphia: Temple University Press, 2005); Juan Francisco Martínez, *Los Protestantes: An Introduction to Latino Protestantism in the United States* (Santa Barbara: Praeger, 2011); Timothy Matovina, *Latino Catholicism: Transformation in America's Largest Church* (Princeton, N.J.: Princeton University Press, 2011); Hjamil A. Martínez-Vázquez, *Made in the Margins: Latina/o Constructions of U.S. Religious History* (Waco, Tex.: Baylor University Press, 2013); Felipe Hinojosa, *Latino Mennonites: Civil Rights, Faith, and Evangelical Culture* (Baltimore: Johns Hopkins University Press, 2014); and Gastón Espinosa, *Latino Pentecostals in America: Faith and Politics in Action* (Cambridge, Mass.: Harvard University Press, 2014). The recent sociological work of Mulder et al. also does not consider Brazilian Protestantism in the United States deeply. See Mark T. Mulder, Aida I. Ramos, and Gerardo Martí, *Latino Protestants in America: Growing and Diverse* (Lanham, Md.: Rowman & Littlefield, 2017).

[22] There is a wide range of studies on Latin American and Brazilian Protestantism providing a good general narrative of the presence of Protestantism in the region and tracing broad religious and political trends. For examples, see Rubem A. Alves, *Protestantism and Repression: A Brazilian Case Study* (Maryknoll, N.Y.: Orbis, 1985); Antônio Gouvêa Mendonça and Prócoro Velasques Filho, *Introdução ao Protestantismo Brasileiro* (São Paulo: Loyola, 1990); Rowan Ireland, *Kingdoms Come: Religion*

The few histories written by and about US missionaries to Brazil focus overwhelmingly on the contribution of these individuals to the numeric growth of Brazilian Baptists and thus do not pay attention to the process of the brazilianization of the Baptist denomination in Brazil as it relates to the Southern Baptist presence—which in terms of Brazilian Baptist denominational leadership was mostly administrative.[23] When it comes to the presence

and Politics in Brazil (Pittsburgh, Pa.: University of Pittsburgh Press, 1992); André Corten, Le Pentecôtisme au Brésil (Paris: Karthala, 1995); Paul Freston, "Pentecostalism in Brazil: A Brief History," Religion 25, no. 2 (1995): 119–33; R. Andrew Chesnut, Born Again in Brazil: The Pentecostal Boom and the Pathogens of Poverty (New Brunswick, N.J.: Rutgers University Press, 1997); Clara Cristina Jost Mafra, Os Evangelicos (Rio de Janeiro: Jorge Zahar, 2001); Andre Corten and Ruth R. Marshall-Fratani, eds., Between Babel and Pentecost: Transnational Pentecostalism in Africa and Latin America (Bloomington: Indiana University Press, 2001); Paul Freston, Evangelicals and Politics in Asia, Africa and Latin America (Cambridge: Cambridge University Press, 2001); Duncan Alexander Reily, História Documental do Protestantismo no Brasil (São Paulo: ASTE, 2003); Phillip Berryman, Religion in the Megacity: Catholic and Protestant Portraits from Latin America (Eugene, Ore.: Wipf & Stock, 2006); Paul Freston, Religião e Política, Sim; Igreja e Estado, Não: Os Evangélicos e a Participação Política. (Vicosa: Ultimato, 2006); R. Andrew Chesnut, Competitive Spirits: Latin America's New Religious Economy (Oxford: Oxford University Press, 2007); Gedeon Alencar, Protestantismo Tupiniquim (São Paulo: Aret Editorial, 2007); Paul Freston, ed., Evangelical Christianity and Democracy in Latin America (Oxford: Oxford University Press, 2008); and Todd Hartch, The Rebirth of Latin American Christianity (Oxford: Oxford University Press, 2014).

[23] In terms of published academic manuscripts, there are only a few exceptions to the encyclopedic and/or pro-missionary tendency in analyses of the Southern Baptist presence in Brazil; most of these are recent publications. In his book on Brazilian Protestantism, French scholar Émile Léonard provided an exceptional account of the Southern Baptist presence in Brazil, looking at some of the tensions between locals and missionaries. But since Léonard's concern was providing a general account of all major denominations, he did not pay exclusive attention to Baptists. See Émile G. Léonard, O Protestantismo Brasileiro: Estudos de Eclesiologia e Historia Social (São Paulo: ASTE, 1963). Jorge Pinheiro and Marcelo Santos edited a volume of short essays signaling a critical analysis of several themes in Brazilian Baptist history that remain understudied, such as the presence of nationalism in grassroots Baptist movements, controversies surrounding the ordination of women, and the issue of the correct date of the official beginnings of Brazilian Baptist history. See Jorge Pinheiro and Marcelo Santos, eds., Os Batistas: Controvérsias e Vocação para a Intolerância (São Paulo: Fonte Editorial, 2012). On the issue of Brazilian Baptist beginnings, Marcelo Santos and Alberto Yamabuchi uncovered problematic aspects of the Brazilian Baptist attempt to establish the date of the beginning of Brazilian Baptist work. See Santos, Marco Inicial Batista; and Alberto Kenji Yamabuchi, O Debate Sobre a História das Origens do Trabalho Batista no Brasil: Uma Análise das Relações e dos Conflitos de Gênero e Poder na Convenção Batista Brasileira nos Anos 1960–1980 (São Paulo: Novas Edições Acadêmicas, 2015). João Araújo authored two volumes that were published in 2015 and touch on the domination of Southern Baptist missionaries over Brazilian Baptists in general. In Histórias, Tradições, e Pensamentos Batistas

of Brazilian immigrants in the United States, the most helpful resources have been produced by social scientists who, though they recognized the importance of religious communities to immigrant life, devoted only limited attention to the history of immigrant religious communities.[24]

(São Paulo: Fonte Editorial, 2015), Araújo argued that contextualizations of Southern Protestantism by Brazilian locals were very limited and generally done against missionary desire. It is in *Batistas: Dominação e Dependência* (São Paulo: Fonte Editorial, 2015), however, that Araújo laid out his argument that Brazilian Baptists were by and large dominated by Southern Baptist missionaries institutionally and still are dominated ideologically. Although Araújo focused mostly on the two-volume work by A. R. Crabtree and Antônio Mesquita as primary sources and only consulted sources in Portuguese, he was correct in his observation that a compelling narrative of Southern Baptist missionary domination is lacking in the literature. Araújo was convinced that his book represented the first scholarly counterpoint to the available Americophile literature. For Araújo, "After the writings of A. R. Crabtree and Antônio Mesquita, all the books that were written about Baptists in Brazil had the same tendency of praising missionaries, their mission, and the churches of the United States. Therefore, over 130 years after the first Baptists churches were planted in Brazil, there has been little literary production and, all of the few works that exist deal with the issues in the same way. There are no counterpoints, criticisms, re-readings, or disagreements. Such attitudes are rejected and silenced" (13). Araújo is correct in pointing out a lack of criticism in the literature on Brazilian Baptist history. His own welcome contributions to the conversation about missionary domination, however, are informed by a limited source selection both in terms of primary sources and language. In many aspects of Araújo's research, his conclusions are more stated than demonstrated.

[24] Many sociological and anthropological works recognize the importance of church communities but do not include a central analysis of Brazilian immigrant church life. These include José Victor Bicalho, *Yes, Eu Sou Brazuca ou a Vida do Imigrante Brasileiro nos Estados Unidos da América* (Governador Valadares: Fundação Serviços de Educação e Cultura, 1989); Maxine L. Margolis, *Little Brazil: An Ethnography of Brazilian Immigrants in New York City* (Princeton, N.J.: Princeton University Press, 1993); idem, "Transnationalism and Popular Culture: The Case of Brazilian Immigrants in the United States," *Journal of Popular Culture* 29, no. 1 (1995); idem, *An Invisible Minority: Brazilians in New York City* (Gainesville: University Press of Florida, 2009); idem, *Goodbye, Brazil: Émigrés from the Land of Soccer and Samba* (Madison: University of Wisconsin Press, 2013); Teresa Sales, *Brasileiros Longe de Casa* (São Paulo: Cortez, 1999); and Sylvia Duarte Dantas Debiaggi, *Changing Gender Roles: Brazilian Immigrant Families in the U.S.* (New York: LFB Scholarly Publishing, 2001). A few manuscripts do pay closer attention to the religious life of Brazilian imigrants in sections, but not as a central concern. See Bernadete Beserra, *Brazilian Immigrants in the United States: Cultural Imperialism and Social Class* (New York: LFB Scholarly Publishing, 2006); Ana Cristina Braga Martes, *New Immigrants, New Land: A Study of Brazilians in Massachusetts* (Gainesville: University Press of Florida, 2011); Annie McNeil Gibson, *Post-Katrina Brazucas: Brazilian Immigrants in New Orleans* (New Orleans, La.: University of New Orleans Press, 2012); and Kara B. Cebulko, *Documented, Undocumented, and Something Else: The Incorporation of Children of Brazilian Immigrants* (El Paso, Tex.: LFB Scholarly Publishing, 2013).

Despite the gaps in scholarly analysis of Brazilian Protestantism in the United States, a few scholars have paid attention to this group in shorter contributions published in edited volumes and book sections.[25] The focus of this research has been more on the phenomenon of Brazilian transnational religiosity than on the presence of any particular religious network in the United States. The major contributions of these works in terms of Brazilian religion include the recognition of the connection between religious affiliation and the decision to migrate among Latinxs in general and Brazilians in particular, the consideration of Brazilian religious networks as an analytical tool that may replace the elusive idea of "Brazilian community," and the comparison between religious trends in Brazil itself and those among Brazilian Christians in the United States.[26]

One manuscript fully devoted to Brazilian religion in the United States, *Jesus in Sacred Gotham*, by Donizete Rodrigues, is an ethnography of a specific Brazilian Neo-Pentecostal church in the New York metropolitan area.[27] Despite the book's accomplishments, to my mind it has two interconnected limitations: the lack of a deeper historical focus, and the fact that Rodrigues' analysis is more

[25] See Philip J. Williams, Timothy J. Steigenga, and Manuel Vasquez, eds., *A Place to Be: Brazilian, Guatemalan, and Mexican Immigrants in Florida's New Destinations* (New Brunswick, N.J.: Rutgers University Press, 2009); Peggy Levitt, *God Needs No Passport: Immigrants and the Changing American Religious Landscape* (New York: New Press, 2007); idem, "Religion on the Move: Mapping Global Cultural Production and Consumption," in *Religion on the Edge: De-centering and Re-centering the Sociology of Religion*, ed. Courtney Bender et al. (Oxford: Oxford University Press, 2012), 159–76; Clémence Jouët-Pastré and Leticia J. Braga, eds., *Becoming Brazuca: Brazilian Immigration to the United States* (Cambridge, Mass.: David Rockefeller Center for Latin American Studies, 2008); and Manuel Vazquez and Cristina Rocha, eds., *The Diaspora of Brazilian Religions* (Boston: Brill, 2013). Most recently, Cristina Maria de Castro and Andrew Dawson edited a volume that focuses on Brazilian religion and migration. However, they decided to emphasize non-Christian groups despite the comparatively rare place of Brazilian denominational Protestantism in the literature. See Castro and Dawson, eds., *Religion, Migration, and Mobility: The Brazilian Experience* (New York: Routledge, 2017).

[26] Jacqueline Hagan has provided a helpful study of the role of religion in the decision to migrate. Although she recognizes the priority of economic considerations in this decision, she demonstrates that "often religious factors, embedded in strong cultural and local practices, ultimately guide and support decision-making and leave-taking." See Hagan, *Migration Miracle: Faith, Hope, and Meaning on the Undocumented Journey* (Cambridge, Mass.: Harvard University Press, 2008), 20–58. See also Levitt, *God Needs No Passport*; idem, "Religion on the Move"; Williams, Steigenga, and Vasquez, *Place to Be*; and Jouët-Pastré and Braga, *Becoming Brazuca*.

[27] Donizete Rodrigues, *Jesus in Sacred Gotham: Brazilian Immigrants and Pentecostalism in New York City* (Amazon, 2014). Rodrigues also published an expanded version of his English work in Portuguese. See Donizete Rodrigues, *O Evangélico Imigrante: O Pentecostalismo Brasileiro Salvando a América* (São Paulo: Fonte Editorial, 2016).

interested in comparative religions than in the history of Brazilian presence in the country. When it comes to Brazilian Baptists in the United States, a recent doctoral dissertation and master's thesis approach the topic, without, however, paying sufficient attention to the history of this group.[28]

All things considered, despite the scarcity of material on Brazilian transnational religion, interest in Brazilian religiosity outside Brazil in general and in the United States in particular is increasing among sociologists, anthropologists, and religious scholars. Approaches that tell historical narratives and trace the theological development of Brazilian transnational religious traditions remain needed. This book, therefore, fills a significant gap in existing scholarship by narrating underexplored aspects of the history of a Latinx-immigrant Baptist network in the United States through the lens of transnational scholarship.

Methodological Approach

Migrational Religion adopts a transnational approach to history, by which I mean it uses an international perspective of historical inquiry that focuses on networks and interactions that take place across nations and between cultures and languages. Central to transnational history is the attempt to deprovincialize approaches that limit their analysis to national boundaries.[29] As in the case of a number of other religious groups, limiting the histories of Brazilian Baptists or Baptists in the United States to their national borders does not yield an adequate understanding of the networks of communication and cooperation developed by Baptists in these two nations. A transnational methodology, therefore, is particularly fitting to illuminate often-neglected aspects of immigrant religious networks in general and Baptist history in particular. Such a methodology aims to, in the words of Daniel

---

[28] See Luiz C. Nascimento, "Religion and Immigration: Towards a Transformative Prophetic Spirit" (Ph.D. diss., Princeton Theological Seminary, 2012); and Rodrigo Serrão De Jesus, "A Igreja Como Pedacinho do Brasil: Migrações e Religião na Capital do Texas" (master's thesis, Federal University of Paraíba, 2014). Serrão's doctoral dissertation also deals with Brazilian religion in the United States, although his focus is on racial and ethnic construction among Brazilian immigrants who attend Protestant churches. In addition, Matt Reis is currently writing on Brazilian Evangelicals in Florida; his doctoral dissertation and forthcoming book chapters should be out in 2021.

[29] See Ian Tyrrell, "Reflections on the Transnational Turn in United States History: Theory and Practice," *Journal of Global History* 4, no. 3 (2009): 453–74; idem, *Transnational Nation: United States History in Global Perspective since 1789*, 2nd ed. (New York: Palgrave Macmillan, 2015); and Thomas Bender, ed., *Rethinking American History in a Global Age* (Berkeley: University of California Press, 2002).

Ramírez, "emancipate itself from epistemic boundaries set by nation-states and powerful knowledge production systems."[30]

Because this study is located at the intersection of Latinx religious history and the history of transnational religious movements, it is at the center of vigorous and current research agendas, which are informed by global migrations in general and the resulting diversification of academic demographics and interests in particular.[31] Today, it is widely recognized that many Latin American, Asian, and African Christians have created powerful global networks and are reenergizing the religious landscapes in Europe and the United States.[32] Brazilians play an important role in this dynamic not only because many Brazilians migrate, taking their faiths with them, but also because of the appeal of Brazilian culture and religions across the globe. I will revisit issues related to how positive US perceptions of Brazilian culture inform the peculiar ways in which the Brazilian immigrant experience can be differentiated from that of other Hispanic or Latinx peoples in chapter 5.[33] It is important to note, however, that this appeal is so apparent that some scholars have argued for the existence of a diaspora of Brazilian religions that is partially informed by the international attraction of romanticized notions of "Brazilian culture." Manuel Vasquez and Cristina Rocha, for example, suggest that there are two main reasons for the appeal of Brazilian religions: (1) the attempt on the part of non-Brazilians to consume an imagined projection

[30] Ramírez, *Migrating Faith*, 207.

[31] This is not the first work to inhabit this particular intersection; scholars such as Gastón Espinosa, Daniel Ramírez, Arlene Sanchez-Walsh, Edwin Aponte, and Timothy Matovina have explored similar tendencies in relation to Latinx Pentecostalism and Catholicism. More broadly, a look at the programs of the American Academy of Religion and American Historical Association, as well as a search of the indices of the *American Historical Review* and the *Journal of American History*, should suffice in establishing the importance of research on the dynamics of religions and migration.

[32] For a few examples, see Philip Jenkins, *The Next Christendom: The Coming of Global Christianity* (Oxford: Oxford University Press, 2007); Alejandro Portes and Rubén G. Rumbaut, *Immigrant America: A Portrait* (Berkeley: University of California Press, 2014); and Levitt, *God Needs No Passport*.

[33] Edwin Aponte's observation regarding Brazilians in his work on Latino/a spirituality sheds light on the complex positionality of Brazilians in terms of pan-ethnic characterizations of Brazilian immigrants. He writes, "Moreover, sometimes people from Brazil have been included in this collective U.S. group even though the common language of that nation is not Spanish but Portuguese, reflecting its colonial history and the broader history of Europe and the Atlantic world. Curiously, while Brazilians may or may not be included in the Hispanic/Latino grouping, people with direct roots in Portugal usually are not included in the Hispanic or Latino/a category." See Aponte, *Santo*, 60. This book argues that Brazilians are both Hispanic and Latinx; however, it also recognizes the complexities that pan-ethnic terms evoke, to varying degrees, for peoples of all nationalities.

of Brazilian culture and (2) the aggressiveness and creativity of Brazilian religious entrepreneurs.[34] Brazilian Baptist immigrant churches are, in a qualified way, part of this dynamic and I tell their story here for the first time.

The particular case of Brazilian religious representation and appropriation points to the need to abandon traditional assumptions in which the nation-state is the locus of religious activity and to adopt an approach sensitive to the fact that religious authority, authenticity, piety, and practice are negotiated across borders.[35] In the words of Peggy Levitt, "American religious life is no longer just American;"[36] developments in the home country may affect immigrant religious communities as much as the structural realities they face in the host country. What Moses Biney wrote about African immigrants in North America is also true of many Latinx immigrants: "The immigrants often shuttle personally and through proxies between their 'host' and 'home' countries and are simultaneously immersed in the affairs of both."[37]

In addition, Brazilian religious life has never been merely Brazilian. The imprint of different forms of African religions, Portuguese Catholicism, and American Protestantism are widespread in Brazil, but all of these religious dispositions have adapted themselves in response to context-specific challenges. Therefore, since the second half of the twentieth century, the religions that Brazil has exported to places like the United States are not just translations of the versions that reached Brazilians in earlier generations but adaptations made in response to the existential anxieties generated by local sociopolitical events. In the case of Brazilian Baptists, however, such adaptations were mostly administrative. Although in the context of the BBC institutional power was eventually transferred to Brazilians, theological tendencies correlated closely to those of the SBC.

---

[34] Manuel Vazquez and Cristina Rocha, eds., "Introduction: Brazil in the New Global Cartography of Religion," in Vazquez and Rocha, *The Diaspora of Brazilian Religions*, 1–42.

[35] Courtney Bender et al., eds., *Religion on the Edge: De-centering and Re-centering the Sociology of Religion* (Oxford: Oxford University Press, 2012); H. B. Cavalcanti, *Almost Home: A Brazilian American's Reflections on Faith, Culture, and Immigration* (Madison: University of Wisconsin Press, 2012); Corten and Marshall-Fratani, *Between Babel and Pentecost*; and Carlos Ribeiro Caldas, "O Papel da Igreja Universal Brasileira do Reino de Deus na Globalizaçao do Neopentecostalismo Atual," *Ciências da Religião* 8, no. 2 (2010): 107–21.

[36] Levitt, *God Needs No Passport*, 2.

[37] Moses Biney, "Transnationalism, Religious Participation, and Civic Responsibility among African Immigrants in North America," in *Migration and Public Discourse in World Christianity*, ed. Afe Adogame, Raimundo Barreto, and Wanderley Rosa (Minneapolis: Fortress, 2019), 59.

Elsewhere, I have provided the historical context for the denominational culture into which leaders of the Brazilian Baptist churches in the United States have been socialized and/or educated.[38] That task was important because the secondary sources that deal with Brazilian Baptist history are generally uncritical of how Southern Baptist missionaries were intentionally engaged in implementing structural and ideological domination of Brazilian Baptists. The Southern Baptist missionary success in Brazil ensured that the BBC remained closely related to the SBC in its theopolitical dispositions.

This project focuses on the history of the Brazilian Baptist presence in the United States, and unlike the case of the history of Southern Baptist missions or the BBC, there are no archives housing key primary sources.[39] With the exception of articles published in the denominational publications in Brazil, such as the *Jornal Batista*[40]—which are readily available in digitized form through the website of the BBC—the history presented in this book is based on data I collected over six years of research. These sources include the minutes and bylaws of pioneering Brazilian Baptist churches on the American East Coast, the minutes of the Fellowship of Brazilian Baptist Pastors in North America, bulletins and newsletters of Brazilian Baptist churches on the East Coast, internal Sunday school material used by churches in California and in Florida, interviews with pastors and church leaders across the United States, and participant observation of services at Brazilian Baptist churches located in the states of Florida, New York, Connecticut, New Jersey, Massachusetts, California, Texas, and Maryland as well as in annual meetings of the OBBPNA and one Annual Meeting of

[38] Chaves, *Global Mission*; Chaves, *Racismo na História Batista Brasileira*.

[39] The issue of sources is a recurring difficulty in researching the history of minoritized groups in the United States. Derek Chang's history of Baptist missions to Chinese immigrants and Southern Black Americans illustrates this difficulty. Chang has noted that "recovering (minority) voices—their intentions, their goals, their thoughts, their beliefs—remains an exercise in informed guesswork," and he is right. See Derek Chang, *Citizens of a Christian Nation: Evangelical Missions and the Problem of Race in the Nineteenth Century* (Philadelphia: University of Pennsylvania Press, 2010), 12. Too often, the voices of minoritized groups are relegated to an author's projection of a suspicious reading of white texts, which are approached "against the grain" in an attempt to recover the subaltern silence of the nonwhite proselyte. In this project, however, I have avoided this approach by including an array of representative voices of nonwhite subjects, although such a move came with the risks inherent in multidisciplinary approaches—which become prominent in several chapters of this book.

[40] The *Jornal Batista* is the major Baptist denominational publication in Brazil. Regarding the importance, influence, and doctrinal and political tendencies of the journal until 1964, see Israel Belo de Azevedo, "A Palavra Marcada: Teologia Política dos Batistas Segundo o *Jornal Batista*" (master's thesis, Seminário Teológico Batista do Norte do Brasil, 1983). The *Jornal Batista* has functioned as a powerful tool for Southern Baptist ideological dissemination since before the foundation of the BBC.

Brazilian Religious Leaders in North America. This project, therefore, although historically rooted, includes interdisciplinary elements—particularly oral history and ethnographic work—especially when describing the beliefs and practices of Brazilian Baptist churches in the United States.

In the following pages, I foreground the voices of the actors of this story. Whereas the history of minoritized immigrant groups is often told in impersonal ways, relegating the names and words of immigrant agents to faceless generalizations, *Migrational Religion* spotlights the voices of usually voiceless immigrants, who are extremely important to the religious landscape in the United States. In places in which perceptions of legal and ethical issues may present challenges, I keep the identities of such actors anonymous for their protection. Immigrant life is messy, many times undocumented, and most times volatile. Immigrant pastors and parishioners cannot give themselves the luxury of playing the game of life by the book. The book was not written for them!

Chapter Summaries

In the following two chapters, I lay the historical groundwork for Brazilian Baptist work in the United States before moving on to exploring more intentionally how the experiences of migration and adaptation to the United States have affected this Latinx religious network. I begin in chapter 2 by telling the story of how Baptist missionary work emerged in the United States. The chapter focuses on the place of the United States in Brazilian Baptist life until 1981, when the first official missionary of the BBC was sent to Newark, New Jersey. Partially because the BBC was founded and led by Southern Baptist missionaries for many decades, the United States became an integral part of Brazilian Baptist life. The *Jornal Batista* has documented the presence of Brazilian and Portuguese immigrant Baptists in the United States since the end of the nineteenth century. In 1981, however, things changed. With the arrival of Humberto Viegas Fernandes, one century after pioneering missionaries William Buck Bagby and Anne Bagby arrived in Brazil, the Brazilian mission to Portuguese immigrants in the United States was launched. After noticing the significant influx of immigrants from Brazil, however, the mission to reach the Portuguese soon morphed into an attempt to cater to this latter population.

The third chapter deals with the development of specific Brazilian Baptist churches and networks in the United States. This story depends on a variety of sources: reports written by Baptists in the United States for the *Jornal Batista*, interviews with the pioneers of Brazilian Baptist work in the United States, internal minutes and bulletins of several churches, and histories of individual churches that were written by members of these communities. Here, religious actors help tell their own stories, which are connected to a broader narrative that not all of them saw clearly. The history of Brazilian Baptist churches in the United States began as an effort of the BBC but soon became diffuse, decentralized, and multifaceted. Yet particular central themes guide the progression of Brazilian Baptist work in the United States: the shift from a focus on Brazilian immigrants to a focus on becoming a multiethnic church, the growing zeal among these communities for international missions, and social involvement that benefits both immigrants and the US-born population.

After telling the broad story of these immigrant churches, I turn my gaze to aspects of their history that show how features of their immigrant experiences affect them more intentionally. Brazilian Baptists in the United States began noticing early on that the number of Brazilian Baptist churches across their new nation was growing. They also realized that the SBC, to which most of these churches were affiliated, did not satisfy their need for what they understood as authentic partnerships and cooperation. Chapter 4 deals with the association created by Brazuca churches to fill this gap. I call this development "ethnic denominationalism," which is the organization of ethnically based associations that act as the de facto places of denominational activity for immigrant communities. This is neither exclusive to nor even original among Brazilian Baptist immigrants. Yet these churches are fully aware that the practices and beliefs they contemplate from within the boundaries of their ethnic denominationalism represent a potential threat to the relationship between them and their official denomination, namely, the SBC.

The way in which the overwhelming presence of undocumented parishioners shapes the beliefs and practices of these communities is the topic of chapter 5. The great majority of Brazilian immigrants in the United States are undocumented, a fact that challenges their pastors—who are sometimes undocumented themselves—to change their perception and stance on immigration policy and associated legal issues.

The influx of Pentecostal migrants into Brazilian Baptist churches in the United States and the prominence of woman leaders in these communities also challenge these churches to revisit the traditional beliefs and practices of their denomination. Chapter 6 documents how these issues have been changing Brazilian Baptist churches in the United States in comparison to both the BBC and the SBC. In significant ways, Brazilian Baptists in the United States are pentecostalized and have signaled acceptance of the ordination of women, differentiating them from their previous and current official national convention. Although the disposition of Brazilian Baptists in Brazil is already more Pentecostal-friendly and more accepting of the ordination of women than that of the SBC, the migration dynamics resulting in a stronger acceptance of Pentecostalism and women's ordination are peculiar to Brazilian Baptists in the United States.

In the seventh and last chapter, I argue that *Migrational Religion*, beyond contributing the narrative of an important transnational religious network, offers a more ambitious input to the scholarly literature. By looking closely at a particular transnational religious network—paying special attention to people dealing with the crises of labor migrations—this work shows how incipient immigrant theologies arise in religious communities as responses to practical, quotidian struggles of unbelonging. Academic contextual theologies that are produced in relative isolation from these struggles tend to construct ideas that incorporate the experiences of others into an individual's articulation of theological truth. But theological development in immigrant communities on the ground does not follow the same pattern. Without leisure, academic training, and access to vehicles of cultural production, the incipient theologies that take shape within these communities try to balance their appreciation for their theological traditions with practical challenges that have to be negotiated within a volatile, unknown world from which spring both much suffering and much creativity. As such, *Migrational Religion* speaks not only of transnational religious movements but also of elements of theological development.

The always-changing landscape of immigrant life pushes immigrants to look for theological maps that may guide them in their new countries. More often than not, they do not find satisfactory maps drawn by the cartographers who articulated the official theologies of their respective traditions. The unanswered longings of immigrant Christians in the United States do not necessarily drive them to write traditional theology. Rather, sometimes even without noticing, immigrants develop incipient theologies that are directly correlated to their experiences of migration. These immigrants, itinerant cartographers themselves, are faced with the need to make sense of their new reality, which includes personal and communal dynamics. The following pages trace the history of how migration and theological unbelonging feed each other in a particular religious network of the Latinx diaspora.

2
REVERSING

The United States in the Latin American Evangelical Story

As a matter of reality, American missionaries and representatives of the Rockefeller Foundation have done more than any other group of people from this country to represent the better elements of our culture to the Brazilian people and win their admiration and friendship for the United States. The Baptist Foreign Mission Board, which represents five million Baptists, has invested millions of dollars in buildings for colleges, schools and churches, and this has been done under the direction of the missionaries who have lived among the people on a meager salary, learned their language and won their love and respect.

Asa R. Crabtree[1]

While the missionaries were here in Brazil, they ruled as they pleased. Part of this domination came to them in the form of "instruction" from the churches in the Southern United States, for which they were emissaries.

João Pedro Gonçalves Araújo[2]

The story of the Italian-born former Roman Catholic priest Giuseppe Piani is a poignant example of how aggressively the Southern Baptist gospel crossed borders. Piani converted to the Baptist faith in Brazil, and Southern

---

[1]   Letter from A. R. Crabtree to the Honorable Cordell Hull, secretary of state, November 29, 1941, International Mission Board Archives, Richmond, Va.
[2]   João Pedro Gonçalves Araújo, *Batistas: Dominação e Dependência* (São Paulo: Fonte Editorial, 2015), 14.

Baptist missionaries of the early 1900s saw in him not only the symbolic value of having a former Catholic priest among their ranks but also the value of having a well-educated individual with much potential. They helped Piani go to William Jewell College in Liberty, Missouri, with the intention of training him into the Southern Baptist mentality. From the United States, Piani wrote a number of letters that were published in the *Jornal Batista*—the most important publication in Brazilian Baptist life.

In a letter sent in 1906, published in a section of the journal dedicated to his numerous descriptions of his experiences in the United States, Piani showed how he had internalized notions of US exceptionalism that were common not only in the that country but also in Southern Baptist missions in Latin America. He wrote:

> What can I tell you? Oh, beloved brothers, there are so many wonders I see that my pen refuses to describe. . . . Oh! Brothers, I would like all of you to come to the United States so that you could understand what it means to be faithful to God and to be a humble and faithful Christian who is dedicated to the cause.[3]

Piani would go on to study at Southern Baptist Theological Seminary in Louisville, Kentucky, and to join the SBC's Home Mission Board. As a highly educated, multilingual convert from Catholicism, Piani became an influential voice in Southern Baptist life in the United States.

Piani's work on the Home Mission Board focused on the SBC's efforts to convert/Americanize European immigrants to the United States. Never wavering from his commitment to US exceptionalism, Piani, who changed his name to Joseph Plainfield, wrote in his 1938 book *The Stranger within Our Gate*:

> Let us discover the fields of foreign concentration in our Southland. Let us localize and immunize the foci of possible moral and spiritual poisoning and infection that are undermining the stamina of our native population and lowering the standards of American life. Finally, let us determine what ought to be the approach of the Home Mission Board and of the churches to the problems confronting America and the Gospel among the foreigners. The answer to the above will determine the right of America to continue to exist as a great spiritual democracy in the midst of a world that is seething and foaming in the shoals and vortex of human passions and the right of Christianity to march forward in the name of Christ.[4]

[3]   José Piani, "Carta de Liberty," *Jornal Batista* VI, no. 24 (1906): 6
[4]   Joseph Frank Plainfield, *The Stranger within Our Gates* (Atlanta: Home Mission Board of the Southern Baptist Convention, 1938), 100.

This perception of the United States as the strongest locus of authentic Christianity was the rule in Southern Baptist missions, not the exception.

Both the alleged superiority of Southern Baptist seminaries, English-speaking intellectuals, and translated literature and the presence of Southern Baptist men in positions of leadership in the United States and abroad became normalized features of the modus operandi of the Brazilian Baptist Convention. Viewed through this prism, the United States was a promised land, a place that represented not only an ideal geographical location for theological education but also an idealized example to be followed by all. As time went on, however, the United States began to be perceived increasingly as a growing mission field. This perception did not develop suddenly in the BBC. The long history of Brazilian Baptist activity in the United States primed the imagination of both the BBC and Southern Baptists in such a way that by the time the Brazilians sent their first missionary to the United States in the 1980s, the event was perceived as a momentous but natural development. Transnational religious entrepreneurs who were trained to see the SBC as a beacon of light in a fallen world, as Giuseppe Piani had, became more common in the US religious market around the last decades of the twentieth century. Unlike Piani, however, not all remained committed to an unqualified appreciation of the SBC during the course of their pilgrimage within the United States.

In this chapter I trace the presence of Brazilian Baptist transnationals in the United States from the time when the majority were individual ministers in primarily national communities to the official appointment of the first Brazilian Baptist missionary to the country. More specifically, I trace the presence of Brazilian Baptists who studied and worked in the United States before the WMB appointed a missionary to Newark in 1981. The various articles published in the *Jornal Batista* both helped to shape the Brazilian missionary imagination in regard to Brazilian presence in the United States and to bring awareness to the massive presence of Portuguese immigrants on the East Coast. By providing an account of these articles, I show how the denomination perceived Brazilian Baptist presence in the United States before 1981.

The presence of Brazilians in the United States is not something new. Brazilian social, religious, and intellectual elites have been traveling to the United States for business, pleasure, and education for over a century. Brazilian Baptists have, at times, been part of these elites and as such benefited from the mobility generally associated with privileged groups. Perhaps the most famous instance of this phenomenon is former Baptist intellectual Gilberto Freyre, whose father taught at North Brazil Baptist Theological Seminary and whose Baptist connections landed him a scholarship at Baylor

University in 1918. After attending Baylor, Freyre studied anthropology at Columbia University and became one of Brazil's leading intellectuals. He left the Baptist ranks while studying at Baylor because of his negative impression of the way in which Southern Baptists treated African Americans, but his presence in the United States was facilitated by his initial Baptist affiliation.[5] Brazilian Baptists also came to the United States specifically to attend Baptist seminaries; some subsequently stayed on to work for denominational institutions and local churches as music ministers, youth pastors, and even senior pastors.

Despite the presence of Brazilian Baptist elites in the United States before the mass migration of Brazilians to the country in the 1980s, the rise in the numbers of Brazuca Baptist churches is a direct result of this later phenomenon.[6] At the same time, the connections and networks that were created before Brazilian mass migration are important in their own right. The *Jornal Batista* often showcased Brazilian Baptist success—even if only individual success, such as Freyre's—in the United States. Such exposure, in turn, encouraged the intentional involvement of Brazilian foreign missions in the country. Central to the appointment of the first official Brazilian missionary to the United States, for instance, were articles published in the *Jornal Batista* that documented the overwhelming presence of Portuguese immigrants on the East Coast. The Brazilian mission to reach the Portuguese in Canada was another element in this enterprise. The increase in the numbers of Brazilian Baptist transnationals thus was undeniably paved by the presence of the Portuguese in the Brazilian Baptist missionary imagination—one whose

---

[5] João B. Chaves, *O Racismo na História Batista Brasileira: Uma Memória Inconveniente do Legado Missionário* (Brasília: Novos Dialogos, 2020).

[6] For the purposes of this project, the term "Brazuca" will be used to name Brazilian and Brazilian American individuals and communities that are in the United States but whose identity is strongly informed by aspects of Brazilian culture. The term was first used by José Victor Bicalho in his pioneering 1989 work on Brazilian immigrants in the United States (see Bicalho, *Yes, Eu Sou Brazuca ou a Vida do Imigrante Brasileiro nos Estados Unidos da América* [Governador Valadares: Fundação Serviços de Educação e Cultura, 1989]). Since the publication of Bicalho's work, a number of other academic pieces have used the term in their analysis and even in publication titles (see Annie McNeil Gibson, *Post-Katrina Brazucas: Brazilian Immigrants in New Orleans* [New Orleans, La.: University of New Orleans Press, 2012]; Clémence Jouët-Pastré and Leticia J. Braga, eds., *Becoming Brazuca: Brazilian Immigration to the United States* [Cambridge, Mass.: David Rockefeller Center for Latin American Studies, 2008]; A. Tosta, "Latino, Eu? The Paradoxical Interplay of Identity in Brazuca Literature," *Hispania* 87, no. 3 [2004]: 576–85). The term originated within the community itself, with Brazilian immigrants in New England using it to self-describe as Brazilians living in the condition of hybridity in the United States.

central disposition can be encapsulated in a hypothetical battle cry: "Save the Catholic colonizer!"[7]

This initial desire to reach the Portuguese immigrant community eventually dissipated, and the search for Portuguese proselytes soon gave way to the desire to make new Brazilian church members. While Brazilian mass migration was not on the BBC's radar when they sent their missionary in 1981, once it became a significant and noticeable phenomenon, the means through which Brazuca Baptist faith communities arose became differentiated and transcended a strict denominational genealogy. Soon after their initial emergence, Brazuca Baptist churches stopped being closely managed either by the convention in Brazil or by other initiatives that had the Portuguese as their primary object; at the same time, they ceased limiting their modus operandi to the quotidian machinations of the US denominations to which they became affiliated. Thus, an initiative of traditional missionary character, channeled through the centralized missions agency of the BBC, began to be more powerfully informed by looser migrant networks, which included but were by no means limited to the denominational affiliations that regimented aspects of their ambiguous belonging to United States denominational bodies. These communities emerged in different ways and at times functioned as a magnet for Brazilian immigrants from various backgrounds who sought, in these faith communities, relief from their anxieties of displacement. Here, the mystical, the psychological, and the social needs of the parishioners were addressed in ways that placed the immigration experience at the center of the communities' mission. As time progressed and the immigration of Brazilians to the United States diminished because of global economic dynamics, Brazuca Baptist churches began to negotiate their "Brazilianness" and to move toward the implementation of a multinational vision.

Brazilian Baptist Presence in the United States before Mass Migration

Brazilian Baptists have been coming to the United States to study and to preach since the first decades of Southern Baptist presence in Brazil. Denominational leader F. F. Soren, for instance, was already studying at Southern Baptist Seminary in Louisville in the late 1800s and, upon his return to Brazil, became a

---

[7] Although I have not emphasized the theme of anti-Catholicism in this manuscript, it is important to recognize the long history of mutual Catholic-Protestant antagonism in Brazil. As a matter of fact, a significant drive in Protestant missions to Latin America presupposed competition with Roman Catholics. For a recent history of Catholic/Protestant conflict, see Erika Helgen, *Religious Conflict in Brazil: Protestants, Catholics, and the Rise of Religious Pluralism in the Early Twentieth Century* (New Haven, Conn.: Yale University Press, 2020).

major player in Brazilian denominational life.[8] C. D. Daniel, who migrated to Brazil as child as part of the Confederate groups who emigrated after the Civil War, came back to the United States to work among Mexicans and Mexican Americans in Texas.[9] The aforementioned former priest Giuseppe Piani came to the United States in the early 1900s and wrote many letters to the *Jornal Batista*.[10] Three leaders of the nationalist movement that led to the split in the denomination in the 1920s—Adrião Bernades, Orlando Falcão, and Antônio Mesquita—were graduates of Baptist schools in Texas.[11] Also in the 1920s, missionary João Loja began writing chronicles of Baptist work among Portuguese-speaking immigrants in New England.[12] Key Brazilian Baptist figures, such as João Soren and Nilson Fanini, not only studied but also traveled to the United States several times as presidents of the Baptist World Alliance. Still, despite the continuous presence of the United States in Brazilian Baptist life, it is only in the late 1960s that consistent reports on the whereabouts and accomplishments of Brazilian Baptist leaders in the United States begin to appear in the *Jornal Batista*.

Brazilian Baptists who showed promise as preachers or potential scholars were at times recruited by SBC missionaries to study in the United States.[13] They were given scholarships to pursue master's, doctoral, or doctor of ministry programs. Upon their return, these graduates were often

---

[8] Catalogue of Southern Baptist Theological Seminary (Louisville, 1900), 11. F. F. Soren became so prominent in Brazilian Baptist life—primarily as a pro-missionary figure—that SBC missionary L. M. Bratcher wrote a biography of the Brazilian pastor. See Bratcher, *Francisco Fulgencio Soren: Christ's Interpreter to Many Lands* (Nashville: Broadman, 1938).

[9] David J. Cameron traced C. D. Daniel's career in Texas and argues that although Daniel was the first president of the Mexican Baptist Convention, he was also a member of the KKK who learned in Brazil to think about Latin Americans as inferior peoples. See Cameron, "Race and Religion in the Bayou City: Latino/a, African-American, and Anglo Baptists in Houston's Long Civil Rights Movement" (Ph.D. diss., Texas A&M University, 2017).

[10] Piani, "Carta de Liberty," 6; idem, "Impressões de um Ex-Catholico nos Estados Unidos II: O Colégio William Jewell," *Jornal Batista* VII, no. 15 (1907): 2; idem, "Carta dos Estados Unidos," *Jornal Batista* VII, no. 39 (1907): 3; idem, "Observações de um Ex-Catholico nos Estados Unidos," *Jornal Batista* VII, no. 21 (1907): 5; idem, "Carta dos Estados Unidos," *Jornal Batista* VIII, no. 2 (1908): 5.

[11] See João Chaves and C. Douglas Weaver, "Baptists and Their Polarizing Ways: Transnational Polarization between Southern Baptist Missionaries and Brazilian Baptists," *Review & Expositor* 116, no. 2 (2019): 160–74.

[12] João G. Loja, "Cronica Norte-Americana," *Jornal Batista* XIX, no. 23 (1920): 8–10; João G. Loja, "Cronica Norte-Americana: O Movimento Mundial entre as Egrejas," *Jornal Batista* XIX, no. 27 (1920): 13–14.

[13] João Chaves, *The Global Mission of the Jim Crow South* (Macon, Ga.: Mercer University Press, forthcoming).

considered to be the future of the denomination because of their training in the United States. By the late 1960s the presence of Brazilian Baptists at these denominational schools was so habitual that an article in the *Jornal Batista* claimed that

> the presence of Brazilian students in the United States is already common. They are young workers who want to be better prepared to serve the Cause. They go there to study—many with much sacrifice—specialize, and come back. They come back with a broader vision of the Baptist work and with more competence to serve the cause of Jesus Christ.[14]

Students in Baptist schools in the United States sent reports with information about their progress and graduation that were printed in the *Jornal Batista*. Studying in the United States was, for Brazilians in general and Brazilian Baptists in particular, a badge of honor, and the *Jornal Batista* printed news coming from schools such as Southern Baptist Theological Seminary, Baylor University, William Jewell College, Southwestern Baptist Theological Seminary, New Orleans Baptist Theological Seminary, and Ouachita Baptist University.[15]

The Brazilian Baptist presence before mass migration, however, was not limited to students in Baptist institutions. Évio Oliveira, for instance, had been a music minister in the southern United States since 1951; in 1968, while serving as music minister of Eastside Baptist Church in Marietta, Georgia, he released an album entitled *He Leadeth Me*.[16] Pastor Valdeci Alves da Silva also ministered in the United States, but unlike Oliveira, he served as lead pastor in Mexican churches in the Corpus Christi area between 1967 and 1971, when, upon graduating from Corpus Christi University, he planned to go to Southwestern Baptist Theological Seminary for his master's degree.[17] In the 1960s Dylton Francioni pastored the Spanish-speaking Misión Bautista in Itasca, Texas, while pursuing his master's degree at Southwestern Seminary.

---

[14] "Estudantes Brasileiros nos Estados Unidos," *Jornal Batista* LXVII, no. 48 (1967): 1.

[15] Werner Kaschel, "Brasileiros em Louisville," *Jornal Batista* LXVIII, no. 29 (1968): 7; "Brasileiros Se Formam em Fort Worth–U.S.A," *Jornal Batista* LXXI, no. 2 (1970): 2; Joelcio Rodrigues Barreto, "A Colônia Brasileira em Arkaddelphia," *Jornal Batista* LXXI, no. 43 (1971): 12; Daniel Paixão, "O Maior Número de Fromandos na História do Southwestern Seminary," *Jornal Batista* LXXIV, no. 31 (1974): 8; Joelcio Rodrigues Barreto, "O Maior Seminário do Mundo," *Jornal Batista* 70, no. 11 (n.d.): 8; Roberto Alves de Souza, "Seminário de Louisville: Quinze Anos de Crescimento," *Jornal Batista* LXXV, no. 46 (1975): 8; Adlai de Freitas Pacheco, "Posse do Pastor Dr. Dylton Francioni de Abreu, na Igreja Batista Dois de Julho," *Jornal Batista* LXXX, no. 27 (1980): 6.

[16] "Brasileiro Grava L.P. Nos EE. UU.," *Jornal Batista* LXVIII, no. 12 (1968): 5.

[17] Joelcio Rodrigues Barreto, "Um Brasileiro, Pastor de Igrejas Mexicanas," *Jornal Batista* LXXI, no. 7 (1971): 12.

He then moved to New Orleans to pursue a doctorate at New Orleans Baptist Theological Seminary. While in New Orleans, Francioni founded the Spanish-speaking Iglesia Bautista Latino Americana, which he pastored until 1972.[18] In 1974 he was called to pastor the Portuguese Evangelistic Baptist Church in Fall River, Massachusetts. When he visited the church, he preached in Portuguese and English but ultimately declined the invitation to pastor the community.[19] Francioni then pastored two English-speaking churches in Louisiana; namely, New Hope Baptist Church in Folsom and First Baptist Church in Abbeville. When Francioni returned to Brazil to pastor Igreja Batista Dois de Julho in 1980, he had accumulated a number of honorary titles: honorary citizen of New Orleans, honorary citizen of New Iberia, and honorary colonel of the state of Louisiana.[20]

Brazilian Baptist pastors, at times, toured the United States, preaching in churches and conducting evangelistic crusades. In 1969 Ben Pitrowsky reported various evangelistic efforts by seven Brazilian Baptist pastors. The *Jornal Batista* published eight reports authored by Pitrowsky, who understood their preaching events in the United States in terms of returning the favor of evangelism to the Southern Baptists who had done missions work in Brazil. He wrote that the seven Brazilian Baptist preachers "entered the United States to preach the same Gospel that, around eighty years ago, was announced to us for the first time by a North American."[21] Nilson Fanini, the famous Brazilian denominational leader, was mentioned in a number of reports to the *Jornal Batista* that told stories of his experiences in the United States to the Brazilian Baptist audience.[22] In one of these reports, correspondent Daniel Paixão, then a doctoral student at Southwestern Seminary, wrote of an event at which Fanini was the keynote speaker, during which seminary president Robert Naylor proclaimed that Brazil was the new Antioch, the place from where missionaries were going out to evangelize the world.[23]

Nilson Dimárzio, who authored a number of reports on Brazilian pastors in the United States published in the *Jornal Batista*, pastored a church in Port

[18] Pacheco, "Posse do Pastor Dr. Dylton Francioni de Abreu," 6.

[19] Nilson Dimárzio, "Na Terra do Tio Sam," *Jornal Batista* LXXIV, no. 31 (1974): 2; Nilson Dimárzio, "Da Terra de Tio Sam X," *Jornal Batista* LXXIV, no. 36 (1974): 2.

[20] Pacheco, "Posse do Pastor Dr. Dylton Francioni de Abreu," 6.

[21] Ben Pitrowsky, "Pastores Batistas Brasileiros Pregam nos Estados Unidos I," *Jornal Batista* LXIX, no. 23 (1969): 5.

[22] "Pastor Nilson Fanini, de Volta aos Estados Unidos, Conta o Que Viu," *Jornal Batista* LXIX, no. 27 (1969): 5; Daniel Paixão, "Nilson Fanini Retorna ao Southwestern," *Jornal Batista* LXXVI, no. 16 (1976): 6.

[23] Paixão, "Nilson Fanini Retorna ao Southwestern," 8.

Lavaca, Texas.[24] Dimárzio mentioned the presence of Dr. Ivan Pitzer de Souza, a pastor and professional counselor who had a counseling practice in Mobile, Alabama, and often preached to sailors in town.[25] Souza was not the only example of Brazilian Baptists performing functions outside traditional church ministry in the United States. The couple Denise and Olavo Feijó, for instance, worked in educational institutions. They arrived in Texas in 1961, and Denise worked as a librarian at Southwestern Seminary while Olavo worked on his doctorate in education. He later taught at Texas Wesleyan College from 1964 to 1966, when he was hired by Weatherford College to teach psychology and philosophy.[26] The *Jornal Batista* also mentioned pastor Amélio Giannetta, who was hired by East Texas Baptist College in Marshall, Texas, to teach evangelism and missions in 1978.[27] But no Brazilian Baptist in the United States got as much attention from the *Jornal Batista* before the first Brazilian Baptist missionary came to the country as pastor Elias Gomes.

Elias Manuel Gomes went to New York City in 1966 to study at New York University (NYU) and, after graduating, started working toward his doctorate in philosophy at Columbia University.[28] Gomes served as a correspondent for the *Jornal Batista*, writing regularly on many topics, including major developments in the SBC; at the same time, he often appeared as the subject of articles, reports, and interviews within the journal's pages.[29]

[24] Dimárzio, "Da Terra de Tio Sam X," 2.

[25] Nilson Dimárzio, "Da Terra de Tio Sam IX," *Jornal Batista* LXXIV, no. 35 (1974): 2.

[26] Paulo C. Porter, "Um Missionário Brasileiro aos Academicos Americanos," *Jornal Batista* LXXI, no. 24 (1971): 2.

[27] William De Souza, "Pastor Amélio Giannetta, um Homem de Deus," *Jornal Batista* LXXVII, no. 36 (1978): 4.

[28] "Entrevista com Nosso Correspondente em Nova Iorque," *Jornal Batista* LXXVI, no. 23 (1976): 1.

[29] Elias M. Gomes, "Onde 'Todo Passado É Prólogo': Visita ao Q. G. de Dwight L. Moody," *Jornal Batista* LXVII, no. 53 (n.d.): 8; idem, "A Mente e os Olhos," *Jornal Batista* LXVIII, no. 20 (1968): 8; idem, "A Convenção Batista do Sul: Últimos Flashes," *Jornal Batista* LXXII, no. 33 (1972): 8; idem, "A Convenção Batista do Sul," *Jornal Batista* LXXIII, no. 29 (1973): 8; idem, "A Convenção Batista do Sul: Fatos e Personalidades Que Impressionam," *Jornal Batista* LXXIII, no. 33 (1973): 8; idem, "Um Preambulo Espetacular (A Convenção do Sul—1974)," *Jornal Batista* LXXIV, no. 27 (1974): 8; idem, "The Southern Baptist Convention: Dallas—Texas—11 a 13 de Junho," *Jornal Batista* LXXIV, no. 28 (1974): 8; idem, "O Primeiro Preto em 129 Anos: A Nova Diretoria da Southern Baptist Convention," *Jornal Batista* LXXIV, no. 29 (1974): 8; idem, "A Convenção do Sul em Fatos e Figuras," *Jornal Batista* LXXIV, no. 30 (1974): 12; idem, "Chales Colson—Um Testemunho Inolvidável," *Jornal Batista* LXXV, no. 29 (1975): 8; idem, "Ressoa o Sino da Liberdade: A 188a Assembéia da Convenção do Sul," *Jornal Batista* LXXV, no. 28 (1975): 7–8; idem, "Fatos Memoráveis: A 188a Assembléia da Convenção do Sul," *Jornal Batista* LXXV, no. 30 (1975): 12.

While in New York, Gomes began to co-pastor an Anglo-American Baptist church in Clifton, New Jersey—an event that was celebrated as "a miracle" by J. Reis Pereira, director of the *Jornal Batista*.[30] In 1971 Gomes was called to be senior pastor of Living Gospel Baptist Church, a predominantly Anglo-American church in Rutherford, New Jersey.[31] In 1974 he wrote to the *Jornal Batista* celebrating his East Coast success but also pointing to the number of Portuguese immigrants in the region. Talking about his experience in Rutherford, Gomes wrote:

> The racial and ethnic makeup [at Living Gospel Baptist Church] is "*bossa nova*." Starting with 12 members three years ago, and now with more than 100—new believers in Christ—the church is mostly comprised of Anglos, but with a good number of Latinos, Asians, Jews, Africans, etc. . . . And it is certainly something strange seeing a pastor with dark skin leading a flock in the United States with a majority of whites. This is also a divine miracle.[32]

He elaborated that "there are around thirty thousand Portuguese and Brazilian people in the close-by city of Newark, and a good number of similar communities around us."[33] Gomes also wrote that his church had ten new Portuguese converts, and that he was going to start a Sunday school class in Portuguese for them.[34]

Although Gomes acknowledged and reported the presence of Portuguese and Brazilian people in his area, he saw himself as a pastor for the nations with a broader appeal and reach in English, rather than as someone who wanted to lead an ethnic congregation. In writing for the *Jornal Batista*, he at times highlighted particular members of his congregation, such as Leo Fichtelberg. Fichtelberg was a Jewish man who directed the Public Library System in Paterson, New Jersey. Gomes dedicated one of his reports solely to Fichtelberg, calling him the Nicodemus of Living Gospel Baptist Church.[35] He saw in Fichtelberg a door to convert Jewish people to Christianity.[36]

---

[30] J. Reis Pereira, "Um Milagre em Nova Jersey," *Jornal Batista* LXXI, no. 39 (1971): 5.

[31] "Pastor Brasileiro de Igreja Batista nos Estados Unidos Visita o Brasil," *Jornal Batista* LXXII, no. 34 (1972): 1–2.

[32] Elias M. Gomes, "Portugal Acontece na Living Gospel," *Jornal Batista* LXXIV, no. 45 (1974): 8.

[33] Gomes, "Portugal Acontece," 8.

[34] Gomes, "Portugal Acontece," 8.

[35] Elias M. Gomes, "Um Novo 'Nicodemus' na Living Gospel: Os Judeus para Cristo," *Jornal Batista* LXXVI, no. 3 (1976): 4.

[36] Gomes, "Um Novo 'Nicodemus,'" 4, 8.

Between 1974 and 1976, Living Gospel Baptist Church doubled its size and offered activities in three languages: English, Portuguese, and Spanish. Gomes reported the new developments thus:

> We have around twenty Brazilians and Portuguese in our Portuguese language department. We offer Sunday School classes in Portuguese for them, and our church has audio phones that allow us to translate English to Portuguese for those who wish to listen to the sermon and other parts of worship in their language. We have at least three Brazilians who are able to do simultaneous translation. We also have many Puerto Ricans and Cubans and a Spanish language department.[37]

In 1977 Gomes went to the Los Angeles area to pastor Village Baptist Church in Norwalk, California.[38] Village Baptist Church had around five hundred members, mostly Anglo-Americans but some Brazilians. In an interview with the *Jornal Batista* in 1979, Gomes was asked what he thought about Baptist work directed to Portuguese and Brazilian immigrants in the United States. He answered that he did not have the time to engage immigrants directly, but that the WMB—the official foreign missionary board of the BBC—should implement such activities, with the board's work in Canada as a model.[39] Gomes, in terms of his explicit self-perception, operated similarly to any other SBC pastor in the area and did not see himself as a pastor for immigrant or even ethnic churches.

The success of Brazilian pastors in the United States as students, itinerant evangelists, senior ministers, music ministers, or college teachers was in evidence in the *Jornal Batista* and certainly had an effect on the imagination of Brazilian Baptists who considered doing missionary work in the land of Southern Baptists. The examples of ministers such as Elias Gomes, Dylton Francioni, Nilson Dimárzio, and others emboldened Brazilian Baptists' sense of potential in regard to their performance in the United States. In addition, reports of the significant Portuguese immigrant communities became a constant feature of the *Jornal Batista* after the late 1960s. Beyond the mention of Portuguese presence in the reports of pastors such as Gomes, Fancioni, and Dimárzio, other articles highlighted the presence of Portuguese immigrants in general and in the East Coast and California regions

---

[37] "Entrevista com Nosso Correspondente em Nova Iorque," 1.
[38] "Um Pastor Batista em Los Angeles," *Jornal Batista* LXXVII, no. 28 (1977): 1; J. Reis Pereira, "Los Angeles, Finalmente!" *Jornal Batista* LXXVIII, no. 41 (1978): 12.
[39] "Pastor Brasileiro de Igreja Norte-Americana," *Jornal Batista* LXXIX, no. 21 (1979): 1, 12.

in particular.[40] Before 1981, however, the success of Brazilian denominational workers in the United States was manifested in SBC ministries that were focused mostly on Anglo-American and Hispanic-American (non-Brazilian, Spanish-speaking) parishioners.

In addition to reports of Brazilian success in the United States and the growing Portuguese migrant presence, between the late 1970s and early 1980s the *Jornal Batista* was intentionally engaged in a twofold propaganda campaign: reporting the success of the Canadian mission to the Portuguese, which began in 1978,[41] and opening up space for making the United States an official WMB mission field. In March 1981, for instance, the journal published an article by missionary Joel F. Oliveira, who lamented the fact that there were so few Brazilian missionaries in the "unbelieving nations" of France and Canada.[42] In February of the same year, also in the *Jornal Batista*, the president of the WMB, Waldemiro Tymchak, attempted to justify Brazilian involvement in mission efforts in developed nations. He wrote:

> Of the 68 workers we have today, 14 are in countries that are considered developed. So, 20% are in countries of better social standing. And the reason we are in at least two of those is the huge Portuguese colony that needs Jesus Christ, and that would not have anyone to preach to them except the Brazilians.[43]

The majority of Brazilian foreign missionaries were in Portugal, which had been appropriated as a suitable missionary field through Southern Baptist influence; when it came to Spain, Brazilian Baptists had been involved in Spanish-speaking missions for many decades, and thus their presence in that country did not draw much criticism. The justification for sending Brazilian Baptist missionaries to developed nations of non-Spanish-speaking populations was then dependent on a convincing argument that established the absolute necessity of Brazilian Baptist missionary action for the sake of the "helpless" Portuguese migrant.

Legitimizing another field in a developed nation was not easy for the WMB, but all the pieces were working together for the establishment of a Brazilian

[40] Herondias N. Cavalcanti, "De New Bedford, Massachusetts, para Portugal," *Jornal Batista* LXXX, no. 31 (1980): 8; Paulo Elias de Sá, "Evangelização dos Portugueses na América, um Desafio Permanente," *Jornal Batista* LXXX, no. 40 (1981): 8.

[41] "Nosso Missionário no Canadá É Notícia," *Jornal Batista* LXXIX, no. 11 (1979): 1; Waldemiro Tymchak, "Porque Estamos Também no Canadá," *Jornal Batista* LXXXI, no. 5 (1981): 2; Erno Engelsdorf, "Por Quê Missões no Canadá?" *Jornal Batista* LXXX, no. 13 (1980): 4.

[42] Joel F. Oliveira, "Missões Mundiais: Uma Obra Incontestável," *Jornal Batista*, March 1981, 13.

[43] Waldemiro Tymchak, "Porque Estamos," 5.

mission in the United States. Copious reports of the success of Brazilian Baptists had been printed in the *Jornal Batista* since the late 1960s, the growing presence of the Brazilians' original foreign missions subject in the United States—the Portuguese—was being constantly reported, and the work among Portuguese immigrants in another developed non-Spanish-speaking country, Canada, was being perceived as a success. The seeds for Brazilian Baptist missionary presence in the United States were sown and would bear fruit on the East Coast.

In 1981 an article in the *Jornal Batista* explained in three easy steps why the WMB should send a Brazilian missionary to the United States. First, Walnut Street Baptist Church in Newark, New Jersey, was asking the WMB for a missionary because it was attempting to reach the local Portuguese population. The neighborhood in which the church was located had become primarily Portuguese, and the church thought that a Brazilian missionary would be ideal for the task of evangelizing them. The WMB just needed to select and test the candidate; the church would pay for the salary, residence, and a car. Second, even before the WMB began to search actively for a candidate, a successful and respected Brazilian pastor came forward and volunteered for the job, an event that the board took as evidence of God's providence. Finally, neglecting to act on the call of the church and the willingness of the pastor—who, according to the article, pastored one of the best churches in the city of São Paulo—was, for the WMB, tantamount to neglecting the Christian responsibility to act on what God commanded. The article stated, "The WMB is more interested in Latin American countries, as all of you know. But we can't neglect a situation that is so clearly an expression of the divine will."[44] In the following month, the board announced that Humberto Viegas Fernandes was going to Newark "in order to work in the evangelization of the Portuguese colony in that city and state."[45]

On September 20, 1981, Fernandes became the nineteenth senior pastor of Walnut Street Baptist Church. According to Fernandes, the celebration of his inauguration was held "in front of a numerous gathering of North Americans, Portuguese, Cubans, Spaniards, and Brazilians, not to mention representatives of other peoples."[46] But Walnut Street was a congregation with a particular migrant history, having been founded as Second Baptist Church of Newark in the first half of the nineteenth century by German immigrants. By 1981 it was time to emphasize the Portuguese language owing to the demographic

[44] J. Reis Pereira, "Missionário Brasileiro nos Estados Unidos?" *Jornal Batista* LXXXI, no. 10 (1981): 3.

[45] "O Primeiro Missionário Batista Brasileiro aos Estados Unidos," *Jornal Batista* LXXXI, no. 23 (1981): 1.

[46] Humberto Viegas, "Missionário Brasileiro na América do Norte," *Jornal Batista* LXXXI, no. 50 (1981): 16.

shifts in Newark in general and in the church's neighborhood in particular. The minutes and documents of the church are a testimony to its contextual creativity. They begin in German, transition into English, move into European Portuguese, and are currently written by Brazilian immigrants.

At Fernandes' inauguration, there was an interesting mix of Baptist representation at Walnut Street. Fred Folkerts, the general secretary of missions for the North American Baptist Conference,[47] was present, as was a former interim Brazilian pastor, Rubens Domingues, who had been affiliated with the Brazilian Regular Baptists. Waldemiro Tymchak, then president of the WMB, an institution historically and ideologically connected to the SBC, sent a letter that was read during the service. And it was certainly the Southern Baptists that Fernandes had in mind, particularly William Buck Bagby, when he said in his report that Walnut Street Baptist Church, "after a century of its organization and, coincidentally, a century after the arrival of the first Baptist missionaries in Brazil, opened its doors under the leadership of a Brazilian Baptist pastor for the sake of the evangelization of the millions of Portuguese people living in the United States."[48] The official Brazilian Baptist mission in the United States had started, and it was a thoroughly Southern Baptist–inspired endeavor.

Fernandes wrote several reports to the *Jornal Batista* from New Jersey letting the Brazilian Baptist audience know of his progress at Walnut Street. One of the first letters showed how he perceived the new mission field of the WMB. The piece was entitled "Letters from New Jersey: Missions in Return."[49] In it, Fernandes talked about the Bagbys, who had gone to Brazil a century before he arrived at Walnut Street, and highlighted the fact that he saw his presence in the United States as a new phase in the history of Brazilian Baptists. Fernandes echoed the words of Waldemiro Tymchak, in writing that "the arrival of a missionary couple in the United States of America inaugurates a new era in our Brazilian Baptist history: 'Mission in Return,' as it was well described by our president."[50] Fernandes later wrote that most of the Anglo-American families who had historically attended the church had moved away, and that those who

---

[47] The North American Baptist Conference was founded in 1865 by German Baptist churches. Originally called the General Conference of German Baptist Churches in North America, it dropped its ethnic identification and adopted its current name in 1944.

[48] Viegas, "Missionário Brasileiro," 10.

[49] Humberto Viegas Fernandes, "Cartas de Nova Jersey: Missões em Retribuição," *Jornal Batista* LXXXII, no. 4 (1982): 16. The Portuguese word *retribuição*, which was used by Fernandes in the article, could be translated as "retribution." However, in Portuguese this word does not necessarily have the connotation of vengeance. In order to translate Fernandes' intentions better, I chose to translate *retribuição* here as "return."

[50] Fernandes, "Missões em Retribuição," 16.

stayed wanted to reach Portuguese immigrants, rather than English-speaking people. While the church provided translation from Portuguese to English, the great majority of the members spoke Portuguese.[51]

Although Fernandes was the official WMB missionary to the United States, there were other Brazilian ministers trying to reach the Portuguese community in California. In 1981 Paulo Elias de Sá reported the struggle of doing so in Chino where he went to join forces with Pr. Gerson Furtado and his wife. Furtado had gone to California to study and had joined First Portuguese Baptist Church in Chino. There, he conducted some work directed at the Brazilian community, but he was concerned primarily with Brazilian university students in the area temporarily, as well as their parents.[52] De Sá wrote to the *Jornal Batista* to ask for prayers so that they could preach the good news to the Portuguese in accordance with the mission "that we received in Brazil, thanks to the missionary vision of our beloved North American brothers."[53] In de Sá's report, one can see glimpses of Brazilian Protestant anti-Catholicism—an element of his Southern Baptist heritage—and Portuguese Catholic anti-Protestantism struggling against each other in the United States religious market. Talking about a Portuguese Catholic procession he had witnessed in California, de Sá stated, "It was a strong manifestation of beauty, elegance, luxury, and money. But what a terrible thing! Too much idolatry! Such paganism! It was St. Fatima's day, and in the heart of an evangelical nation, one could witness a pronounced pagan manifestation. What a difficult challenge for the people of God."[54] Ecumenism was not a Brazilian Baptist strength, and the anti-Protestant violence that was present in Brazilian religious history didn't help in this regard.

In the same report, de Sá told the story of a Portuguese man who converted to the Baptist faith but had his business boycotted by his Catholic Portuguese clientele who were warned by a Portuguese radio program that the "Protestant and communist influences had dominated" the new convert's place of

---

[51] Humberto Viegas Fernandes, "Cartas de New Jersey: Fim de Ano com Boas Novas," *Jornal Batista* LXXXII, no. 8 (1982): 7–8; "Missionário Brasileiro Batiza em New Jersey," *Jornal Batista* LXXXII, no. 8 (1982): 1.

[52] Paulo Elias de Sá, "Pastor Brasileiro Coordena Estudos Religiosos para Estudantes Internacionais," *Jornal Batista* LXXXII, no. 2 (1982): 8. The NBC also reported the presence of a Pr. Joel Ferreira in the United States. Ferreira went back to Brazil in 1982, but he left two Portuguese-speaking churches that he formed while in an unspecified place in the United States. See "Pr. Joel Em Florianópolis," *Batista Nacional*, October 1982, 5.

[53] Paulo Elias de Sá, "Evangelização dos Portugueses na América, um Desafio Permanente," *Jornal Batista* LXXXI, no. 40 (1981): 8.

[54] De Sá, "Evangelização dos Portugueses na América."

business.[55] De Sá's report showed some of the early challenges of reaching the Portuguese community in the United States, but soon Brazilian Baptist missionaries would notice the influx of Brazilian immigrants coming to the country, which would provide new opportunities for Brazilian religious entrepreneurs: they would be able to cater to their own people.

Brazilian Baptist Churches in the United States: The Possibility of Brazilian Members

Brazilian Baptist work in the United States, as the examples of Fernandes and Furtado illustrate, had a multifaceted beginning. Although officially Fernandes was indeed the first denominational missionary sent from Brazil,[56] Furtado and others had already engaged in some ministerial work among Portuguese and Brazilian immigrants without the financial backing of the WMB or explicit support of the SBC. Therefore, one may have to speak of the polygenesis of Brazilian Baptist work in the United States. But one thing is clear in the history of the group: most pioneer Brazilian Baptist missionary-pastors came to the United States (while under Southern Baptist ideological influence) in order to reach the Portuguese community, and only then did the Brazilians—because of their mass migration due to economic and ideological factors—become the focus of Brazilian Baptist missionary and pastoral efforts.

Despite the influx of Brazilian immigrants in the 1980s, the history of Brazuca Baptist churches does not begin with the concerted efforts of the BBC to follow the flow of Brazilian immigrants who were, to quote the famous movie title, "coming to America." As a matter of fact, the BBC never consolidated its institutional presence in the United States as an official mission field of the WMB—as it did with other developed countries such as France, Spain, Portugal, and Canada. In addition, the affiliation of Brazuca Baptist churches with denominational bodies in the United States was characterized more by symbolic importance than by actual cooperation, as their engagement in ethnic denominationalism—which I will narrate later—illustrates.

In their book on Brazilian immigration to the United States, Álvaro Lima and Alanni Castro document the estimated number of Brazilian immigrants in the United States from 1990 to 2014. They reported that, according to the US Census and the American Community Survey, there were 80,485 Brazilian immigrants living in the United States in 1990—mostly concentrated

---

[55] De Sá, "Evangelização dos Portugueses na América."

[56] There were at least two other missionaries sent to the United States by the WMB, but they came to the country only after many Brazuca Baptist churches were formed and, as such, had a limited role in the history of the group.

on the East Coast. This number grew to 212,428 by 2000 and to 359,149 by 2009, the peak year of Brazilian immigration to the United States.[57] These estimates, however, are highly contested, as Lima and Castro themselves admit. The number of undocumented Brazilian immigrants in the United States makes it impossible to provide an official count, and researchers are sometimes accused of underestimating the presence of Brazilian immigrants by as much as 80 percent. The Inter-American Development Bank and the Brazilian Ministry of Foreign Relations, however, generally agree on estimating the number of Brazilians as between 800,000 and 1.4 million people.[58] According to the ministry of foreign relations, as of 2014, Florida, Massachusetts, New York, New Jersey, and California are the states with the largest concentration of Brazilian immigrants; more than 60 percent of Brazilian immigrants live in these states. Florida has an estimated 260,000 Brazilians, Massachusetts has 218,000, New York and New Jersey have 212,000 (more than half of them live in and around the city of Newark), and California has around 125,000 Brazilians.[59] In addition to the complications involved in these estimates, however, one must not lose sight of the fact that Brazilian immigrants also return to their home country in largely unknown numbers. Both estimates of the number of Brazilian immigrants in the United States and of Brazilian Baptists in the country are complicated further by the fact that they do not account for returning migrants, even though the latter are an indispensable part of the networks and interactions they energize.

The most important aspect of wider Brazilian immigration for Brazilian Baptists is that the influx of Brazilian immigrants allowed for the development of religious networks that came to characterize the history of the group.[60] This story is, therefore, characterized more by a network-informed than by an institutionally controlled presence. In other words, the religious entrepreneurial spirit of Brazilian Baptists mostly replaced, in the United States, what was historically the responsibility and monopoly of denominational bodies such as the BBC'S WMB, the Home Mission Board of the SBC, and the SBC's International Mission Board (IMB). What dominated

---

[57] Álvaro Eduardo de Castro Lima and Alanni de Lacerda Barbosa Castro, *Brasileiros nos Estados Unidos: Meio Século (Re)Fazendo a América (1960–2010)* (Brasília: Fundação Alexandre de Gusmão, 2017), 53.

[58] Lima and Castro, *Brasileiros nos Estados Unidos*, 54.

[59] Lima and Castro, *Brasileiros nos Estados Unidos*, 56.

[60] Maxine L. Margolis, *An Invisible Minority: Brazilians in New York City* (Gainesville: University Press of Florida, 2009). Margolis, for example, quotes documentation provided by the Brazilian government and argues that the first wave of immigration began around 1984.

the institutional imagination of these churches was not traditional denominationalism but Brazuca ethnic solidarity, even when such solidarity was practiced from within the resources and language provided by the traditional denominations that informed the self-understanding of leaders and members who named their religious initiatives "Baptist."

This shift is noticeable within Fernandes' trajectory, to which I will return in looking more closely at the group of interconnected Brazuca Baptist churches in the northeastern US states, which I will call the "East Coast Lineage." This group is particularly important and representative because it includes the oldest and most influential churches among Brazilians in the United States. The most prominent ways in which Brazilian Baptist churches have started, historically, take one of five forms: (1) at the initiative of the WMB in conjunction with a US church; (2) spontaneously, that is, a group is formed without formal leadership and only after it is well established does it hire a pastor and become Baptist; (3) a group of Brazilians become members of a predominantly Anglo-American, African American, or Hispanic American church, and the host church helps structure the Brazilian congregation; (4) as a mission or congregation of another Brazilian Baptist church; and (5) as a division of another church. The history of Brazilian Baptists in the United States, therefore, is neither bounded by an easily identifiable genealogy nor limited by a uniform affiliation to institutional structures. It is, however, a function of broader migration dynamics that, beginning in the 1980s, resulted in great numbers of Brazilian people moving to the United States. The story of Brazuca Baptist churches is also dominated by the presence of leaders once affiliated with the BBC, although leaders affiliated with the alternative National Baptist Convention of Brazil (NBC) have had a minor presence in the United States.[61]

---

[61] There are only three mentions of pastors affiliated with the NBC working among Brazilians or Portuguese in the United States in the official periodical of the denomination, the *Batista Nacional*, between the periodical's founding in 1967 and 2010. These mentions speak of Pr. Joel Ferreira's return to Brazil in 1982, after founding two Portuguese-language churches in the United States; of the role of Pr. Rosival de Araújo as keynote speaker in the first Congress of Spiritual Renewal, held in Framingham, Massachusetts, in 1992; and of a twenty-five-year celebration of Rev. Dr. Antônio Barbosa de Lima at First Missionary Baptist Church of the Great Boston in 1994 (the article does not specify whether the celebration was for Lima's ministry in general, his marriage, or his time in that church—the Portuguese allows for all of these possibilities). See "Pr. Joel em Florianópolis," 5; "Estados Unidos," *Batista Nacional*, December 1992, 6; "Igreja Batista de Boston Comemora Jubileu de Prata do Seu Pastor," *Batista Nacional*, June 1994, 8. The NBC was not as centralized as the BBC, its foreign missionary efforts not as broad, and its ecumenical dispositions more pronounced. The possibility of other NBC trained pastors in the United States was, however, already hinted at in

When Brazuca Baptist churches were organized, they by and large became part of the SBC denominational structure through the communities' affiliation to SBC-related associations and state conventions. A significant number of these churches, however, were not particularly satisfied with this Baptist common arrangement, as I will show later.

---

one of the above-mentioned articles, which ends with the following note: "To the Pastors who are in the United States, we send our desire that the Lord may continue to use you powerfully." See "Estados Unidos," 6.

3
GROWING

Histories of Immigrant Churches

Latino Protestant churches grow in three ways: through converts, through Latin American immigrants, and through biological growth. These three represent very different experiences and framings of Protestantism. . . . The Latin American connection is maintained through the constant movement of peoples, whose role is often unseen in descriptions of the developments of Latina Protestantism.

Juan Francisco Martínez[1]

This rise of Latino Protestants will be significant not only for their own churches but also for denominational leaders who strive to reach and minister to a diversifying population, for political leaders who confront issues and craft alliances, for educational leaders—of religious and non-religious institutions—assessing needs for curriculum and training, for business leaders providing training and expanding services, and for average citizens in understanding and accepting this diffuse and growing portion of their everyday lives.

Mark Mulder, Aida Ramos, and Gerardo Martí[2]

I n winter 2016, a few months after I visited a Brazuca megachurch in Pompano Beach, Florida, that had been established in the 1990s, I entered a

---

[1] Juan Francisco Martínez, *The Story of Latino Protestants in the United States* (Grand Rapids: Eerdmans, 2018), 9.

[2] Mark T. Mulder, Aida I. Ramos, and Gerardo Martí, *Latino Protestants in America: Growing and Diverse* (Lanham, Md.: Rowan & Littlefield, 2017), 135.

Brazilian church in Newark, founded by German immigrants in the late 1800s. A Portuguese bakery across the street reminded me that Portuguese immigrants had transformed this neighborhood, once heavily populated by German immigrants. The Brazilian churrascaria just a few blocks away and the many other Brazilian establishments and churches in the area created an environment in which it was possible to live, work, pray, sing, and engage in many social activities in the New Jersey community without needing to speak any other language than Portuguese.

Newark and Pompano Beach are different places in many ways. Yet they share a high concentration of Brazilian immigrants that have not only made Brazilian culture and language a common feature in their public spaces but which have also made Brazilian churches important institutions for a significant number of local inhabitants.

Walnut Street Baptist Church in Newark is a beautiful red brick structure that at one point housed over four hundred Portuguese and Brazilian members. According to the current pastor, this number has since diminished by more than half, partially because the growing number of Brazilian immigrants in the area has increased ecclesiastical competition. The Newark of today indeed offers a Brazilian religious menu characterized by more church and denominational options than are available in many Brazilian towns! Increased migration can mean many things to immigrant church communities. On the one hand, such growth in one area means more potential parishioners for existing churches; on the other, it can also mean that different kinds of churches will be created to cater to new immigrants. Older immigrant churches that once had little competition for parishioners are often affected by this dynamic. Yet Walnut Street Baptist Church has remained strong, relevant to the Brazilian community in Newark, and engaged in many transnational connections. The church's experience also illustrates a broader pattern of migrations and segmented assimilations in the United States. Walking around that once German-inhabited space listening to adults speaking in Portuguese and children speaking in English reminded me that religious communities have always been central to the history of migration to the United States.

As with the particular case of Walnut Street Baptist Church, Brazuca Baptist churches have a rich history in general. Similar to other immigrant churches, however, their stories are often not officially recorded and are preserved mostly in oral histories kept and nurtured by leaders and older members who have been part of the community for a long time. That historians only seldom pay attention to the history of immigrant churches with the intention of constructing their official narrative means that secondary historical sources for

Brazuca churches are rarely available. Nevertheless, for the purposes of tracing the historical traditions of immigrant churches, it remains crucial to look for ways in which their memories are written down, preserved, and appreciated.

This chapter traces the history of Brazuca Baptist churches by examining a combination of official church documents, interviews with church leaders, articles printed in the *Jornal Batista*, and the rare instances of available secondary literature.[3] I begin by looking at the East Coast Lineage, a group of older and influential Brazuca Baptist churches located in the northeastern region of the United States.[4] I then tell the story of other important Brazuca Baptist churches across the country and conclude the chapter by focusing on the missionary zeal and work performed by these immigrant churches. This will set the stage for the following chapter, which deals with the cooperative work among Brazuca Baptist churches, a phenomenon I call "ethnic denominationalism."

The East Coast Lineage: A Paradigm for Understanding Histories of Brazuca Churches

The history of Brazuca Baptist churches is diffuse rather than centralized. While the most prominent Brazuca Baptist leaders estimate that there are over 150 Brazuca Baptist churches, congregations, and ministries, many of them began independently from one another. Furthermore, the ongoing efforts to create a Brazuca Baptist denomination have not completely succeeded, as we will see in the following chapter. These ministries originated in diverse ways. For example, in 1990, the historic First Baptist Church of Dallas had a Brazilian ministry that later became a church; the same happened at First Baptist Church of Austin, Texas. In addition, in the late 1980s, Georgetown Baptist Church in Washington, D.C., had a strong and highly educated Brazilian membership that participated enthusiastically in the church without the absolute necessity of services being held in Portuguese. The East Coast Lineage, however, gives us the most vivid example of the richness of immigrant churches' narratives. The group is made up of four churches—one in New York City; one in the Greater Boston area; one in Elizabeth, New Jersey; and one in Danbury, Connecticut—that are directly connected to the work of the first Brazilian Baptist missionary to the United States, Humberto Viegas Fernandes. Either

---

[3] It is important to note that the bulk of my interviews and ethnographic work was conducted between 2013 and 2016. The ways in which these communities have developed after 2016, therefore, are not considered in many of my observations.

[4] I don't include Florida under the descriptor "East Coast." Although Florida is an important center for Brazilian migration to the United States, I use this term to mark northeastern states—particularly New Jersey, Massachusetts, New York, and Connecticut.

directly or indirectly, these four churches launched or helped consolidate over twenty other churches. Some of these communities, in turn, started their own congregations that eventually became churches. Here I uncover their stories by focusing on the four oldest communities of the lineage, beginning with the church in Jamaica, Queens.

Primeira Igreja Batista Brasileira de New York

In September 1981 Manuel Cunha, a Portuguese Baptist who lived in New York City, visited Walnut Street Baptist Church with the intention of asking Fernandes to start a work in Jamaica, Queens. Cunha had left his SBC-affiliated church because it had become charismatic, and he reported that a number of Portuguese and Spanish speakers were leaving the church for similar reasons.[5] The disillusioned group was composed of immigrant members of Highland Baptist Church in Jamaica. A *Jornal Batista* article from 1976 mentions that Brazilian Baptist Chapel of Manhattan had dissolved and its members joined Highland Baptist Church that year.[6] Little is known about Brazilian Baptist Chapel, but it was pastor Rubens Domingues—formerly affiliated with Brazilian Regular Baptists, who served as pastor at Walnut Street Baptist Church before Fernandes' arrival and after Fernandes left—who led the group in the mid-1970s.[7] Fernandes wrote that after the group began meeting as an independent congregation in the buildings of Highland Baptist, "the North America brothers called us Brazilian Baptist Chapel,"[8] perhaps failing to differentiate properly between the two groups.

In response to the request, in October 1981 Fernandes began leading a Bible study group in Jamaica on Saturday nights. The group met at Cunha's residence, which Fernandes imagined as a representatively ethnic home: "a Portuguese husband, a Brazilian wife, and an American son."[9] The initial meeting included

[5] Humberto Viegas Fernandes, "Primeira Igreja Batista de Língua Portuguesa nos Estados Unidos," *Jornal Batista* LXXXIII, no. 4 (1983): 6, 8.

[6] João Martis Ferreira, "Os Batistas Brasileiros em New York," *Jornal Batista* LXXVI, no. 46 (1976): 4, 8.

[7] Ferreira, "Os Batistas Brasileiros em New York," 4, 8. The 1981–1988 minutes of Walnut Street Baptist Church are lost or misplaced, as are the 1983–1992 minutes of First Portuguese-Speaking Baptist Church of New York City. The incomplete documentation in these churches, and many others, made it difficult to confirm some of the claims made by interviewees and in articles published in denominational periodicals—which themselves were often based on an individual's account of events.

[8] Fernandes, "Primeira Igreja Batista," 6, 8.

[9] Humberto Viegas Fernandes, "Cartas de Nova Iorque: Primeira Igreja Batista de Língua Portuguesa nos Estados Unidos, Cresce," *Jornal Batista* LXXXIII, no. 31 (1983): 12.

seventeen people, among whom were "Portuguese, Brazilians, Venezuelans, Chinese, and possibly people from other nationalities."[10] The group grew, and Fernandes decided to leave Walnut Street Baptist Church after the Baptist Convention of New York (SBC) invited him to start a Portuguese-language work in the New York City area. Rubens Domingues then assumed the pastorate of Walnut Street Baptist Church. Under Domingues, that church began to consider expanding its services by changing portions of Sunday worship from Portuguese to English, in order to favor the second generation of parishioners (some now US-born).[11] Soon after, the church also contemplated the possibility of a multinational ministry.[12] But it was Fernandes' move to New York that most strongly affected the history of Brazilian Baptists on the East Coast and, consequently, the story of many Brazilian Baptists in the entire country.

When Fernandes moved to New York, he forfeited his official affiliation with the WMB and, in November 1982, organized Primeira Igreja de Língua Portuguesa de New York (First Portuguese-Language Baptist Church of New York, henceforth FPLBC New York) in Jamaica.[13] While FPLBC New York and other churches of the East Coast Lineage adopted the descriptor "Portuguese-Language" in an attempt to include Portuguese, Brazilian, and other Lusophone peoples in their communities, historically these churches have been overwhelmingly Brazilian in membership. FPLBC New York is possibly the oldest continuously operating Brazilian-founded Baptist church in the United States.[14]

Fernandes' firsthand experience among immigrants in the United States gave him a keen view of the shortcomings of the WMB's original vision of reaching the Portuguese by using a strategy similar to the one used in Canada. For him, the start of FPLBC New York signaled a needed change of course. He wrote several reports to the *Jornal Batista* highlighting the peculiar contributions of a missionary work with broader horizons, not only in terms of nationality but also in terms of immigration status. In regard to nationality, Fernandes wrote that the organization and early success of FPLBC New York

> came to change part of the original plan of the World Mission Board, which initially wanted to give priority to the evangelization of the Portuguese people.

[10] Fernandes, "Primeira Igreja Batista," 6, 8.

[11] *Atas da (Minutes of) Walnut Street Baptist Church*, 1997, 174.

[12] *Atas da (Minutes of) Walnut Street Baptist Church*, 2001, 237.

[13] "INÍCIO," *PIB Family Church*, accessed November 2, 2015, http://www.pibfamily .church/. In terms of the name of many Brazuca Baptist churches, it is important to note that they don't always translate into English closely. Although a close translation of some of these churches' names is "Portuguese-Language," they have often translated this section of their name as "Portuguese-Speaking."

[14] Levy Penido, interview on New York ministry, phone interview, October 26, 2015.

What happens is that America does not only shelter Portuguese people from Portugal and [the] Azores. There are Portuguese-speaking peoples here who came from Europe, Africa, and also Brazil. All of them need salvation the same. The newest convert of our church, named João de Souza, only speaks Portuguese, but Portuguese from Guinea-Bissau, which is in the heart of Africa. He is the private driver of his country's ambassador. . . . No missionary work can be done in unilateral terms. FPLBC New York will take the message of salvation to people who speak Portuguese and also other languages.[15]

Fernandes' entrepreneurial spirit, energized by the richness immigrants brought to the US religious landscape, manifested itself in his aggressive initiatives. Within one month of the creation of the church, he had already started two Bible study groups with an evangelistic purpose—one in Portuguese and one in Spanish—and planned to start two more soon.[16] The president of the WMB, who constantly wrote to the *Jornal Batista* about his international trips, said that Fernandes had made FPLBC New York the base of operations for reaching Portuguese-speaking migrants in other East Coast communities.[17]

Fernandes was also involved in the dynamics of difference in the SBC. When he reported to the *Jornal Batista* about a regional Southern Baptist conference he attended, he demonstrated a keen proficiency at highlighting the power of ethnic groups in US religious life in general, and the northern presence of the SBC in particular. He wrote:

In order to show the power of ethnic groups, it is enough to mention that of the 243 churches that compose the Baptist Convention of New York, 120 are concentrated in the Metropolitan Association of New York, and of these 120 churches, seventy are churches of foreigners; churches that are recognizably Hispanic, Slavic, Polish, Ukrainian, Chinese, Greek, German, and one of Portuguese language.[18]

Although the SBC was beginning to expand its activity among different groups of immigrants in the United States in the 1980s, Fernandes thought that the convention was still narrow minded regarding the kind of immigrants it considered to be significant to its mission and strategy. He recalled that an SBC pamphlet distributed at the meeting informed participants about the three kinds of foreign immigrants in the United States: immigrants (who had valid

---

[15] Humberto Viegas Fernandes, "Cartas de Nova Iorque: Primeira Igreja Batista de Língua Portuguesa nos Estados Unidos," *Jornal Batista* LXXXIII, no. 5 (1983): 8.

[16] Fernandes, "Cartas de Nova Iorque," 8.

[17] Waldemiro Tymchak, "Duas Grandes Experiências, Muitas Lições," *Jornal Batista* LXXXIII, no. 7 (1983): 8.

[18] Humberto Viegas Fernandes, "Cartas de Nova Iorque: Uma Assembléia Convencional Diferente," *Jornal Batista* LXXXIII, no. 8 (1983): 12.

visas or were citizens), nonimmigrants (temporary workers), and refugees. But, as Fernandes noticed, the SBC had omitted "the world of the illegals, whose size is impossible to determine. The ethnic groups in the United States, therefore, are divided in[to] two great groups: visible and invisible."[19] As we will see later, the group that Fernandes called "invisible" has nonetheless exercised a great deal of influence in Brazuca Baptist churches.

Fernandes' quick-paced initiatives on the East Coast had lasting effects on the history of Brazuca Baptists, but things did not always go the way he planned. The first church to start from one of Fernandes' initiatives was an FPLBC New York congregation in Manhattan pastored by Paulo Cappelozza. Cappelozza's group met in the building of the Metropolitan Baptist Association, but the group became an independent church after some irreconcilable differences between Cappelozza and Fernandes came to light.[20] Cappelozza then started Metro Brazilian Baptist Church in 1986, with the help of Metro Baptist Church in Manhattan.[21] Gene Bolin, then senior pastor of Metro Baptist Church, helped Cappelozza not only by providing a place for the initial meetings of the Portuguese-speaking group but also by serving as a sponsor for Cappelozza's legalization, after the latter had first pastored in the United States with a tourist visa.[22] Cappelozza stayed at Metro Brazilian Baptist Church until 2011, when he retired to Orlando, but Metro Brazilian still continued its ministry to Portuguese-speaking peoples in Manhattan after his retirement.

Fernandes also faced some opposition at FPLBC New York. According to his successor, Levy Penido, Fernandes was no longer with the church in 1986 when Penido was called to lead the community. Penido had been the first Brazilian Baptist missionary in Ecuador, a pioneer of the denomination in that country, and when he came to the United States for the meeting of the Baptist World Alliance (BWA) in 1985 he met a Brazilian friend, Pr. Daniel Paixão,[23] who at the time worked for the SBC. Penido recalled that Paixão told him that if he moved to New York to work with the New York Baptist Convention (SBC), he would bring Penido with him.[24] Paixão went

---

[19] Humberto Viegas Fernandes, "Cartas de Nova Iorque: Congress of Ethnic Evangelism," *Jornal Batista* LXXXIII, no. 30 (1983): 11–12.

[20] Paulo Cappelozza, interview, October 12, 2016.

[21] Paulo Capelozza, "Pastor Brasileiro nos States," *Jornal Batista* XCII, no. 33 (1992): 4.

[22] Cappelozza, interview.

[23] Paixão would become pastor of several Brazuca Baptist churches, including the one in New York and First Portuguese-Language Baptist Church in Elizabeth, which was a congregation of FPLBC in New York. Today, Paixão is pastor of a Brazuca Baptist church in Orlando.

[24] Levy Penido, interview, October 29, 2015.

to New York, and soon after, Penido arrived in Jamaica to pastor the group Fernandes had previously led. According to Penido, he never saw a group "so small and yet so full of problems." He attempted to articulate the source of the problems he faced: "Half of the group was Baptist and the other half was not . . . and, the vice president of the church was a Portuguese man, he was very firm. The deacons were Portuguese, the treasurer was a woman from Venezuela, and 95 percent of the membership was Brazilian from different places and different religious backgrounds."[25] The clashes that arose as a result of the different ethnic, denominational, and cultural differences, Penido recalled, made many want to give up. By the time he left the church nine years later in 1994, however, the community not only had a healthy membership but had helped to start two other congregations that in turn became strong churches. In addition, the church assisted in the consolidation of another faith community once led by Fernandes.[26] These churches were Primeira Igreja de Língua Portuguesa de New Jersey (First Portuguese-Language Baptist Church of New Jersey, henceforth FPLBC New Jersey), Primeira Igreja Batista de Língua Portuguesa de Danbury (First Portuguese-Language Baptist Church in Danbury, henceforth FPLBC Danbury), and Primeira Igreja Batista Brasileira da Grande Boston (First Brazilian Baptist Church of Greater Boston).[27] As readers will see, all of these churches eventually changed their names to English ones as a sign of their desire to become multinational (rather than narrowly Brazilian-focused) churches. In addition, these churches had their own effect in starting congregations, helping consolidate churches, and training leaders who would become pastors of other Brazuca Baptist churches and other communities abroad.

After Penido left FPLBC New York in 1994, the church called Francisco Izidoro as its next senior pastor.[28] Izidoro had pastored Brazilians who migrated to New York and were members of FPLBC New York when Penido left. These members were key to the church's invitation to Izidoro and his acceptance of the New York pastorate.[29] The church is still pastored by Izidoro and meets in its own building in Astoria, New York. The church also has a congregation in Garden City, New York. In the mid-2000s, the church

[25] Penido, interview.
[26] Penido, interview.
[27] Penido, interview.
[28] *Atas da (Minutes of) Primeira Igreja Batista de Língua Portuguesa de New York*, 1994, book 2, 13.
[29] Francisco Izidoro, interview, January 5, 2017.

changed its name to PIB Family Church, to broaden its appeal beyond Portuguese-speaking immigrants.

Primeira Igreja Batista Brasileira da Grande Boston

My second example comes from the Greater Boston area. In 1986 a group of Brazilian immigrants led by lay leader Gessuy Freitas started meeting in the Boston area in hopes of forming a Brazuca Baptist church. By December of the same year, Huberto Viegas Fernandes, who was still on the East Coast, met with the group at Tremont Baptist Church in Boston.[30] He had been invited by the Greater Boston Baptist Association to start the work in an area that had a considerable number of Brazilian immigrants. The group soon began meeting at Metropolitan Baptist Church in Boston.[31] Fernandes returned to Brazil in early 1987 in order to teach at a small seminary, but the church in Boston, like the one in New York City, prospered.[32] The Boston group then called Pr. Marcos Soares da Silva to lead the work, but he had to return to Brazil at the end of 1989 because he was unable to secure the documentation needed to comply with US immigration laws.[33] During Silva's short tenure, however, the group started another Brazilian Baptist mission in Framingham, Massachusetts.[34] After he left, Gessuy Freitas once again assumed the group's leadership for a few years.

A BBC denominational leader named Isaltino Gomes Filho, on a visit to Boston, observed that though Freitas was leading the community, he was not yet ordained and the church urgently needed a pastor.[35] Eduardo Lacerda visited the church in 1991, by which point the church's leadership had been assumed by Cléber Machado and Freitas had become the group's vice president.[36] Later, both Machado and Freitas were ordained and became Baptist pastors of other Brazuca Baptist communities.

---

[30] Antônio Marques, "Histórico da Primeira Igreja Batista da Grande Boston," unpublished manuscript, n.d.

[31] Leonina Henringer, "Brasileiros nos Estados Unidos: Missão Batista Brasileira em Boston," *Jornal Batista* LXXXVII, no. 20 (1987): 12.

[32] Karl Janzen, "De Nova Iorque para Dourados," *Jornal Batista* LXXXVIII, no. 18 (1988): 12.

[33] Marques, "Histórico."

[34] Marques, "Histórico."

[35] Isaltino Gomes Coelho Filho, "Impressões de uma Viagem Missionária," *Jornal Batista* XC, no. 30 (1990): 16.

[36] Eduardo Lacerda, "Impressões de uma Viagem Missionária," *Jornal Batista* XCI, no. 16 (1991): 9.

In June 1991 Pr. Jorge Bezerra[37] became the pastor of Primeira Igreja Batista Brasileira da Grande Boston (First Brazilian Baptist Church of Greater Boston).[38] Under Bezerra's leadership, the church started a radio program in Portuguese, seconded its choir to sing at the annual meeting of the New England Baptist Convention, and held a service celebrating the official organization of the group as a church.[39] By the time Cleber Machado wrote to the *Jornal Batista* in 1993 and reported on the great number of Brazilian migrants coming to the region, Bezerra was contributing regular articles on Christianity to a major periodical of the Brazilian community in Greater Boston, the *Brazilian Times*.[40] In addition to a weekly radio show, he also had a TV show in Portuguese with a focus on preaching to the Portuguese-speaking population in the area.[41]

First Brazilian Baptist Church in Boston was the first Brazuca Baptist church to have its own facilities. According to Machado's report, the transaction was made without any help from Anglo-American Baptist churches. They bought buildings that had been used previously as Boston University's Jesuit Center and saw the move as one that would benefit the region's entire Brazilian community. The leadership of the church celebrated this milestone with the Brazilian Baptist audience by saying that "in front of the main building there is a sign in English and Portuguese that reads: First Brazilian Baptist Church of Greater Boston—we cooperate with the Southern Baptist Convention."[42] The responsible employee of the bank that financed the buildings to the Brazilian group, which perhaps agreed to do so because of the noticeable increase in Brazilian businesses in the region, was reported to have said that it was the first time in his forty years working at the bank that he had seen

[37] Ana Martes interviewed leaders of this church—including Bezerra—in the 1990s and considered them fundamentalists partially because of Bezerra's criticism of homosexuality and of what he saw as the immoral US society. See Martes, *Brasileiros nos Estados Unidos: Um Estudo Sobre Imigrantes em Massachusetts* (São Paulo: Paz e Terra, 2000), 123.

[38] *Atas da (Minutes of) Primeira Igreja Batista Brasileira da Grande Boston,* 1991, book 1, 7.

[39] *Atas da (Minutes of) Primeira Igreja Batista (Boston),* 1991, book 1, 10–15.

[40] For an assessment of the influence of the Brazuca media on Brazilian transnational networks, see Elsa R. P. Vieira, "The Formative Years of the Brazilian Communities of New York and San Francisco through the Print Media: The Brazilians/ The Brasilians and Brazil Today," in *Becoming Brazuca: Brazilian Immigration to the United States,* ed. Clémence Jouët-Pastré and Leticia J. Braga (Cambridge, Mass.: David Rockefeller Center for Latin American Studies, 2008), 81–102.

[41] Cleber Machado, "1a. Igreja Batista Brasileira em Boston: Um Desafio Missionário," *Jornal Batista* XCIII, no. 5 (1993): 7.

[42] Cleber Machado, Jairo Dias, and Mariluce Araújo, "A Primeira Igreja Batista Brasileira da Grande Boston Agora Tem Seu Templo Próprio," *Jornal Batista* XCIV, no. 44 (1994): 2.

the institution providing financing to an ethnic group of any kind.[43] In 1995 the Greater Boston Baptist Association announced that First Brazilian Baptist Church of Greater Boston was the fastest-growing church to cooperate with them, regardless of distinctions between immigrant churches and predominantly Anglo-American congregations.[44]

After disagreements with the church's leadership in 1999, Bezerra left the church and founded Igreja Evangélica Batista do Amor (Evangelical Baptist Church of Love) in Boston. By 2001 he was in Florida, as a pastor for Brazilian members of Glendale Baptist Church, a predominantly African American community.[45] The Boston church then had two senior pastors, Edson Queiroz (2000–2002) and Nivaldo Nassif (2002–2010), and in 2012 Antônio Marques arrived from Brazil to lead the congregation, which he continued to do as of this writing. During Queiroz' tenure the church began a mission in Brockton, Massachusetts, and ordained one of its lay leaders, John Galgoul, to pastor it. Galgoul had been born in Brazil to Southern Baptists missionaries. Now he was being ordained in a Brazuca church in Boston to minister to Brazilians in the United States—yet another testimony to the richness of migration narratives and SBC influence.[46]

Timeline of Leadership Transitions at First Brazilian Baptist Church of Greater Boston

Pr. Nivaldo Nassif came to Boston from São Paulo on the recommendation of Queiroz, to be inaugurated in February 2002.[47] Under Nassif, the church helped solidify a Brazilian church in New Bedford, sent one of its associate pastors to pastor the Brazuca Baptist church in Worcester, and organized a mission in Newton and one in Ipswich.[48] The Boston church, however, suffered significant losses at the end of the first decade of the twenty-first century, a time when the United States economy crashed and the Brazilian economy showed signs of strength, thus affecting the flow of Brazilian migration to and from the United States. Between 2007 and 2009, the church's financial struggles were so significant that the US Immigration Services denied its application for a religious visa for a worship leader the church wanted to

---

[43] Luiz Paulo Moraes, "Igreja Brasileira em Boston É Luz numa Cidade em Trevas," *Jornal Batista* XCV, no. 42 (1996): 13.

[44] *Atas da (Minutes of) Primeira Igreja Batista (Boston)*, 1995, book 1, 86.

[45] Rickey Armstrong, "Deus Expande Seu Reino no Sul de Miami," *Jornal Batista* C, no. 44 (2001): 4.

[46] *Atas da (Minutes of) Primeira Igreja Batista (Boston)*, 2001, book 2, 233–34.

[47] *Atas da (Minutes of) Primeira Igreja Batista (Boston)*, 2002, book 2, 238–41.

[48] *Atas da (Minutes of) Primeira Igreja Batista (Boston)*, 2002–2005, book 2, 247–402.

1986 — Bro. Gessuy Freitas (Leader)

13/Dec/1986 – Mar/1987 — Pr. Humberto Viegas Fernandes (Consultant)

Mar/1987– May/1988 — Bro. Gessuy Freitas (Leader)

06/Jun/1988– Aug/1989 — Pr. Marcos Soares (Senior Pastor)

Aug/1989– 15/Jun/1991 — Bro. Gessuy Freitas (Leader)

15/Jun/1991– 22/Mar/1999 — Pr. Jorge Bezerra (Senior Pastor)

01/Aug/1999– 10/Jun/2000 — Pr. Sebastião Carlos Batista (Interim Pastor)

10/Jun/2000– 02/Feb/2002 — Pr. Edson Queiroz (Senior Pastor)

2/Feb/2002– 6/Jul/2010 — Pr. Nivaldo Nassiff (Senior Pastor); Pr. Josias Souza (Associate Pastor); John Galgol (Associate Pastor)

Jul/2010– Apr/2011 — Pr. Roberto Alves de Souza (Interim Pastor); Pr. André Queiroz (Associate Pastor)

09/Jun/2011– 26/Aug/2011 — Pr. Marcone Correa (Substitute Pastor)

11/Mar/2012– 26/Aug/2012 — Pr. Eladio Alvarez (Interim Pastor)

26/Aug/2012– Present Day — Pr. Antônio Marques (Senior Pastor)

hire.[49] The church subsequently rented its facilities to a Brazilian Pentecostal church, a Korean church, and a Nepalese church in the area, each of which used the building at a different time on Sundays.[50] Faced with a financial and numeric drought, the leadership of First Brazilian Baptist Church of Boston started to think more seriously about a multiethnic ministry in an attempt to broaden their appeal. Nassif left the church in July 2010 and later joined the staff of First Baptist Church of Orlando, where he served as the Brazilian ministry pastor.

After the congregation spent two years without an official senior pastor, in August 2012 Antônio Marques arrived to lead the Boston church. Marques' story is another example of the fluid dynamics of migration. His grandfather was a Portuguese migrant to Massachusetts who eventually decided to move to Brazil with his young family. Marques' father was also a border crosser. He was born in the Greater Boston area; was raised in Brazil; served in the US Army during World War II; returned to Brazil to get married; came back to the United States, where Marques' sister was born; and returned again to Brazil, where he died. In 2012 his middle-aged son arrived in Boston on a religious visa and, without being able to speak much English, began to pastor a Brazuca church in the region where his father had been born.[51]

Marques first visited Boston in 2010, when he came to the United States for the Leadership Summit conference—a global phenomenon among evangelical leaders—for the development of his leadership skills. This trip was an initiative of Marques'; along with his church in Brazil, he had sponsored his trip himself, evidence of the value that Brazilian Protestant churches give to such events. After the conference, he visited the Boston area to get to know the region of his father's birth. Marques had friends in Boston, some of whom had worked with him in Brazilian Baptist institutions. A few months after he returned to Brazil, he received a phone call from the leaders of First Brazilian Baptist Church of Greater Boston, a contact that was presumably facilitated by his Brazilian friends in Massachusetts, inviting him to return to Boston to pastor the church.[52] Following Marques' arrival, in 2013 the church sold its $2.5 million building, moved to a new $1.1 million facility in 2014, and changed its name to Baptist Church of Greater Boston: A Lovely Place, in order to broaden their reach. It continues its effort to become a strong multinational church, despite all the challenges involved in such an endeavor.[53]

---

[49] *Atas da (Minutes of) Primeira Igreja Batista (Boston)*, 2010, book 2, 451–53.
[50] *Atas da (Minutes of) Primeira Igreja Batista (Boston)*, 2010, book 2, 443–49.
[51] Antônio Marques, interview, March 20, 2017.
[52] *Atas da (Minutes of) Primeira Igreja Batista (Boston)*. 2011, book 3, 487.
[53] *Atas da (Minutes of) Primeira Igreja Batista (Boston)*, 2014, book 3, 31–36.

Primeira Igreja Batista de Língua Portuguesa de New Jersey

Our East Coast journey takes us next from Massachusetts to New Jersey. When Levy Penido arrived to pastor FPLBC New York in 1987, he shared something in common with his predecessor—an aggressive desire to expand Brazilian Baptist work on the East Coast. He had extensive missionary experience in Ecuador, where he was the WMB's pioneering missionary. He also had a childhood friend and denominational ally in Dr. Daniel Paixão, a Southwestern Baptist Theological Seminary graduate whose instrumentality as an officer of the Baptist Convention of New York was key for Penido's acceptance of his new mission field.[54] Soon after Penido arrived at FPLBC New York, he challenged people to start two new churches. Aloísio Campanha, then a lay leader who would later become pastor of another church in New York City, took the lead in the New Jersey congregation that became Primeira Igreja Batista de Língua Portuguesa de New Jersey (First Portuguese-Language Baptist Church of New Jersey, henceforth FPLBC New Jersey).[55]

While on vacation from his regular job in Brazil, Campanha came to the United States in the mid-1980s to work in the construction industry. Soon he discovered that he could make much more money working in construction in New Jersey than in Brazil, and so he stayed on the East Coast, where he later met the woman who would become his wife—also a Brazilian immigrant.[56] Campanha was originally a member of Walnut Street Baptist Church but left the community because, according to him, the church was too liberal.[57] He then joined FPLBC New York and was now, under Penido's leadership, returning to help lead another Baptist group in New Jersey. The group's initial meetings were in the house of Judson and Rosane Souza, who lived on Walnut Street in Newark, just two blocks away from Walnut Street Baptist Church.[58]

In 1992 the group rented a meeting space in Newark and called as their pastor Daniel Paixão, who, as a denominational official, had helped bring Penido from Ecuador to New York.[59] In the late 1990s, under Paixão's leadership, the church moved to its own building in Elizabeth, New Jersey. Benefiting from the boom in Brazilian migration to the New Jersey region, FPLBC New Jersey grew

---

[54] Penido, interview.

[55] *Atas da (Minutes of) Missão Batista Brasileira em New Jersey*, 1991, book 1, 1.

[56] Aloísio Campanha, interview, October 18, 2015.

[57] On this point, Campanha seemed to have judged the stance of the church according to standards not based on the community's official beliefs. The bylaws and minutes of the community do not indicate that the church was doctrinally liberal by any measure.

[58] *Atas da (Minutes of) Missão Batista*, 1991, book 1, 1.

[59] *Atas da (Minutes of) Missão Batista*, 1992, book 1, 10–11.

rapidly. In 1997 Paixão left to pastor a group in Orlando, and when the church failed to bring a well-known Brazilian pastor to Elizabeth, it invited the young Baptist pastor Josias Bezerra to head the community.[60] (We will return later to Bezerra's reflections on the meaning of immigration narratives to pastoral theology and practice, for they represent some of the most insightful articulations of theological responses to the existential anxieties with which immigrant parishioners in Brazuca Baptist churches confront Brazilian pastors.)

In 2002 Bezerra returned to Brazil in order to complete a psychology degree; that December, Pr. José Calixto, a former BBC missionary in Latin America, became pastor.[61] In 2006 Aloísio Campanha, who had been a lay leader in the community since its inception, was ordained and remained part of the church staff until he began pastoring the newly founded Igreja Batista da Liberdade em New York in 2012.[62] Calixto left the church in 2010, and Campanha led the community as an interim pastor until 2012 and helped the community sporadically until the new pastor, Sérgio Freitas, was hired in 2014.[63] Under Freitas' leadership, the church changed its name to the English PIB New Jersey: Church of the City.

With that, we move east to Connecticut and to our fourth church.

Primeira Igreja Batista de Língua Portuguesa de Danbury

Primeira Igreja Batista de Língua Portuguesa de Danbury (First Portuguese Language Baptist Church of Danbury, henceforth FPLBC Danbury) began at the initiative of Levy Penido. Penido recalled that he wanted to start a congregation in Danbury, Connecticut, even if it meant going against the wishes of his family and of FPLBC New York, who did not want him to be involved in yet another initiative.[64] Penido did not know that there were many Brazilians in Danbury, but he knew there were many Portuguese immigrants. Nevertheless, he went to Danbury looking for Brazilians.[65] He narrated the beginnings of the work in Danbury in the early 1990s by relating that when he arrived in the city he went to a grocery store's entrance to see whether he could spot compatriots:

> I knew that Brazilians needed to buy groceries, so I said to myself: "I am going to a grocery store." The first Brazilian I found was an older lady leaving

---

[60] *Atas da (Minutes of) Primeira Igreja Batista de Língua Portuguesa de New Jersey*, 1999, book 1, 159.
[61] *Atas da (Minutes of) Primeira Igreja Batista (New Jersey)*, 2002, book 2, 44, 66.
[62] *Atas da (Minutes of) Primeira Igreja Batista (New Jersey)*, 2012, book 2, 185.
[63] *Atas da (Minutes of) Primeira Igreja Batista (New Jersey)*, 2014, book 2, 201.
[64] Penido, interview.
[65] Penido, interview.

the grocery store while I was standing up outside. I asked her the following question: "Do you speak Portuguese?" She had just arrived from Brazil and didn't know a word of English, so she answered with a clear "*não*." Then I told her: "So you are exactly who I am looking for." It was very interesting. Then I found Pr. José Monteiro. He was not yet a pastor but he was a Christian and there were some brothers and sisters who met in his house. Then we found an American church that sheltered us.[66]

In 1992 the Danbury congregation called Pr. Gerson Furtado as their pastor. Furtado had been in the United States since the early 1980s, having come to study at California Baptist University. In 1992 he was pastoring in Washington, D.C., and he commuted from the national capital to Danbury for a significant period of his tenure—a significant drive of about five hours each way.[67]

Under Furtado, the congregation became a church in 1993, cooperating with the SBC.[68] That same year, Furtado left, recommending his friend, Pr. Damy Ferreira, who had been a pastor of First Portuguese-Language Baptist Church in San Francisco, to go pastor the Connecticut community.[69] In 1987 Ferreira had left San Francisco to work as executive secretary of the Carioca Baptist Convention, in Rio de Janeiro, but eventually returned to the United States to pastor Brazilian Baptist Church of Queens, a church that started as a congregation of a predominantly Spanish-speaking church in New York City.[70] Ferreira then went to pastor in Danbury, from where he contributed to the *Jornal Batista* and often presented reflections about his time in Danbury to a Brazilian audience. In the first such article, Ferreira described Danbury as a place of great opportunity for a Brazilian church. He noted that in 1994 Danbury had a population of sixty-five thousand people, of whom seven thousand were Brazilian and another higher but unspecified number were Portuguese. The Portuguese language was so prominent in the city that "in some streets here, instead of using the greeting 'hi,' in English, people use the Portuguese 'oi.' They are the 'oi' streets."[71] The Brazilian presence in Danbury was so prominent that even Afro-Brazilian religions like Candombé and Umbanda were already being practiced in the city. According to Ferreira, local newspapers reported on Afro-Brazilian rituals being performed in the local cemetery.[72]

[66] Penido, interview.
[67] *Atas da (Minutes of) Primeira Igreja Batista de Língua Portuguesa de Danbury,* 1992, book 1, 17.
[68] *Atas da (Minutes of) Primeira Igreja Batista (Danbury),* 1993, book 2, 26.
[69] *Atas da (Minutes of) Primeira Igreja Batista (Danbury),* 1993, book 2, 83.
[70] See Damy Ferreira, "Posse em New York: Mais uma Tarefa a Cumprir," *Jornal Batista* XCIII, no. 13 (1993): 4; and Damy Ferreira, "Primeira Igreja Batista de Danbury Empossa Novo Pastor," *Jornal Batista* XCIV, no. 15 (1994): 9.
[71] Ferreira, "Primeira Igreja Batista de Danbury," 9.
[72] Ferreira, "Primeira Igreja Batista de Danbury," 9.

Between 1994 and 1996, when Ferreira decided to leave the church, FPLBC Danbury won "Best of the Year" for its television program, ordained lay leader José Monteiro, and supported two Brazilian Baptist congregations in Connecticut, one in Rockland, and one in Bridgeport.[73] In 1997 Pr. Ophir de Barros arrived from Brazil to lead the Danbury church and remained its senior pastor until his retirement in 2011. Leaders in the Danbury church who had known him when he pastored them over a decade earlier in Brazil wanted to be pastored by him again, now in the United States.[74]

In 1999 FPLBC Danbury started a Spanish-language work, and around 2005 it launched a service in English.[75] The Portuguese service, however, remained the most prominent one throughout its history. In 2002 the church bought a building in downtown Danbury, where once a Chase Bank franchise operated. The building was purchased for a little over $1 million, with $700,000 being financed by Union Bank.[76] In 2007 the church began the process that eventually culminated in the change of its name from the Portuguese Primeira Igreja Batista de Língua Portuguesa de Danbury to All Nations Baptist Church.[77] This move coincided with the already-mentioned correlation between the diminishing migration flow and the awakening of the desire for multinational churches in the vision of Brazuca Baptist pastors. Barros mentioned that after the shift in the church's name and focus, people from Jamaica, Barbados, and other nations joined its membership.[78] Barros left the church in 2011, and the church had several interim pastors until the 2015 arrival of a missionary of the BBC, Pr. Girlan Silva. The church contacted the WMB in order to find a missionary to lead the community forward and selected Silva, who began trying to advance the relatively new church vision of building a multinational community.[79] Silva, however, did not remain long as a missionary of the WMB, for when he accepted the church's offer he became an employee of the community and his link to the WMB had a two-year limit. He decided to stay with the church in Danbury rather than being reassigned to another field.

• • •

The story of the East Coast Lineage shows that strong chains of church planting characterized the Brazuca Baptist pioneer churches. Nevertheless, it was

[73] *Atas da (Minutes of) Primeira Igreja Batista (Danbury)*, 1994–1996, book 2, 75–130.
[74] Ophir de Barros, interview, October 26, 2015.
[75] *Atas da (Minutes of) Primeira Igreja Batista (Danbury)*, 1999, book 3, 34.
[76] *Atas da (Minutes of) Primeira Igreja Batista (Danbury)*, 2002, book 3, 52.
[77] *Atas da (Minutes of) Primeira Igreja Batista (Danbury)*, 2007, book 3, 84.
[78] Barros, interview.
[79] *Atas da (Minutes of) Primeira Igreja Batista (Danbury)*, 2013, book 3, 169.

the broader religious networks, not denomination-centralized initiatives, that moved these chains forward beyond their genesis. Fernandes came to the United States as a WMB missionary and then changed institutional affiliations to the New York Baptist Convention, moving from New Jersey, where he was originally working, to New York City. He did so, however, in response to the needs of an already-present group that took the initiative of asking for his intervention. Penido, on the other hand, was a missionary in Ecuador and left the WMB to come to the United States as a result of his friendship with Daniel Paixão, who worked for the New York Baptist Convention. The convention, however, was never Penido's employer; he was an employee of the Brazuca Baptist church in New York City. Paixão in turn eventually pastored a congregation that Penido's New York City church started in New Jersey, whose founding members also took the initiative in asking for pastoral leadership.

In Boston, Fernandes helped lead a group of immigrants who were already meeting in the city and who eventually chose their pastor, Jorge Bezerra, independently from either the WMB or the SBC; the same happened in the Brazuca Baptist church in Danbury under Penido's leadership. Josias Bezerra, Ophir Barros, Sérgio Freitas, Antônio Marques, and other pastors ended up in the United States as a result of people they knew or had previously pastored who were immigrants to the East Coast at the time they were offered their pastoral positions. The level of denominational institutional reliance of different congregations and religious leaders varies widely, but the common thread in the narrative of these communities is the presence of migrant networks that have energized the particular form taken by their presence in the United States.

Another common characteristic of these communities is the presence of Brazuca Baptist leaders who were trained and ordained in BBC institutions. When these leaders were called to pastor Brazuca Baptist churches, they still felt as if they were part of their original denomination. The churches they pastored, however, were usually, at least on paper, a part of the SBC apparatus, and, because of this affiliation, their loyalties were torn between two institutions that, despite their doctrinal proximity, transmitted different regional flavors of Baptist dispositions. This denominational ambiguity eventually gave way to a new form of denominationalism.

Beyond the East Coast Lineage: Stories of Church and Migration

If the centrality of migrant networks is already seen in the churches of the East Coast Lineage, they are even more evident in the freedom, entrepreneurial spirit, and creativity with which Brazuca Baptist churches beyond the lineage were formed. Before taking a closer look at the transition from a Brazilian to a multinational character that is typical of most of the Brazuca Baptist churches, as well as at the global missionary presence that permeates many of these communities, I will trace the narratives of Brazilian Baptist communities in California; the Washington, D.C., metropolitan area; and Florida to illustrate that the history of immigrant denominational presence in the United States in general and Brazuca Baptist history in particular is heavily informed by the history of labor migrations. As such the emergence of Brazuca Baptist communities does not always fit the mold of popular understandings of denominational missions and immigrant church planting.[80] In the history of Brazuca Baptists, the migration dynamic is the mighty elephant and denominational loyalty the overpowered rider.

Stories from California

Beyond the developments of the East Coast Lineage, the multifaceted beginnings of Brazuca Baptist work were evident as early as 1982. Gerson Furtado, who worked in First Portuguese Baptist Church in Chino, California, began concentrating on the Brazilians who migrated to the area for educational reasons. Furtado saw his ministry to Brazilians as one that gave assistance to temporary students and their parents, who came to California from Brazil to visit their college-attending sons and daughters.[81] Furtado himself was studying at California Baptist University and saw his role as one of ministering to international students who would return to their countries.[82] No Brazuca Baptist church came out of Furtado's work in Chino, but soon another Brazuca Baptist community would blossom in California.

In San Francisco, 413 miles north of Chino, another Brazilian Baptist church emerged independently from the developments in Fernandes' work on the East Coast. The formation of FPLBC San Francisco was serendipitous; Geriel de Oliveira, a Brazilian pastor who was serving as the executive secretary of the San Francisco Baptist Association and who had been living

---

[80] Afe Adogame has provided a helpful and concise assessment of theories of migration and their applicability to the study of religious networks. Although Adogame is correct that human agency is at times diminished by theories that emphasize economic and structural reasons for migration, the economic motif is the major factor in the Brazilian presence in the United States either directly (poor and lower middle-class Brazilian immigrants wanting to make money) or indirectly (middle-class and rich Brazilians wanting to benefit from the context of a more affluent society). See Afeosemime U. Adogame, *The African Christian Diaspora: New Currents and Emerging Trends in World Christianity* (London: Bloomsbury, 2013), 11–19.

[81] Paulo Elias de Sá, "Pastor Brasileiro Coordena Estudos Religiosos para Estudantes Internacionais," *Jornal Batista* LXXXII, no. 2 (1982): 8.

[82] Geriel de Oliveira, interview, February 13, 2017.

in the United States for over twenty years, was involved in a car accident in 1983. He learned at the body shop to which he took his car for repair that the mechanics were Brazilian and that the wife of one of the mechanics was Baptist.[83] Oliveira subsequently began a Bible study group in his house in San Francisco. Technically, he could not pastor a church because of the policies of the San Francisco Baptist Association, so when the group grew large enough to warrant a pastor, he reached out to his friend and former classmate at California Baptist University, Gerson Furtado, then pastoring in Brazil. Furtado did not want to come to California, but he recommended his friend Damy Ferreira, who in time became the founding pastor of FPLBC San Francisco.[84]

When the church was formed, in 1984, there were an estimated ten thousand Brazilians and one hundred fifty thousand Portuguese in the city. Ferreira was quick to notice that English-speaking and Spanish-speaking churches in the Bay Area were ineffective in appealing to Portuguese-speaking people in general and that, unlike their counterparts in Brazil, the evangelical churches in San Francisco did not practice aggressive evangelism.[85] The group moved their meeting from Oliveira's house to one of the oldest Baptist churches in California, First Baptist Church of San Francisco (FBC San Francisco), in January 1984. Pastor Ferreira celebrated the fact that the same year FBC San Francisco let FPLBC San Francisco use its buildings, the new community began cooperating with the SBC.[86]

A number of people who had experience in church work in Brazil and in the United States assisted Ferreira in his ministry. For example, John Timothy Kunkel helped Ferreira in his California mission. Kunkel was born in the United States, had a college degree in Portuguese, and was married to a Brazilian woman. In 1986, when Ferreira started a congregation in Oakland, Ferreira gave Kunkel, who also had a master of divinity degree and was working on his doctorate, the responsibility for leading the work.[87]

A more striking example of the complexities of Brazuca Baptist networks, however, is that of Pastor Arnaldo Pessoa, who also helped Ferreira at FPLBC San Francisco. Pessoa left Brazil in 1969, crossing South America, Central America, and the Mexican border (largely on foot) and reaching the United

---

[83] Damy Ferreira, "A Sombra do Portão Dourado: Uma Igreja Batista de Língua Portuguesa na Califórnia," *Jornal Batista* LXXXIV, no. 18 (1984): 11–12.

[84] Oliveira, interview.

[85] Ferreira, "Igreja Batista de Língua Portuguesa na Califórnia," 11–12.

[86] Damy Ferreira, "A Sombra do Portão Dourado: Igreja Batista Mais Antiga da Califórnia," *Jornal Batista* LXXXIV, no. 34 (1984): 12.

[87] Damy Ferreira, "A Sombra do Portão Dourado: Contando as Bençãos," *Jornal Batista* LXXXVI, no. 9 (1986): 12.

States in 1972.[88] On the way from Brazil to the United States, Pessoa lived in places like Panama, Colombia, and Mexico; in 1972 he arrived in San Antonio, Texas, and enrolled in the Baptist Bible Institute in town, now called the Baptist University of the Américas. There, he learned English, became Baptist, and married a Cuban refugee before enrolling in the psychology program at Wayland Baptist University.[89] When Ferreira founded FPLBC in San Francisco, Pessoa was pastoring Hispanic churches in town, studying at Golden Gate Baptist Theological Seminary, and helping FPLBC as much as he could as a member of the congregation.[90] When Pessoa graduated from the seminary in 1987, he was appointed as a Southern Baptist missionary—to Colombia. By then Geriel de Oliveira, who was key to the founding of FPLBC San Francisco, was a secretary of the FMB in Richmond, Virginia; he was partially responsible for Pessoa's appointment.[91] According to Ferreira, Pessoa's appointment made FPLBC San Francisco feel like the church in Antioch, sending one of its own to reach foreign nations.[92]

In 1987, in a somewhat parallel move, Ferreira accepted a position as executive secretary of the Carioca Baptist Convention, in Rio de Janeiro. Kunkel became the senior pastor of the church with Ferreira's departure.[93] Before he left, however, FPLBC San Francisco left FBC San Francisco and partnered with a Southern Baptist Hispanic church called Primera Iglesia Bautista de Sur.[94] Soon after Ferreira departed for Brazil, Kunkel was appointed by the FMB to be a missionary in Paraguay, and Pr. Billy Wesley Larrubia Rios became the senior pastor of FPLBC San Francisco, where he would pastor for over a decade.[95] During Rios' tenure, the church's ministry reached a young Brazilian migrant named Ribamar Monteiro Jr., who was working without proper documents in the United States. In time he returned to Brazil for theological training and then become a pastor of a multisite Brazuca Baptist ministry in the Bay Area.

[88] Damy Ferreira, "A Sombra do Portão Dourado: A Aventura de um Brasileiro Que Viajou Quase a Pé para os Estados Unidos—II," *Jornal Batista* LXXXV, no. 41 (1985): 12.

[89] Ferreira, "Sombra do Portão Dourado: A Aventura II," 12.

[90] Damy Ferreira, "A Sombra do Portão Dourado: A Aventura de um Brasileiro Que Viajou Quase a Pé para os Estados Unidos," *Jornal Batista* LXXXV, no. 40 (1985): 11–12.

[91] Oliveira, interview.

[92] Damy Ferreira, "A Sombra do Portão Dourado: Um Fim-De-Ano com Muitas Festas," *Jornal Batista* LXXXVII, no. 9 (1987): 12.

[93] Damy Ferreira, "A Sombra do Portão Dourado: Despedida," *Jornal Batista* LXXXVII, no. 31 (1987): 12.

[94] Damy Ferreira, "A Sombra do Portão Dourado: Um Ano Novo de Mudanças," *Jornal Batista* LXXXVII, no. 11 (1987): 12.

[95] Silva Edinete, interview, March 18, 2016; Sandra de Souza, "Pastor Brasileiro na Califórnia," *Jornal Batista* XCI, no. 37 (1991): 12; and Oliveira, interview.

Monteiro first came to the United States in 1988, accepting the invitation of one of his migrant friends who had been in California since 1982.[96] He visited FPLBC San Francisco on the invitation of a Brazilian colleague from work, a visit that would change Monteiro's trajectory. His family had raised him in the Presbyterian church in Brazil. Now, away from church life, the only Brazilian church he knew was FPLBC San Francisco. There, he had a conversion experience, was baptized in December 1989, and soon after began to work at the church. In May 1990 he felt a call to become a pastor.[97] In 1992 Monteiro, now married, returned to Brazil to attend seminary. He stayed in Brazil until 1997, when he became a youth minister at FPLBC San Francisco and began a mission in Marin County. In 2001 that mission work became independent, the pastor of FPLBC San Francisco left the church, and so Monteiro stepped in and pastored both works for about two years. When a new FPLBC San Francisco pastor was appointed in 2003, Monteiro expanded his reach and founded churches in two other locations. Today, Monteiro's work is the strongest Brazuca Baptist ministry in California, and he is the senior pastor of three locations in the Bay Area: Corte Madera, Brisbane, and San Pablo.[98]

Stories from the Washington, D.C., Metropolitan Area

Far away on the other coast in Washington, D.C., in June 1984, Joe Underwood, a former Southern Baptist missionary to Brazil, became the associate pastor at Georgetown Baptist Church, eager for the appointment partly because the church was filled with Brazilian members. He commented in the *Jornal Batista* in 1985 that "the Brazilian Baptist residents of the capital of the United States [had] discovered a comfortable shelter in Georgetown Baptist Church," adding, "actually, it is more than a shelter: it is their church."[99] Indeed, the Brazilian members were an integral part of the church's life; many held leadership positions, and together they brought to Georgetown "a new life and enthusiasm."[100] With Underwood on the staff, Georgetown Baptist began a service in Portuguese on Sunday afternoons that, a year later in 1985, had fifty regular participants. The church also offered immigration counseling and planned on "creating an office that helps (Brazilians) search for jobs, switch jobs, look for housing, etc."[101] Underwood was the first to advertise his services

---

[96] Ribamar Monteiro Jr., interview, January 6, 2016.
[97] Monteiro Jr., interview.
[98] Monteiro Jr., interview.
[99] Joe Underwood, "Batistas Brasileiros em Washington," *Jornal Batista* LXXXV, no. 3 (1985): 16.
[100] Underwood, "Batistas Brasileiros em Washington," 16.
[101] Underwood, "Batistas Brasileiros em Washington," 16.

to a Brazilian Baptist audience in Brazil; having noticed the flux of Brazilian migration to the United States in the mid-1980s, he told readers of the *Jornal Batista* that "the churches and people in Brazil who know Brazilians living in Washington and surrounding areas, or those who are yet to migrate here, are invited to write to Pr. Joe Underwood, Georgetown Baptist Church, 31st and N Streets, NW, Washington D.C., 20007, U.S.A."[102]

In the same year that Underwood arrived in D.C., another group of Brazilian Baptists was meeting in homes in the area until, in January 1985, they organized Igreja Batista Brasileira em Washington D.C. (Brazilian Baptist Church in Washington, D.C.), in a room rented from Wheaton Presbyterian Church, in Maryland.[103] Pastor João Petrowitz and his wife, Ruth, led the founding group. They resided in the D.C. area, where Petrowitz worked as a car mechanic and had noticed the need for a Brazuca Baptist work in their region.[104] In the same year that the Brazuca church began, it debuted a fifteen-minute radio program in Portuguese called *Minutos de Esperança* (Minutes of Hope) aimed at local Portuguese-speaking immigrants. Presumably bolstered by this outreach, the church grew considerably and by the early 1990s, had quadrupled in size to 120 members. In 1992 Geriel de Oliveira, formerly employed by the FMB in Richmond, became interim pastor of Brazilian Baptist Church in Washington, D.C. (henceforth BraBC in D.C.).[105]

Oliveira's tenure was brief, and in 1995 the church began looking for a pastor to lead the community, there having been a split in the church and Oliveira having left with a group of parishioners. Together, they formed a predominantly Brazilian church called Igreja Batista Nações Unidas (United Nations Baptist Church) that today meets in Silver Springs, Maryland.[106] Meanwhile, BraBC in D.C. began looking for a pastor to replace Oliveira. Its process of pastoral recruitment illustrates the power that moving to and pastoring in the United States has in the imagination of Brazilian Baptist leaders. In July 1995 BraBC in D.C. sent two representatives to observe a pastor of one of the most prominent churches in Brazil, to find out whether he would be a good candidate for the church. They went to Liberdade Baptist Church, in São Paulo, in order to draw up a report on Pr. Eli Fernandes, a longtime leader of the São Paulo megachurch.[107] Fernandes did show interest in coming to D.C. but asked for the church to wait several months before he could leave his prominent post

---

[102] Underwood, "Batistas Brasileiros em Washington," 16.
[103] *Atas da (Minutes of) Igreja Batista Brasileira de Washington D.C.*, 1988, 1–2.
[104] Carlos Mendes, interview, July 18, 2016.
[105] *Atas da (Minutes of) Igreja Batista Brasileira de Washington D.C.*, 1992, 48.
[106] Mendes, interview.
[107] *Atas da (Minutes of) Igreja Batista Brasileira de Washington D.C.*, 1995, 101.

in Brazil. The church decided not to wait and instead extended an invitation to one of the pastors on Fernandes' staff, Pr. Carlos Mendes.[108] As of this writing, Mendes has been the pastor of BraBC in D.C. for the past two decades and is a prominent leader among Brazilian Baptists in the United States.

In May 1999 another church was founded in the area. Igreja Batista de Língua Portuguesa em Arlington (Portuguese Language Baptist Church in Arlington, Virginia) began under the leadership of Pr. João Rocha, an employee of the Brazilian embassy. This Brazilian group was sponsored by Westover Baptist Church, along with the Mount Vernon Baptist Association and the Baptist General Association of Virginia.[109] Rocha wrote to the *Jornal Batista* in 2001 saying that though the church was mostly Brazilian, it was actually international and had members who had migrated from several countries. In that same letter he helpfully listed the Brazilian churches in the D.C. metropolitan area, which by then were seven: "1) United Nations Baptist Church (Pr. Geriel de Oliveira), 2) Brazilian Baptist Church of Gaithersburg, Maryland (currently without a pastor), 3) BraBC in D.C. (Pr. Carlos Mendes), 4) Portuguese Language Baptist Church in Arlington, Virginia (Pr. João Rocha), and three other churches of other denominations."[110]

Stories from Florida

The northeastern states did not have a monopoly on Brazuca Baptists—far from it. Florida is presently the home of the biggest Brazilian Baptist church outside of Brazil, Primeira Igreja Batista Brasileira da Flórida (First Brazilian Baptist Church of Florida). In 2016 it had almost two thousand (mostly Brazilian) members. The pioneer Brazilian Baptist missions in Florida began in 1987, when Giovani and Neuba Régia began a mission in Orlando with the help of the Home Mission Board of the SBC and a predominantly Spanish-speaking church called Primera Iglesia Bautista de Orlando.[111] In December 1987 another Brazilian Baptist mission started in Miami under the pastoral leadership of José Heleno da Silva. Silva had been in the United States in 1982, when he preached at several churches in Texas; on a visit to Florida, he noticed the great number of Brazilians and Portuguese in the region. In 1985 Silva returned to Florida, now to do an internship at First Baptist Church of Orlando. Once more he noticed the great number of Brazilian and Portuguese migrants,

---

[108] *Atas da (Minutes of) Igreja Batista Brasileira de Washington D.C.*, 1996, 120.

[109] João Correa Rocha, "Igreja Batista de Língua Portuguesa, em Arlington, Virginia," *Jornal Batista* C, no. 1 (2001): 9.

[110] Rocha, "Igreja Batista de Língua Portuguesa," 9.

[111] José Heleno Silva, "Missões na Flórida," *Jornal Batista* LXXXVIII, no. 16 (1988): 12.

as well as migrants from Angola and Mozambique. When he returned to Brazil, Silva arranged to come back to Florida with his wife and start the First Portuguese-Brazilian Baptist Mission in Miami.[112]

The most impressive example of Brazilian Baptist success in the United States, however, began in 1990, again in a serendipitous way. That year, Pr. Ivan de Souza and his wife came to South Florida in order to visit their son, who was attending college there and seemed to need help adapting to college life. They decided to stay in the region for three months.[113] That was enough for Souza to realize that the Pompano Beach area could use a Portuguese-speaking church, and he began a mission with the help of First Baptist Church of Pompano Beach. When he returned to Brazil, Souza convinced his son-in-law, Silair de Almeida, a pastor in a small town in northeastern Brazil, to go to Florida to take over the group. Almeida accepted the challenge, and using soccer, entertainment, and initiatives that helped struggling Brazilian families in the region, helped form a church that, in 2006, made the *Outreach Magazine* list for the hundred fastest-growing churches in America; the community was also recognized by Saddleback Church as one of the healthiest churches in the world.[114] By the time I conducted interviews and did ethnographic and archival work at Almeida's church, it not only had an impressive missionary presence across the globe but also helped underprivileged US-born peoples and immigrants through its many social initiatives. The church also often hosted the Brazilian consulate in its multibuilding property—where immigrants could benefit from a number of services provided by the Brazilian government, such as renewing passports or applying for dual citizenship for US-born children of Brazilian parents. Almeida is now an influential leader in South Florida. Among other things, he has served as a representative of the Brazilian Council of Representatives of Brazilians Living Abroad (a part of the Brazilian Ministry of Foreign Relations) and has been involved in numerous initiatives involving local businesses and governments.

First Brazilian Baptist Church in Orlando also had a peculiar beginning. It started as a Bible study group that wanted to be generically evangelical and nondenominational. Without a pastor, it called itself Brazilian Christian Community and met in a building of First United Church of Christ in Curry City.[115] The group then invited Pr. Dr. Daniel Paixão, a retired pastor who had been an officer of the SBC's FMB, to be their pastor. Only after Paixão joined the church

---

[112] Silva, "Missões na Flórida," 12.
[113] Silair Almeida, interview, March 2, 2016.
[114] Almeida, interview.
[115] "Nossa Historia," *PIBBORLANDO Church*, accessed February 12, 2021, http://www.pibborlando.org/nossa-historia/.

did the members decide to become Baptist.[116] There is another Brazuca Baptist church in Orlando, Memorial Brazilian Baptist Church, which split off from First Brazilian Baptist Church, and both communities reflect a genealogy in which initially nondenominational groups evolved into Baptist communities.

Continuity and Discontinuity: Once Brazilian, Now Multinational, Always Missionary

Despite the diffuseness of the history of Brazuca Baptist churches such as these, there are a few characteristics that unite them. I explore the doctrinal, institutional, and ideological commitments that generate a sense of solidarity among these churches in the following chapter, but here it is appropriate to mention two common characteristics: (1) the move from a focus on being a Brazilian church to being a multinational church, and (2) the missionary impulse that characterizes Brazuca Baptist communities and reveals the worldwide impact that their presence in the United States represents.

The first of these traits manifests itself in an environment characterized by a twofold tension between the weakening in the influx of Brazilian migrants on the one hand and the challenges stemming from a concern for second-generation Brazilian Americans on the other. While the initial high influx of Brazilian immigrants justified the drive toward the maintenance of a Brazilian identity threatened by US society, Brazuca Baptist churches toward the end of the first decade of the twenty-first century had to come to grips with the fact that migration patterns are fluid. The crash in the US economy during the 2007–2008 financial crisis and the apparent strength of the Brazilian economy during the Workers Party's administration changed the migration pattern drastically. With more Brazilians leaving the United States than coming to the country, Brazuca Baptist communities had to be creative to survive in a changing religious market and to become more attentive to ministering effectively to the growing—and primarily English-speaking—second generation. When it comes to the Brazuca Baptist missionary impulse, a legacy of their Southern Baptist heritage, the discussion below shows how effective these communities have been through their investment in world missions.

Migration Influx and the Multinational Church

The general shift in focus among Brazuca Baptist churches from a Brazilian membership to a desire to broaden their appeal to a larger audience coincided with the slowing down of Brazilian immigration to the United States and the

[116] Daniel Paixão, interview, July 13, 2016.

increase in the return of Brazilian migrants to Brazil due to the fluctuations of the global economy. This shift was felt more strongly in some regions of the United States, such as the northeastern states, than in others. Florida, for example, was less negatively affected by the migration flux, in part because of its popularity among Brazilians both in Brazil and in other US states. As such, Florida benefited from both international and internal migration in exceptional ways.[117] Other factors, such as the toughening of immigration enforcement and the challenge brought by a second generation of Brazilian Baptists coming of age in these communities, are also significant, but fluctuations in first-generation migration patterns are central to the change in focus. After over two decades of prioritizing Brazilians as members and potential parishioners, as a strategy for survival most Brazuca Baptist churches are becoming less Brazilian, although the effectiveness of this strategy is yet to be proven and not all Brazuca Baptist pastors admit that they are making the shift.[118]

Some of the Brazuca Baptist pastors who have spearheaded the transition in the name of their congregations have had a clear rationale for doing so. Ophir Barros, for example, said that he had in mind the churches started by German immigrants to Brazil when he suggested changing the name of Primeira Igreja Batista de Língua Portuguesa de Danbury to All Nations Baptist Church. In fact, he sought a full transition from an immigrant church to a national church, based on his observations of German churches in Brazil itself. He worked with the Baptist state convention of Paraná, a Brazilian state to which many German immigrants went to perform agricultural jobs.[119] During his time with the convention, he dealt with the issues raised by the properties of German churches that died as a result of failing to transition beyond the German identity, and he feared for the fate of Brazuca Baptist churches unwilling or unable to expand their appeal across ethnic lines. Today, the worship hall of All Nations Baptist Church has the flags of countries like Honduras, Russia, Mexico, Puerto Rico, Barbados, and Israel hanging on the two sides of the square room where the cashiers and tellers of Chase Bank once sat. The worship space itself was designed to further the vision of a multinational church. Yet Barros' substitute as All Nations Baptist Church's senior pastor

---

[117] See Matt Reis, "Brazilian Evangelicos in Diaspora in South Florida: Identity and Mission" (Ph.D. diss., University of Edinburgh, forthcoming 2021).

[118] A notable exception to this trend is Silair Almeida's PIB Florida, the largest Brazuca church. Almeida continues to emphasize Brazilianness, and other pastors claim that he can afford to do that because of the dense Brazilian population in South Florida. Other Florida pastors also have told me that maintaining Brazilianness is very important.

[119] Barros, interview.

laments that though this vision is widely shared among pastors, parishioners have sometimes challenged it. When he arrived in the United States, he

> noticed a strong ethnocentrism among Brazilians. We talk about multiethnic churches, but they don't work in practice. We have a church that is predominantly Brazilian, we know that we have a Hispanic community, and if we start to reach the Hispanic community, that is, if we open the church to a more missionary vison, deep inside the Brazilians want to always be in control of everything. They don't want to share, don't want to share leadership in a multiethnic church. So we see this strong ethnocentrism. "We want to be Brazilian and to live as Brazilians," they say. And they close doors to a heterogeneous church, so we live in a homogeneous church. Homogeneous churches in the world in which we live as immigrants, they have a hard time growing. Why? Because this vision comes with the members, it is in the head of the first generation. And if you want to change that, you will have to be very patient and work very carefully in order avoid divisions.[120]

Translating the leadership's vision of transitioning from being Brazilian to being multiethnic presents challenges in an environment in which new immigrants continue to arrive, even if in smaller numbers, with the expectation that churches function as mechanisms and spaces for the maintenance of their national and ethnic cultures.

In 2015 Sérgio Freitas, of PIB New Jersey: Church of the City, noted that the signs and Brazilian and Portuguese flags that then identified the church no longer represented the community's identity. Freitas was extremely bothered that only Portuguese speakers could read the church signs and was working to change this reality. Freitas said that immigrants could not afford to close themselves off in their "ethnic ghettoes" and that "the immigrant churches are closing, they are closing."[121] But he denied—and denied "in the name of Jesus"— that his openness to reach peoples from all nations was a survival strategy. "I am working," he said, "to be a church of people who do not like the church, and of people who the church doesn't like, regardless of nationality and flag."[122] In short, he understood this disposition as a clear theological, rather than strategic, option. By January 2017, when I visited the church after a few years from Freitas' arrival in New Jersey, there were no signs in Portuguese and no identification of the church building that would call attention to its ethnic roots.

The shift in outlook in these and other Brazuca Baptist communities, however, came only with the shift in the Brazilian migration patterns. It was during

---

[120] Girlan Silva, interview, January 4, 2017.
[121] Sérgio Freitas, interview, October 29, 2015.
[122] Freitas, interview.

the mid- to late 2000s, when Brazilian immigration was diminishing in numbers, that many Brazuca Baptist churches became more aggressive about widening their horizons. First Baptist Church of Greater Boston: A Lovely Place, for instance, contemplated developing a partnership with Gordon-Conwell Seminary so that young seminary students could come to the church to preach in their English services; the church also attempted to merge the Korean and Nepalese communities that rented their space with the Brazilian parishioners.[123] In addition, not only did the East Coast Lineage churches in New York, Boston, Elizabeth, and Danbury change their names and reach; other churches did so too, among them the multisite Bridge Ministry in the California Bay Area, Evangelical Church of the Nations in New Bedford, Walk Worthy Baptist Church in Austin, and a number of other communities that have Brazuca Baptist DNA but have negotiated their Brazilianness, their explicitly Baptist identification, or both.

In addition, English-speaking and/or bilingual youth, who, despite their love for aspects of Brazilian culture, are much more acculturated to US society than their parents could ever imagine, increasingly populate Brazuca Baptist churches, causing great concern among the leadership—not only about their attendance but also about how to accommodate their desire for a predominantly English-speaking church. Although there is no unanimity regarding the need for transitioning from an immigrant community to a multinational one with English as a primary language, the great majority of Brazuca Baptist leaders are experimenting with ways to make this transition. These churches are, therefore, hoping to be incorporated into the US religious landscape in a way similar to that in which many German, Irish, Italian, and Spanish churches once transitioned from immigrant to national churches. Time will tell whether they will succeed, and how possible changes in migration patterns will inform these churches' future strategies. Until now, however, variations in migration patterns seem to have had little impact on a commitment that Brazuca Baptists leaders learned from their Southern Baptist founding fathers: wherever the church community is located, it must be committed to missionary work.

Immigrant Churches, Missionary Churches

The great majority of Brazuca Baptist pastors who immigrated to the United States to lead faith communities saw themselves as missionaries, even when they came to the country on their own initiative. Initially, they saw themselves mostly as missionaries to their own people abroad but also to all peoples

---

[123] *Atas da (Minutes of) Primeira Igreja Batista (Boston)*, 2009, book 3, 432–34.

across the globe. The means through which the world was to be affected by the ministry of their immigrant churches were the financial contributions of immigrant parishioners, whether documented or undocumented. Brazuca Baptist churches, therefore, were aggressive in contributing to world missions.

The First Brazilian Baptist Church of Greater Boston, for instance, was supporting missionaries in Mozambique, Angola, Cuba, and Brazil by the mid-1990s, soon after Jorge Bezerra's arrival.[124] The Boston church also supported missionaries in São Paulo, Rio de Janeiro, Luanda, and Guinea-Bissau.[125] Under Nivaldo Nassif, the church added missionaries in eastern Europe, Turkey, Kenya, and Senegal to its initiatives.[126] Primeira Igreja Batista Brasileira da Flórida supports hundreds of missionaries across the world, has built orphanages in Haiti and Cuba, has helped build and support health clinics among Native Brazilians in the Amazon, provides education for 123 ministers in Cuba, and engages in constant mission trips to the Global South.[127] The proportion of the financial and personal investment into world missions, of course, varies from church to church, depending on its size and budget. Yet Brazuca Baptist churches that do not invest in world missions beyond their contributions to the cooperative programs of the SBC are the rare exception.

Why such deep commitment? No doubt part of the reason is that many of the pastors who founded churches in the United States had personal experience working as foreign missionaries. For example, Humberto Viegas Fernandes came to the United States through the WMB, Levy Penido was a WMB missionary in Ecuador before coming to the East Coast, Josias Bezerra served as a temporary missionary in Guinea-Bissau, and José Calixto had been a coordinator of Bolivarian countries (Venezuela, Bolivia, Colombia, Peru, and Ecuador) and of the North Area (Caribe, North America, and Central America) for the WMB, as well as a missionary in Costa Rica. In addition, the memory that the BBC was the result of world mission efforts of the SBC's FMB remains firmly entrenched in the Brazuca Baptist imagination.

The strategies through which the missionary zeal of Brazuca Baptist leaders has been disseminated and maintained in Brazuca Baptist churches are generally not very different from those used in Southern Baptist churches. A closer look at the way in which this dynamic played out at PIB New Jersey: Church of the City will help illustrate this dynamic. The pastors of PIB New Jersey faced some resistance in raising money for missions in Brazil and abroad. In 2002 Josias Bezerra

[124] Moraes, "Igreja Brasileira em Boston," 13.
[125] *Atas da (Minutes of) Primeira Igreja Batista (Boston)*, 1999, book 2, 122–23.
[126] *Atas da (Minutes of) Primeira Igreja Batista (Boston)*, 2002–2005, book 2, 247–402.
[127] Almeida, interview.

wrote a justification for the practice in the *Folha da Primeira*, the internal news-letter of the church. People who thought that the church's campaign for world missions in general, and the mediation of the WMB in particular, was a waste of time and money may be correct logically but not necessarily theologically, said Bezerra. He challenged the community by writing that

> before you talk or even think that raising money in America so that Brazilian institutions can do the work of missions is absurd, pray so that God can show you what is his will concerning this issue. If you become convinced of the worth of this work, don't look just to the financial sum that will be invested, but to the lives that will enter into a new life-dimension by participating in a real encounter with the message of Jesus Christ.[128]

Bezerra was not alone in trying to implement this endeavor, of course. His leadership team also espoused the vision and denominational background into which many members had to be educated. Márcia Garcia, the minister of missions of PIB New Jersey also wrote to the church exhorting it to embrace the work of world missions. "God could send his angels to preach," she said, "but he trusted us with this work of taking the good news of the kingdom to those who have no hope. Remember the words of Jesus in Matthew 28:19 20: 'go and make disciples of every nation.'"[129]

In addition to the theological justifications for world missions printed on the front page of the *Folha da Primeira*, PIB New Jersey constantly advertised its world mission efforts and asked for prayers for specific missionaries.[130] The church also printed letters it received from its missionaries in Brazil and abroad. Regardless of the where such missionaries were stationed, almost all were Brazilian and had connections to the WMB. As the missionary corre-spondence shows, the ministries with which PIB New Jersey was involved var-ied. For example, Damivan and Marinete Santos worked in the port of Parana-guá, trying to minister to sailors; Luis and Orleusa Silva conducted evangelism

---

[128] Josias Bezerra, "Por Que Missões?" *Folha da Primeira*, February 24, 2002, 1.

[129] Márcia Garcia, "Há um Clamor Agora?" *Folha da Primeira*, March 10, 2002, 1.

[130] Márcia Barrientos, "A Tarefa Missionária da Igreja," *Folha da Primeira*, July 10, 2001, 1; Bezerra, "Por Que Missões?" 1; Garcia, "Há um Clamor Agora?" 1; Márcia Garcia, "Missões, Oportunidade de Servir," *Folha da Primeira*, October 6, 2002, 1; José Calixto, "O Plano de Deus para a Obra Missionária," *Folha da Primeira*, October 27, 2002, 1; José Calixto, "Por Que uma Campanha de Missões Mundiais na Igreja?" *Folha da Primeira*, April 27, 2003, 1; idem, "Brasil: um País a Ser Conquistado," *Folha da Primeira*, October 12, 2003, 1; "Campanha de Missões Nacionais," *Folha da Primeira*, September 23, 2001, 2; "Pedidos de Oração por Missões," *Folha da Primeira*, December 16, 2001, 2; "A Primeira Faz Missões," *Folha da Primeira*, March 24, 2002, 3; "Nossos Novos Missionários," *Folha da Primeira*, November 3, 2002, 2; and "Ore por Nossos Missionários," *Folha da Primeira*, March 9, 2003, 3.

in China; Eliezer Pinheiro de Souza planted churches in rural Brazil; and Rosângela Teck helped train pastors in Huambo, Angola.[131]

In 2002 this one church sent $32,216.25 to support mission in Brazil alone. At that time, the dollar was estimated at around 3.60 reais (the Brazilian currency), and the above total was enough to help support twenty-four missionaries, most of whom were located in rural and impoverished areas of the country.[132] To give a sense of the scope of the church's ministry, some of the WMB's goals for world missions beyond Brazil in 2003 were sending out one hundred new missionaries, enrolling five thousand new people to pray for missions, getting twelve thousand new people to support missions financially, generating partnerships with two hundred new businesses, and raising $3 million in the annual offering. Clearly PIB New Jersey and other Brazuca Baptist churches, despite not being in Brazil or being official members of the BBC, were seen and saw themselves as part of this plan.[133] In the previous year, PIB New Jersey claimed to have helped send seventy-nine new missionaries to the mission field, enroll over two thousand to pray for missions, and raise a considerable sum of money for missions in Brazil and beyond.[134] The importance of churches such as PIB New Jersey for the financial goals of the WMB was so great that Waldemiro Tymchak, then president of the WMB, was the keynote speaker of the second missionary conference hosted by the church.[135]

Igreja Batista Brasileira de Washington D.C. also advertised its missionaries' activities in its weekly bulletin. In 2002 this church was involved in initiatives such as the support of a missionary in Africa; ministries of social assistance in Brazilian Baptist churches in Brazil; and support for Baptist Seminary of Havana, Cuba.[136] By 2007 the church had engaged in support for ministries in Mozambique, Somalia, different parts of Brazil, and an undisclosed location in Asia.[137] The D.C. church posted most of its missionary correspondences on the church news board and thus did not print them in bulletins and newsletters,

[131] Eliézer Souza, "O Senhor de Missões Tem Feito Maravilhas," Folha da Primeira, October 13, 2002, 1; "Biografia Missionária," Folha da Primeira, May 8, 2001, 1; Damivan Santos, "Relatório Missionário," Folha da Primeira, April 1, 2001, 1; Rosângela Teck, "Carta Missionária," Folha da Primeira, March 16, 2013, 1.

[132] "Uma Oferta Inesquecível," Folha da Primeira, February 16, 2003, 1.

[133] "Veja os Resultados do Nosso Inversitmento na Obra Missionária," Folha da Primeira, March 23, 2003, 2.

[134] "Veja os Resultados," 3.

[135] "Anunciai Paz as Nações: Segunda Conferência Missionária da Primeira," Folha da Primeira, May 15, 2003, 1.

[136] "Campanha Missionária," Boletin da Igreja Batista Brasileira em Washington, June 30, 2002, 2.

[137] "Ministérios e Avisos," Boletin da Igreja Batista Brasileira em Washington, January 7, 2007, 2.

but the community was clearly active in supporting missions throughout its history. The missionary they supported in Africa, Calvin Brain, had been a member of the church since its early years. World missions continue to be a given in Brazuca Baptist churches, and the financial advantages of giving in US dollars greatly magnifies their potential global impact.

The spirit of this commitment to world missions can be clearly identified in the enthusiastic and creative description of the pastor of a Brazilian megachurch in Florida. When asked about his church's investment in missions, he shared:

> We have our PIB-shop here, that has about thirty thousand clothing items, each of them costs $2.00, and everything we sell goes to missions work. Today we have over thirty voluntary workers working on this initiative. We have in our church today 450 volunteers in all ministries—Brazilians who volunteer to help. . . . We learned many things. First, I have a very strong missionary presence in the Brazilian Amazon region. So, in Brazil, we chose two places, one close to [the city of] Manaus and the other in the [tribe of the] Ticunas. Why? Because nothing represents Brazil better than the forest. The Amazon. So in taking Brazilians back to Brazil in our missionary trips, I give them this Brazilian identity—"here is your forest." I have been doing this a lot with our teenagers. And the results have been extraordinary, they have fallen in love with Brazil. This is a way of giving and receiving. We have been [helping build] a large church in Jacaré village, the missionary went from here—he lived here for thirteen years. Today he is building; he has already built the temple with air conditioning and everything, it is an area by the river, and now we are building an entire health clinic. As a matter of fact, Pr. Cléber is taking a group there tomorrow until this health clinic, dental clinic, and everything is ready. We have three orphanages in Haiti, including one we just bought—we freed fifty children from slavery and abuse. Today they are well, very well taken care of. A couple from the WMB coordinate this, we have ten employees there. We have been in Cuba for the last twenty years. This is our oldest project. Twenty years. All Cuban pastors of the new generation were helped by the church in terms of support. So, I know all the Cuban pastors. When I go to Cuba I feel at home wherever I go. But the most important thing for me is taking the groups. Last year we took 150 people [there] on mission trips.[138]

As this pastor's testimony suggests, the multidirectional character represented by world missions efforts undertaken by immigrant networks combines a commitment to Southern Baptist–style missions with elements not commonly associated with missionary efforts. Brazuca churches also see missions to Brazil as an aspect of maintaining ethnic identity—especially in new generations of Brazilian Americans—and are engaged in the work of social justice

---

[138] Almeida, interview.

in several countries around the world. The bulk of this work is financed by undocumented parishioners, either through direct financial contributions or through volunteer work in church ministries. What would be the Southern Baptist response to the reality that the commitment to missions and global justice work of immigrant churches is significantly supported by undocumented workers? Praise the Lord but build the wall? One wonders.

Conclusion

The story of Brazuca Baptists is rich and full of surprises. Strictly speaking, Brazilian Baptists have been coming to the United States since the late nineteenth century. Already early on in the history of the Southern Baptist presence in Brazil, promising students, denominational leaders, and able preachers traveled to the United States for a wide range of reasons. In the 1960s the number of Brazilian Baptist students and pastors in the United States was so significant that reports on their whereabouts and accomplishments were regularly printed in the *Jornal Batista*. In 1981 the WMB sent Humberto Viegas Fernandes to the United States as the first Brazilian Baptist missionary. Fernandes came to evangelize Portuguese immigrants, but upon arrival he found that the WMB's vision was tainted by a limited evaluation of the richness of migration to the United States. The churches started by Fernandes became primarily Brazilian, and the mass migration of Brazilians to the United States meant that Brazilian Baptist leaders formed primarily Brazilian, rather than Portuguese, churches. Yet the economic crisis in the United States after 2008, combined with the strengthening of the Brazilian economy and the challenges brought by a growing second generation, affected the demographic and financial situation of these immigrant communities. As a response to this dynamic, the Brazuca Baptist churches have entered a new phase in their history by trying to broaden their appeal to a larger sector of US society. This move represents a next step toward the incorporation—even if not assimilation—of Brazuca Baptist churches into the broader competition of the multifaceted American Sunday.

The role of Brazuca Baptist churches in world missions is a testament to the transgression of the limited idea of reverse missions and of legalistic or romantic imaginings of global proselytism. First, these communities are strong examples of multidirectional missions; that is, they are a living example that missions, in the contemporary environment, go from everywhere to everywhere. Brazilian missionary-pastors came to the United States, and the churches they founded in turn sent and supported missionaries in Brazil and in Africa, Asia, South America, and Europe. In addition, Brazuca Baptist pastors have moved between Brazil, the United States, and other countries as pastors, denominational leaders, missionaries, and teachers. Often they imagine themselves as citizens of the realm of God and live in accordance with that imagination. A substantial and perhaps even majority of the funds supporting world mission efforts have come from the contributions of undocumented immigrants in the United States. As we will see, undocumented immigrants comprise much of the membership of some Brazuca Baptist churches, and there is no evidence that they tithe less often or in smaller amounts than documented parishioners. The history of Brazuca Baptists is therefore one of a group that is not only progressively moving beyond the immigrant dynamics that characterized its beginnings but also one of a community with a proven record of worldwide impact. Now, we turn to look more closely at the ambiguous belonging of Brazuca Baptists to the US denominational bodies with which they are affiliated, an ambiguity for which attitudes to language and culture are partially responsible.

4
CONNECTING

Unbelonging and the Creation of Ethnic Denominationalism

The Brazilian church is a third culture. It is not Brazilian, nor it will be American. It is in between. Brazilian culture is nonnegotiable. People who are in a Brazilian church, [it] is because they have a preference for Brazilian culture. Because those who transitioned to US culture can't stand a Brazilian church.

Pastor Lécio Dornas[1]

Language often gives us clues to a person's socialization, to the communities that have shaped an individual's central mode of communication, which often connects deeply with patterns of thinking. Language is an important element in the dynamics of belonging—in part because it is such a central mediator of culture. The role of linguistic patterns in the ambiguous belonging of immigrant Christians manifests itself in a number of directions. In Brazuca churches, linguistic anxieties appear for instance in concerns that relate to the role of these churches in the maintenance of Brazilian culture in future generations and in issues surrounding the inclusion of songs in Spanish and English in Sunday services. The ambiguity of Brazuca belonging as it relates to language—and the cultures that language helps transmit—sometimes appear in subtle patterns of speech of Brazuca leaders. On the one hand, it is not uncommon to hear immigrant pastors mispronouncing English words or misusing US expressions; on the other, it

[1] Lecio Dornas, interview, October 15, 2015.

is also not uncommon to hear the casual Southern exclamation "Lord have mercy" in the middle of a Portuguese conversation or even the translated version of expressions such as "I am not supposed to"—which sounds odd in Brazilian Portuguese. The liminality of immigrant Christian imagination is reflected by the negotiation of different languages, spaces, and manifestations of community—all of which are in the constant process of negotiation, development, and employment. Institutionally, for the purposes of our understanding of immigrant churches, these deeper sensibilities of liminality are clearly manifested in denominational dynamics.

The denominational identity of Brazuca Baptist churches is, on one hand, an extension of the Southern Baptist ethos. On the other hand, it is characterized by an uneasiness with strict denominational affiliation that is the result of the eclectic experiences so common among Brazilian immigrants. While the Brazuca Baptist leadership cultivates a historically informed appreciation for the SBC, buttressed by the documented affinity between the BBC and the SBC in terms of the overwhelming majority of their explicit theological confessions, their stance on the cooperation between them and the US denominations (often the SBC) with which they are affiliated is highly ambiguous. A retired pastor who worked in Brazuca Baptist churches for over two decades and was strongly involved with the ethnic denominationalism of Brazuca Baptists aptly observed:

> The partnership [with the SBC] is not ideological. We maintain connections with the Brazilian Baptist Convention. Pastors here [in the US] had been pastors there [in Brazil]. We even created a partnership between our fellowship of pastors here and the one in Brazil. We are a section of the one in Brazil. So, we made a connection to the BBC and as the BBC has a connection to the SBC, we consider the SBC to be our big momma. But when we try to work with them, we have issues.[2]

In the mid-1990s, less than fifteen years after Brazuca Baptist churches began forming all over the country, this uneasiness materialized in the formation of the Associação das Igrejas Batistas Brasileiras na América do Norte (Association of the Brazilian Baptist Churches in North America, or AIBBAN). While that formation was the direct result of another Brazuca Baptist event that preceded it, namely the Congresso da Juventude Batista Brasileira na América do Norte (Congress of the Brazilian Baptist Youth in North America, henceforth CONJUBBRAN), once created, AIBBAN became the most

---

[2] For the purposes of this chapter, the identities of pastors whose words can compromise their denominational and congregational work will be kept confidential.

important cooperative work with which Brazuca Baptist churches were affiliated. The creation of the AIBBAN represented a particular form of denominationalism founded on an ethnodenominational solidarity that symbolized the failure of US denominations to incorporate ethnic groups to the satisfaction of the latter. This ethnic denominationalism also shows how institutions such as the SBC—but also the American Baptist Churches USA, to which some Brazuca Baptist churches are affiliated—have sometimes failed to live up to their rhetoric of welcoming diversity and supporting ethnic groups. While the AIBBAN initiative was not a full-fledged, unanimous rejection of previous affiliations, for all practical purposes it was an affirmation that the most appropriate affiliation for Brazuca Baptist churches was explicitly ethnic. The connection of Brazuca Baptist churches to national denominational bodies was imagined by many Brazuca Baptist pastors as being largely symbolic, and for some time the AIBBAN took the form of a robust transnational alternative to common and localized Baptist protocol.

In this chapter, I focus on the history of ethnic denominationalism among Brazuca Baptists. Doing so entails providing a historical narrative of the AIBBAN, and of the Brazuca Baptist anxieties manifested in the formation of this association.[3] To address this properly, I deal with a number of elements of Brazuca Baptist history. First, I show how churches and pastors have historically seen themselves as products of the SBC—a reality that they may articulate in terms of fidelity to the Bible and sympathy for Southern Baptist understanding of the Good Book. Second, I show how Brazuca Baptist transnational networks helped Brazuca Baptist leaders maintain a strong connection to the BBC that informed the formation of the AIBBAN as a potential arm of the BBC in the United States. I then talk about CONJUBBRAN, providing a narrative of its activities among Brazuca Baptists. Finally, I tell the history of the AIBBAN, concluding with a brief discussion of new efforts for implementing ethnic denominationalism among Brazuca Baptists.

Ethnic Denominationalism and SBC Spirit

When the BBC sent its first Brazilian missionary to Newark in 1981, it was as a denomination that complied strictly with the confessions of faith, political dispositions, and social imagination of the SBC as understood at the time. Yet, none of these SBC elements is static and, given the solidification of the divisions in the

---

[3]   According to various past presidents of the AIBBAN, the official documents of the institution are currently lost. The same is true for the CONJUBBRAN. This narrative, therefore, relies on church minutes, church bulletins, interviews, and articles printed in the *Jornal Batista*.

denomination, they have become more pronouncedly conservative since then. Brazuca Baptist churches adopted a number of SBC confessions of faith and, by doing so, judged themselves to be faithful reproducers of the faith of their "founding fathers." Consequently, Brazuca Baptist churches and their leaders were not always fully aware of all the ways in which the migration dynamics worked to nudge them away from the general modus operandi of both the SBC and the BBC. In other words, in terms of their self-understanding and doctrinal articulations, Brazuca Baptist churches have remained mostly faithful to their SBC heritage. At the same time, in terms of their practice and denominational identity these institutions have been greatly affected by migration dynamics. A few leaders have realized this difference but have chosen not to be outspoken about it. Yet the possibility the aforementioned retired pastor raised is realistic: "Perhaps if there were a SBC commission to see if Brazilian Baptists [in the United States] could be a part of the denomination, some Americans would say: 'no, do not include these people among us.'"

The Southern Baptist Ethos in Brazuca Baptist Churches

Beyond loose affiliation, the clearest demonstration of the theological continuum between the SBC and Brazilian Baptist churches in the United States is the presence of SBC confessions in the churches' bylaws. The 1995 bylaws of PIB Family Church, for instance, include not only a mention of its cooperative relationship with the New York Baptist convention and the SBC but also a stand-alone paragraph in the first chapter of the document that reveals anxieties that parallel those of the SBC:

> Members who are excluded from the church by decision[s] made in the church's general assembly lose their rights and privileges as members, and any member whose sexual conduct is contrary to biblical principles, such as: homosexuality, bisexuality, lesbianism, and cohabitation, will be summarily excluded from the church.[4]

The document also states that the church

> adopts the Baptist principles stated in the pact of faith of the churches that cooperated with the Convention of Memphis, Tennessee, [on] May 14, 1925 and has as its goal the celebration of the worship of God and the preaching of the Gospel of Jesus Christ, with all its means and resources, in conformity with what is clearly stated in Holy Scripture, the only rule of faith and practice.[5]

---

[4] *Estatuto da (Bylaws of) Primeira Igreja Batista de Língua Portuguesa de New York*, 1995, 1.
[5] *Estatuto da (Bylaws of) Primeira Igreja Batista (New York)*, 1.

Yet when PIB Family Church revised its bylaws in 2004, their commitment to a doctrinal statement had changed, even though they remained affiliated with the SBC. By then, it was the Doctrinal Declaration of the BBC that for them functioned as the means through which proper scriptural interpretation manifested itself.[6] In the same year, First Brazilian Baptist Church of Greater Boston: A Lovely Place showed its appreciation for both its SBC affiliation and its transnational connection to the BBC. The eighth article of their 2004 bylaws stated:

> A person will lose his or her membership status if he or she is excluded by a decision of the church's general assembly, in which the convocation includes the acceptance or exclusion of members for the following reasons: First—Infringing the ethical, moral, and behavioral principles defended by the church, which is founded in the Holy Scriptures and are in accordance to the Confession of Faith of the Southern Baptist Convention, which is transcribed in an annex of these bylaws. Second—Defending or professing doctrines or practices that are contrary to the Declaration of Faith of the Brazilian Baptist Convention and of the Southern Baptist Convention.[7]

There is no major doctrinal difference between SBC's Baptist Faith and Message 2000 and the Doctrinal Declaration of the BBC, but the shift toward the inclusion of the BBC in the bylaws of these churches is indicative of the emotional distancing from the United States denomination—and approximation to the BBC—that characterizes the history of a number of Brazuca Baptist churches.

Yet the particular ways in which Brazuca Baptist churches expressed their theological affinities varied. First Brazilian Baptist Church of Greater Boston, for instance, chose to use the SBC's Baptist Faith and Message of 1963 in its 2001 bylaws, before omitting the specific Confession of Faith to which it ascribed in its 2004 bylaws.[8] By contrast, PIB New Jersey was more generic in its bylaws, stating that

> the [PIB New Jersey] church accepts the Holy Bible as the only rule of faith and practice, accepting as doctrine the Confession of Faith of the Southern Baptist churches of the United States of America and the Southern Baptist Convention, to which the church is affiliated.[9]

The leadership of PIB New Jersey was not particularly concerned about specifying the particular SBC confession of faith to which they attached their doctrines.

[6] *Atas da (Minutes of) Primeira Igreja Batista de Língua Portuguesa de New York,* 2004, book 1, 79.

[7] *Atas da (Minutes of) Primeira Igreja Batista Brasileira da Grande Boston,* 2004, book 2, 310–11.

[8] *Atas da (Minutes of) Primeira Igreja Batista (Boston),* 2001, book 2, 200.

[9] *Atas da (Minutes of) Primeira Igreja Batista de Língua Portuguesa de New Jersey,* 1993, book 1, 42.

The leaders of Brazuca Baptist churches also have a generally positive perception of the SBC. For example, a pastor of a Brazilian Baptist church in Austin said, "I think [the SBC] continues to be one of the strongest denominations in the United States, independently of [its fragmentation]. I consider it a good denomination compared to the alternatives." A pastor in Florida and former president of a Brazuca Baptist cooperative institution in the United States, said that

> the Southern Baptist Convention is a conservative denomination. Strong and firm in its identity that is renewing some of its aspects in the last twenty years, getting better. But it always maintains its convictions, its firm doctrinal and theological positions. . . . As far as I can see, the Southern Baptists continue to be greatly respected.

Positions such as these are generally representative of Brazuca Baptist churches but not hegemonic. A pastor who works on the East Coast, for instance, has a critical stance toward the SBC, despite having pastored a number of SBC-affiliated churches. For him, the SBC is generally welcoming of people who are "fundamentalists, conservatives, Shiite Republicans and demonizers of any contrary opinion." Another pastor, who has worked in New York City for decades, shared, "My experience with them is zero in quality. I think they are extremely cold, uninterested in what is happening with Brazilians in New York, especially New York. The Southern Baptist Convention, because of their racism, didn't plant churches here in the northern US. They are weak in that. For me, their vision is 150 years outdated." These pastors do, however, recognize that their vociferous digression from the SBC represents a minority voice among Brazilian Baptists both in Brazil and in the United States.

In addition, critics of some aspects of the SBC nonetheless appreciate the SBC presence in the Brazilian past; at times even pastors who are critical of the SBC's conservative bent season their criticism with remarks of appreciation. For example, a pastor in the Washington, D.C., metro area commented that "[the SBC] is a conservative convention. And it is the convention that evangelized us there, in Brazil, they created our Baptist Convention. So, I have a historical and ideological connection to the SBC." The shadow of the SBC looms so large over the Brazuca Baptist churches that even communities that cooperate with the American Baptist Churches USA often have a dual affiliation with the SBC because of their historical connection. But because these churches are quintessentially immigrant churches, they cultivate transnational attachments that tend to transcend their explicit denominational affiliation in ways that official documents do not always reveal. Though they have a perceived ideological and historical connection with the SBC, Brazuca Baptist churches are generally not enthusiastic about their role as potential participants in SBC strategies and initiatives.

Transnational Connections of Brazuca Baptist Churches

A peculiar characteristic of Brazilian Baptists, when the group is seen through a transnational lens, is that when in Brazil, they cannot escape the reach of the SBC; at the same time, in the United States they still feel part of the BBC as well as of other Brazilian-based networks. In other words, they are in the United States, but Brazil is evident in their modus operandi. For our purposes, this means that the identity of Brazuca Baptist churches is informed by Brazilian evangelicalism in general and by the BBC in particular,[10] although these Brazilian expressions of Christianity have themselves been thoroughly informed by US missionaries and institutions of cultural production. The Brazilian Baptist pastors coming to the United States to pastor Brazuca churches have cultivated and expanded their transnational relationships and networks in a number of ways, maintaining their connection to the Brazilian religious and, at times, political environment.

One example of the creativity and power that exist in the networks in which Brazuca Baptist leaders participate is the Global Kingdom Network, which was founded by a Brazilian immigrant to the United States. The pastor of a Brazuca megachurch, when asked about how he decided whom to invite to speak and sing in his church, mentioned the Brazilian chapter of network as source of potential speakers:

> I am part of a network in Brazil called Global Kingdom Network, which gathers the pastors of the largest 120 churches in Brazil, no matter what denomination they belong to. There are many Baptists in this same group. We meet once a year in the Brazilian chapter of Global Kingdom and there is no (official) leadership, we meet for prayer and to discuss contemporary themes—abortion, homosexuality, and each speaks a little, then we split into small groups—and through this we have a network of relationships with this group. Each one knows what the other thinks and believes, so when they get here (in my church) they come knowing what we believe, although the person may have practices in their church that I don't agree with, especially churches that have apostles, I don't even call them apostles when they are

[10] The word "evangelicalism" is often used in Brazil as a synonym for "Protestant." The variations of evangelicalisms in Brazil, therefore, make the word even less precise in Brazil than it is in the United States. For the purposes of this chapter, however, I am using "evangelicalism" to describe groups that are not Baptists and yet share with Brazilian Baptists the characteristics of the Bebbington Quadrilateral (biblicism, crucicentrism, conversionism, and activism), although with a stronger Pentecostal flavor.

here, I call them pastor. But they have many practices that are theirs. They respect our practices, we respect their practices. I bring three levels of people to our church. First the invitees. Who are they? We have several conferences throughout the year, and we are proactive regarding who we want to bring as speakers. Speakers for families, speakers for youth, etc. . . . We are proactive. So, the conferences of the year. Secondly, singers who are vacationing in Florida—which diminishes the cost. For example, [name of singer] is a person that if a church in Brazil invites him for an event, it will be R$20k to R$30k. But when he is in Florida, he comes to us for free. And many others. And preachers as well. If they are in Florida for some reason and our agenda is open, if they want to take the opportunity we connect with them. So, there are those who we invite, those who are in Florida for some reason, and those with specific themes.

The example of this megachurch pastor points to the fact that immigrant churches with denominational connections do not limit their participation in transnational networks to denominationally minded groups. Yet, in terms of how they conceptualize their identity, denominational connections are still central to their self-perception.

One of the ways in which Brazuca Baptist leaders continued their presence in Brazilian Baptist life was by publishing about the developments in their communities in the *Jornal Batista*. First Brazilian Baptist Church of Greater Boston, for instance, used the journal several times as an avenue for making its news and events known to a wider audience. Pastor Jorge Bezerra, the first long-tenured pastor of the church, was a dynamic and aggressive religious entrepreneur who, together with his leadership staff, sustained strong ties between the Boston church and Brazilian religious and political life. His inauguration ceremony was advertised both in Brazil, through the *Jornal Batista*, and in the Brazilian community in Boston, through the *Brazilian Times*, a Massachusetts-based newspaper directed to a Brazilian audience. The invitation published in the *Jornal Batista* read:

> The First Brazilian Baptist Church of Greater Boston has the honor to announce to the denomination the name of its new worker, and it invites all to be present in the inauguration service of Pr. Jorge de Oliveira Bezerra, who after eight months of a rigorous process in the American Consulate received a special visa of American citizen [green card].[11]

In the first year of his tenure, Bezerra sent a letter to Brazilian president Fernando Collor de Mello while the latter was visiting Washington, D.C., letting him know of his support and "also making him aware that there is a

[11] Cleber Machado, "Convite," *Jornal Batista* XCI, no. 21 (1991): 11.

Brazilian group in Boston that is concerned with the political situation of our beloved nation."[12]

First Brazilian Baptist Church of Greater Boston's use of the *Jornal Batista* was so broad that at times even the controversies of the church made their way into the Brazilian publication. In one of these instances, the firing of Pr. Doriscélio Pinheiro, former director of the biblical institute administered by the church and pastor of one of its missions, resonated in Brazil. The report read:

> The First Brazilian Baptist Church of Greater Boston, united in Regular Assembly, on July 15 of 1998, unanimously decided to officially register the recommendation of the Deacons and Trustees for the firing of Pr. Doriscélio de Souza Pinheiro from his functions of Director of the Biblical Theological Seminary of Boston as well as from the directorship of our mission in Nashua, NH, and to cancel the request for his visa with the Department of Immigration and Naturalization of the American Government that we had filed. At the same time, we offered a compulsory letter to him and his wife, considering that his conduct, during his time with us, was extremely reproachable, causing several harms to the Body of Christ. His summary exclusion did not happen because our Pastor recommended to the plenary that we conceded a compulsory letter to attenuate his situation.[13]

As the report illustrates, misbehavior in the United States could have transnational ministerial repercussions. In another instance, which is explored further below, some of the issues that led Jorge Bezerra to leave the church were also featured in the *Jornal Batista*.[14] The Brazilian connection of these institutions in the United States was so strong that even controversies had repercussions in both nations.

Of course it was not exclusively the East Coast Lineage churches that relied on the *Jornal Batista* to maintain transnational ties with the BBC. That practice precedes the post-1980s establishment of Brazuca Baptist churches by many decades. Between the 1960s and 1980s, the publication featured a great number of articles pertaining to the Brazilian presence in the United States.[15] The

---

[12] *Atas da (Minutes of) Primeira Igreja Batista (Boston)*, 1991, book 1, 7.

[13] John Allen Galgoul et al., "Comunicado," *Jornal Batista* XCVII, no. 42 (1998): 5.

[14] Carlos Mendes et al., "Parecer dos Líderes Que Estiveram em Boston Conversando com o Pr. Jorge Bezerra e a Igreja Batista Brasileira da Grande Boston," *Jornal Batista* XCIX, no. 42 (1999): 9.

[15] Some examples include Ben Pitrowsky, "Pastores Batistas Brasileiros Pregam nos Estados Unidos VIII," *Jornal Batista* LXIX, no. 38 (1969): 5; Joelcio Rodrigues Barreto, "Uma Viajem Inesquecível," *Jornal Batista* LXX, no. 7 (1970): 8; Nilson Dimárzio, "Na Terra de Tio Sam," *Jornal Batista* LXXIV, no. 10 (1973): 4; Daniel Paixão, "Carta dos 'States': Compartilhar o Seu Amor É Nossa Tarefa Global," *Jornal Batista* LXXIV, no. 46 (1974): 11–12; and Elias M. Gomes, "Um Culto Memorável: Meu Adeus a New Jersey," *Jornal Batista* LXXVII, no. 26 (1977): 8.

practice continued and indeed expanded as the communities expanded in the 1980s and beyond.[16] Brazuca Baptist churches' use of the BBC's flagship publication was not limited to publishing news and local controversies. In addition to providing information of no particularly strategic nature, some Brazuca Baptist churches advertised their presence in the United States to a Brazilian audience, at times hoping to capitalize on future migrants who would be able to identify religious communities that could help them acclimate to their new country either directly or through their pastors, who presumably were closer readers of the *Jornal Batista* and had a broader denominational network.[17]

Travel agencies targeted Brazilian Baptists as potential customers and sometimes partnered with Brazuca Baptist ministries in programs of ethnic denominational vacationing. In 1993 an ad appeared in the *Jornal Batista* for a trip to Orlando that was exclusively for Baptists and guided by Baptist pastors. One of the denominational tourist attractions was First Baptist Church of Orlando, which had a Brazuca Baptist congregation. The ad read, "We will visit the First Baptist Church of Orlando, and attractions such as Epcot Center, Disney, Sea World, Universal Studios, etc."[18] Organizers of events such as the CONJUBBRAN sent invitations to Brazilian Baptists, letting them know about the speakers and music groups that would attend the meeting.[19] Yet the most prominent form of advertisement of Brazuca Baptist churches in the *Jornal*

---

[16] For example, Dirce Sirazawa Cooper, "A Colônia Brasileira em Fort Worth: Brasileiros e Norte-Americanos Cultuam em Português e Inglês," *Jornal Batista* LXXXIII, no. 5 (1983): 2; Tadeu Godoy, "O Milagre Brasileiro no Texas: Amarillo para Cristo," *Jornal Batista* LXXXVII, no. 44 (1987): 10; Iran de Medeiros Lopes, "Uma Igreja de Brasileiros em Filadélfia," *Jornal Batista* LXXXVIII, no. 12 (1988): 12; Ayde Ferreira Gomes, "Pastor Brasileiro Realiza Abençoada Cruzada em Clinton, Mississippi," *Jornal Batista* LXXXVIII, no. 26 (1988): 7; José Heleno, "De Miami—USA: Aum Sinal do Fim, Escândalos," *Jornal Batista* LXXXVIII, no. 33 (1988): 12; Jamil Ribeiro, "Missão Brasileira em Miami," *Jornal Batista* LXXXIX, no. 16 (1989): 3; Renata Oliveira, "Batistas Brasileiros Fazem Congresso no 'Coração da América,'" *Jornal Batista* XCVI, no. 50 (1997): 16; Ophir Barros, "Pastor Ophir Barros Filho nos Estados Unidos," *Jornal Batista* XCVII, no. 39 (1998): 5; Renato Nogueira, "Orlando: Turismo e Igreja Viva," *Jornal Batista* CII, no. 17 (2002): 16.

[17] This dynamic of Brazilian Baptists qualifies Bernadete Bezerra's insight that Brazilians do not know about American Brazilian church communities until they arrive in the United States. She looked at Brazilian Adventists in California, who seem not to have developed transnational denominational networks as strong as those created by Brazilian Baptists in the United States. See Bernadete Beserra, *Brazilian Immigrants in the United States: Cultural Imperialism and Social Class* (New York: LFB Scholarly Publishing, 2006), 99–100.

[18] "Praia da Costa de Orlando," *Jornal Batista* XCIII, no. 47 (1993): 7.

[19] "VI CONJUBBRAM," *Jornal Batista* XCV, no. 11 (1996): 10.

Batista appeared in the form of simple ads with concise information about an individual community's leadership, street address, and service times. The first church to use the *Jornal Batista* to advertise its services as a clear invitation to potential Brazilian migrants or tourists was Georgetown Baptist Church in Washington, D.C.[20] Yet it was the PIB Florida (formerly Primeira Igreja Batista Brasileira no Sul da Flórida) that used the strategy the most. In 1999 alone, for example, PIB Florida advertised its Pompano Beach services twenty times, that is, at a rate of almost twice a month.[21] The ads were simple: they showed a picture of the church building, of the pastoral family, information about weekly activities, and the church's address and contact information. The Primeira Igreja Batista Brasileira de New Orleans (First Brazilian Baptist Church of New Orleans) also advertised in the *Jornal Batista*[22] and sometimes competed with PIB Florida, their ads running side by side. The ads of the New Orleans church, however, were slightly different and more intentional. They showed the name and contact information of the church, a picture with thirteen people—members and the pastoral family—of different age groups, and the following message: "Our church is at the disposal of the brothers who want to visit New Orleans and we invite you to celebrate Jesus Christ with us." Igreja Batista Brasileira de Boca Raton (Brazilian Baptist Church of Boca Raton) provided an even more compelling invitation. Its ad introduced the pastor and his wife, letting the readers know that the pastor had been the host of the TV show *Reencontro*, which was connected to the ministry of famous Brazilian Baptist pastor Nilson Fanini, a former president of the BBC and of the BWA. It also included the message, "When you come to America, we want to receive you with arms wide open." Below the church's name, the motto

[20] Joe Underwood, "Batistas Brasileiros em Washington," *Jornal Batista* LXXXV, no. 3 (1985): 16.

[21] Examples of the 1999 ad campaign include "Primeira Igreja Batista Brasileira no Sul da Flórida," *Jornal Batista* XCIX, no. 12 (1999): 3; "Primeira Igreja Batista Brasileira no Sul da Flórida," *Jornal Batista* XCIX, no. 22 (1999): 3; "Primeira Igreja Batista Brasileira no Sul da Flórida," *Jornal Batista* XCIX, no. 26 (1999): 13; "O Que São os Protestantes," *Jornal Batista* I, no. 9 (1901): 13; "Primeira Igreja Batista Brasileira no Sul da Flórida," *Jornal Batista* XCIX, no. 31 (1999): 13.

[22] Examples of the New Orleans church's ad campaign in 1999–2000 include "Primeira Igreja Batista Brasileira de New Orleans," *Jornal Batista* XCIX, no. 51 (1999): 10; "Primeira Igreja Batista Brasileira de New Orleans," *Jornal Batista* XCIX, no. 52 (1999): 13; "Primeira Igreja Batista Brasileira de New Orleans," *Jornal Batista* XCX, no. 1 (2000): 4; "Primeira Igreja Batista Brasileira de New Orleans," *Jornal Batista* XCX, no. 2 (2000): 10; "Primeira Igreja Batista Brasileira de New Orleans," *Jornal Batista* XCX, no. 3 (2000): 5.

targeted the loneliness immigrants often feel: "Your Brazilian family in the United States."[23]

Transnational denominational advertising, of course, runs the risk of influencing migration of all forms—legal or otherwise—and Brazuca Baptist pastors were keenly aware of this risk. A pastor of a church in Florida, for instance, used not only ads in the *Jornal Batista* but also his significant social media presence to attract immigrants to his church. In one of his many Facebook posts, a photo appears of the pastor on a Miami pier, gesturing to the camera as if he is calling people to come. The caption reads, "Come to Florida, the Brazil where things work." This pastor said in 2016 that he was diminishing his social media advertising for ethical reasons, since for every one of those posts, he said, "I receive fifty new members in the church, thus potentially weakening other Brazilian churches in the region." But the pastor's goal with this particular post was much more specific:

> My focus was, and I am looking for other ways of doing this, the Brazilians who are American citizens or have green cards and are now living in Brazil. Those who have green cards are risking losing them because they are spending too much time outside of the country, and those who are American citizens, once the Brazilian economy is weakened and the economy here is strengthening, and it is time for them to come back home, they are American citizens. It is time for them to come with their families, recognizing they made a premature decision to leave the country. Many are not doing well financially in Brazil; they are not adapting well and lost all the money they brought back. Most of the Brazilians who returned to Brazil with resources in hand failed in their investments there because they made mistakes. So today we are trying to bring them back to start again, and many returned. Many, many returned.

In addition, a former pastor of the Danbury All Nations Baptist Church, whose presence in the United States was also advertised in the *Jornal Batista*, pointed out some practices of Brazuca Baptist churches that relate to their nonintentional support of undocumented border crossing, a topic addressed more fully in the next chapter.[24]

Brazuca Baptist churches also cultivate their connections to and networks with Brazilian evangelicalism by regularly inviting famous Brazilian preachers and musicians. This practice transcends denominational ties and is based

---

[23] "Quando Vier a América . . . ," *Jornal Batista* XCX, no. 15 (2000): 9; "Quando Vier a América," *Jornal Batista* XCX, no. 16 (2000): 3.

[24] Barros, "Pastor Ophir Barros Filho nos Estados Unidos"; Ophir Barros, interview, October 26, 2015.

thoroughly on the Brazilian evangelical market. PIB New Jersey, for instance, has invited gospel celebrities such as Grammy-nominated singer Cristina Mel, the famous pastor Russell Shed, pastor Estevam Fernandes, reggae gospel band Cia de Jesus, pastor Ed Rene Kivitz, and controversial Brazilian Pentecostal pastor Ricardo Gondim, to name a few.[25] Brazilian Baptist Church in Washington, D.C., has invited people such as singer and author Atilano Muradas, pastor Daniel Camaforte, singer songwriter Paulo Cesar Baruk, Presbyterian pastor Jeremias Pereira, and Brazilian rock star Rodolfo Abrantes.[26] While PIB Florida regularly invites famous Brazilian singers and pastors, First Brazilian Baptist Church of Greater Boston has also invited famous Brazilian guests.[27]

These connections to Brazilian audiences through denominational publications, to the BBC through doctrinal commitments, and to Brazilian evangelicalism through interdenominational guests are common occurrences in Brazuca Baptist communities and represent the fact that the denominational identity of Brazuca Baptist churches has been negotiated transnationally. The constant presence of practitioners from a number of Brazilian denominations at special events of Brazuca Baptist churches has ensured the maintenance of a Brazilian evangelical spirit that shapes the Brazuca Baptist presence in the United States. Given that in the late twentieth century Brazil became the country with the most Pentecostal and charismatic Christians in the world, this means that such influences have crossed borders in the form of sermons and songs opening space for a stronger charismatic bent in Brazuca Baptist churches than in most SBC churches. In addition, this phenomenon has kept the Brazilian religious market, with its forms and contents, in constant evidence, allowing these immigrant communities to imagine themselves as part of a denominational family that transcends their immediate denominational affiliation.

The connection between Brazuca Baptist churches and Brazil, of course, has not been limited to religious or denominational dynamics. Other elements of Brazilian culture have also been maintained in these communities. Although

[25] "Comunicações do Pr. Calixto," *Folha da Primeira*, April 22, 2007; "Cia de Jesus," *Folha da Primeira*, September 2006; "Apresentação da Cantora Cristina Mel," *Folha da Primeira*, November 2, 2002, 2; "II Simpósio de Oração," *Folha da Primeira*, November 1, 2004, 2; "IV Simpósio de Oração," *Folha da Primeira*, May 7, 2006; "Comunicações do Pr. Calixto."

[26] "Ministérios e Avisos," *Boletim da Igreja Batista Brasileira em Washington*, March 4, 2007; "Ministérios e Avisos," *Boletim da Igreja Batista Brasileira em Washington*, October 7, 2007; "Ministérios e Avisos," *Boletim da Igreja Batista Brasileira em Washington*, November 11, 2007; "Ministérios e Avisos," *Boletim da Igreja Batista Brasileira em Washington*, July 13, 2008; "Ministérios e Avisos," *Boletim da Igreja Batista Brasileira em Washington*, January 18, 2009.

[27] *Atas da (Minutes of) Primeira Igreja Batista da Grande Boston*, 1991, book 1, 10.

immigrant religious communities assist in introducing immigrants to the host culture, they also engage in practices that rehearse, perform, and redeploy Brazilianness.[28] For instance, PIB Florida organizes a yearly Brazilian fair at which typically Brazilian foods and music are on offer. They have also invited people involved in Brazilian political life—such as Deltan Dallagnol, the federal prosecutor involved with the task force that made headlines in Brazil and all over the world because of its investigation of political corruption—as well as Brazilian soccer players who come to Florida to play for local leagues. Weekly newsletters of Brazuca Baptist churches often feature news about Brazilian politics, voting, soccer games, and Brazilian music.[29] In addition, practices such as individual and communal prayers and updates on former and current members have kept Brazil constantly in evidence.

Praying for Brazil and for issues related to immigration to the United States from Brazil are commonplace in Brazuca Baptist churches. So are prayers for immigrants crossing the border, flying into the country, the Brazilian economy, and former members who have returned to Brazil. For example, PIB New Jersey has sometimes used a specific place in its weekly newsletter to highlight prayer requests related to Brazil and/or people in Brazil.[30] Brazilian Baptist Church in Washington, D.C., mentioned prayers connected to Brazil in most of its weekly newsletters that I analyzed for this book.[31]

Mission efforts in Brazil have also kept communities focused on the country, and the theopolitical imagination of Brazuca Baptists has connected missions in Brazil to the creation of social dynamics that would allow Brazil to thrive. In other words, Brazuca Baptists have understood the efforts to evangelize Brazil as an investment in a better socioeconomic future for their home country. When the 2002 campaign for missions in Brazil started at PIB New Jersey, it was this imagination that became evident in Marcia Garcia's "call to arms":

> We are once again beginning a new missionary campaign. This time our goal
> is Brazil. According to the latest census research conducted by the Brazilian

[28] Rodrigo Serrão de Jesus, "A Igreja Como Pedacinho do Brasil: Migrações e Religião na Capital do Texas" (master's thesis, Federal University of Paraíba, 2014), 16–17; Donizete Rodrigues, *Jesus in Sacred Gotham: Brazilian Immigrants and Pentecostalism in New York City* (Amazon, 2014).

[29] This is a common feature of weekly newsletters of Brazilian Baptist churches in the United States. For examples, see *Folha da Primeira* (1993–2010) and *Boletim da Igreja Batista Brasileira em Washington* (2002–2009).

[30] For a few examples, see "Para Você Interceder," *Folha da Primeira*, November 8, 1998; "Para Interceder," *Folha da Primeira*, November 28, 1999; "Para Interceder," *Folha da Primeira*, October 3, 1999; "Para Você Interceder," *Folha da Primeira*, August 29, 1999; "Para Você Interceder," *Folha da Primeira*, May 9, 1999.

[31] I had access to the 2002 and 2008–2016 newsletters of the church.

Institute of Geography and Statistics, the Gospel grew 71% in Brazil. But there is much more that needs to be done. Brazil is still a great challenge. There are 150 million Brazilians that still have not had a personal encounter with Jesus. Among these 150 million there are specific groups, which constitute a challenge to the Church of Christ. They are: those marginalized by society, the Indians, the Romeiros, and the Atheists. Today, when Brazilians will be electing their new president, there is new hope in the hearts of this people who has suffered much. And we, who are far away, begin to dream about the possibility of returning and finding a more just and more dignified Brazil. However, we know that what will really change Brazil is the genuine conversion to the lordship of Christ. And it is up to us to participate in part of this change.[32]

Brazilian Baptist Church in Washington, D.C., used the ministry of the Atletas de Cristo (Athletes of Christ) to connect the 2002 Soccer World Cup to the riches of the gospel. In addition, one edition of their newsletter reprinted two short articles that came out in Brazilian newspapers.[33] In short, Brazil has been an indispensable element in the religious and cultural life of these communities.

At times, former members write back from Brazil, and their correspondence illustrates how immigrant communities affect the life of immigrants. Of course, immigrant experiences are quite diverse. Yet I highlight the letter sent by Orivaldo Lopes Jr., printed on the front page of *Folha da Primeira*, because it is particularly rich. Lopes Jr. is a professor in the social sciences postgraduate program at the Federal University of Rio Grande do Norte who lived in New Jersey for six months while doing research at Drew University. While at Drew, Lopes Jr. attended PIB New Jersey. He wrote back to the church from Brazil in September 2000, saying:

> I'll risk becoming extremely repetitive, but I cannot stop from expressing, one more time, my gratitude for all that you did for me in these last six months I lived there. I had the immense privilege of being involved in a church that has, in its natural way of being, the gestures of help and care without having to appeal to sweetened discourses and excessive pampering.
>
> My arrival in São Paulo was great! The reunion with family and friends filled me with joy. The thing was that my wife's birthday coincided with the day of my arrival, so there was much celebration with family and friends. Saturday night the party continued, and we received another group of friends. I noticed how extraordinarily good it is to have friends. By the way, your friendship was the best of my acquisitions in the United States and I anticipate with pleasure moments of reencounter here in São Paulo, in Natal, or there, in New Jersey.

[32] Garcia, "Missões, Oportunidade de Servir," *Folha da Primeira*, October 6, 2002, 1.
[33] Carlos Mendes, "Ecos da Copa," *Boletim da Igreja Batista Brasileira em Washington*, June 7, 2002.

I have not yet returned to the academic activities because the weather is still cold and humid, which guaranteed me a strong cold. These hemispheric changes are difficult.

I was happy to read the *Primeira Online*. The text about Disneyland was very opportune, although what I really liked was Pr. Josias' comments. I take it as something good that the fundamentalist evangelicals are taking the first steps towards a critique of culture. As in all first steps, (and here I am reminded of my little friend Aaron) they are clumsy and full of spectacular falls. The clumsiness should not discourage us from taking these more-than-necessary steps. I suggest we put the devil inside parentheses. Our discourse is not about him, but about the Kingdom of God and the Project. With this effort we will have a number of interesting ideas that will enrich our life in the world in which the Lord stubbornly left us.

A huge kiss and a big hug for everyone,

Pr. Orivaldo P. Lopes, Jr.[34]

Transnational relationships, such as the one cultivated between Lopes Jr. and PIB New Jersey, but also less evident connections between Brazuca Baptist churches and their former parishioners back in Brazil, have helped maintain the communities' connections with the dynamics of Brazil, regardless of their geographical location in the United States. At least as of this writing, they were in the United States, but in terms of their imagination of religious and cultural belonging, not necessarily of it.

CONJUBBRAN (1991-2008):
Giving Birth to Ethnic Denominationalism Proper

CONJUBBRAN began as an effort to bring together the Brazuca Baptist churches in worship events that focused on music and sermons. The initial format of CONJUBBRAN was not atypical for Brazuca Baptists, as it followed the framework of denominational youth congresses common in both Brazil and the United States. In the early 1990s, it was generally known that there were many Brazuca Baptists who had very little contact with each other, given the diffuse history and geographically diverse nature of their churches. Churches on and near the East Coast already engaged in *intercâmbios*—gatherings of people from different churches—before the launch of the first CONJUBBRAN, but the latter took this primarily local disposition and expanded it into a nationwide program.

---

[34] Orivaldo Lopes Jr., "Queridos Irmãos da Primeira," *Folha da Primeira*, September 17, 2000, 1.

There were fifteen CONJUBBRANs: New York City (1991), Boston (1992), Pompano Beach (1993), Elizabeth (1994), Dallas (1995), Pompano Beach (1996), Washington, D.C. (1997), Boston (1998), New York City (1999), San Francisco (2000), Austin (2001), Pompano Beach (2002), Charlotte (2004), Orlando (2006), and Pompano Beach (2008).[35] The events brought together dozens of Brazuca Baptist congregations to worship, in their own tongue, in the Land of Uncle Sam. Together with the other influences internal to church communities that made Brazilianness evident, CONJUBBRAN reinforced the transnational nature of Brazuca Baptist churches.

The place where the CONJUBBRANs took place was decided on the basis of the structure of the church that hosted the event, which explains why some churches were repeat hosts, among them PIB Florida (which hosted CON-JUBBRAN four times), PIB Family Church (twice), and First Brazilian Baptist Church of Greater Boston (twice). For churches that did not own their facilities, such as First Brazilian Baptist Church of Austin, which met in the downtown Austin facilities of FBC Austin, this meant using the facilities of a host Anglo-American church to house the event.

The congress began at PIB Family Church, in New York City, during Levy Penido's tenure. It was not, however, a clerical initiative. It started as an idea in the mind of Hélio Martins, a young migrant who was part of the Brazilian mass migration to the East Coast. Martins had been involved in youth work in his church in Belo Horizonte, Brazil.[36] Soon after arriving in New York City in 1985 and becoming a member of PIB Family Church, Martins became a leader of the church's youth group. Bothered by the lack of options for Brazilian Christian youth gatherings in the United States, Martins conceived of CONJUBBRAN as a remedy for this perceived gap. He recalled:

> I don't know exactly what happened. I just know that Jesus put this idea in my head. He called me to be a channel of blessings. Not that I wanted it, although I always liked Christian youth work. So, the dream of uniting the youth was born. The Brazilian Baptist youth had nowhere to go, in terms of youth gatherings. There were very few Brazilian churches around. There was

[35] None of my interviewees remembered the order and places of the CONJUB-BRANs with confidence, and there are no known official documents of the congresses. The minutes and newsletters of churches, however, provided information of their years and locations. None of the consulted documents show a CONJUBBRAN happening in 2003, 2005, or 2007, and a 2008 issue of the weekly newsletter of Brazilian Baptist Church in Washington, D.C., mentions CONJUBBRAN as being a biennial event (see "Ministérios e Avisos," *Boletim da Igreja Batista Brasileira de Washington D.C.*, July 8, 2008). The evidence leads me to believe that the practice of making CONJUBBRAN biennial began after 2002.

[36] Hélio Martins, interview, December 7, 2015.

one in New Jersey, we had heard of another one in another state, and then pastor Jorge Bezerra came to Boston. Actually, Jorge Bezerra was the first keynote speaker of CONJUBBRAN. He came to pastor the church of Boston, and we contacted other churches and they liked the idea. . . . My idea was to unite the Baptist youth in order to reach others for Christ through this organization—and, as an additional bonus, the churches would be in closer relationship to each other. They would have an opportunity to get together, to strengthen their bond. These events were something that was left behind (in Brazil). Anyone who came looking for those experiences didn't find it, because the American culture is different from our own, and our ethnic group was small compared to what it is today.[37]

At the first CONJUBBRAN, which met in 1991 at PIB Family Church, the meeting's attendees were mostly from East Coast Lineage churches, with Jorge Bezerra preaching. The meeting surprised many attendees because of the presence of churches of which even the leaders of the oldest Brazuca Baptist churches had never heard.[38] In 1991 a board of directors was created for CONJUBBRAN, and it was decided that the CONJUBBRAN meeting would be held regularly.[39]

The widespread yearning to gather with other Brazuca Baptist churches became evident rather early on in the history of CONJUBBRAN. Silair Almeida, for example, drove to Boston in 1992, with numerous members of his then small church, to attend the meeting. He secured the role of host for 1993, and the 1993 CONJUBBRAN became the first of four CONJUBBRAN meetings in Pompano Beach. Almeida's participation in CONJUBBRAN was also an important aspect of the growth of his Florida megachurch. Martins recalled that none of the Brazuca Baptists on the East Coast knew anything about Florida and its beautiful beaches until they went there for CONJUB-BRAN.[40] The way in which Almeida hosted the 1993 CONJUBBRAN, Martins said, was a watershed moment in the history of the event because he helped give it structure and shape. In the early days, attendees stayed in the houses of members of host churches. As the meeting grew, host churches such as Almeida's would include hotels and Christian camps in the meeting, which took place over Labor Day weekend.[41] Although the initial goal of CONJUB-BRAN was to focus on youth, practically speaking it welcomed people from all age groups. Because people made countrywide connections while attending meetings like CONJUBBRAN, networks that facilitated internal migration of

---

[37] Martins, interview.
[38] Aloísio Campanha, interview, October 19, 2015.
[39] Martins, interview.
[40] Martins, interview.
[41] Martins, interview.

immigrants were strengthened as a result of the meeting. Religious events such as these are often an element in the internal migration of foreigners who live in the United States.

CONJUBBRAN was also a vehicle for expanding the ministerial network of Brazuca Baptist pastors. Some of the pastors who spoke at the event included Presbyterian-ordained Caio Fabio (at one time the most well-known Protestant figure in Brazil), Pentecostal pastor Silas Malafaia, Baptist Ed Rene Kivitz, Estevam Fernandes, Oliveira de Araujo, Eli Fernandes, and Pentecostal pastor Ricardo Gondim.[42] For the musical performances, Grammy-winning singer Kléber Lucas was one of the many evangelical celebrities who performed at the event.[43] Yet the organizers' move to showcase the celebrities of the Brazilian evangelical market generated tensions that contributed to the event's eventual demise.

The first CONJUBBRAN was financed partially by the IMB, thanks to the influence of Geriel de Oliveira, who had worked for the SBC for over thirty years before retiring and becoming the pastor of a Brazuca Baptist church.[44] The cost of the events, however, became increasingly high, in part because of the expense of bringing well-known speakers and singers from Brazil. But financial cost was not the only issue. Daniel Paixão recalled that some of the conflicts that arose in CONJUBBRAN were born out of a particular form of Christian zeal: sermons against undocumented immigrants. He said:

> Leaders from Brazil came with a Brazilian mindset and did not understand the circumstances of our Brazilian parishioners in America. Instead of helping, they instilled more guilt and conflict. We had [CONJUBBRAN] keynote speakers who came from Brazil and condemned the fact that people lived here illegally. They approached this topic openly as if it was a sin to come to the United States as undocumented immigrants. These instances generated many conflicts and, because of things like this, the CONJUBBRAN began to deteriorate.[45]

Preachers from Brazil preaching to Brazilian immigrants in the United States generated tensions by reproducing aspects of the theology held by the SBC, the denomination to which Brazuca Baptist churches were affiliated, one of the many ironies of transnational religious networks.

---

[42] Martins, interview; "Conjubbran," *Folha da Primeira*, October 9, 2000, 3.
[43] "A Primeira em Ação," *Folha da Primeira*, July 25, 2004, 2.
[44] Geriel de Oliveira, interview, February 13, 2017.
[45] Daniel Paixão, interview, July 13, 2016.

In addition to the internationalization of the congress, CONJUBBRAN also became a stage for territorial issues among the most prominent Brazuca Baptist leaders in the United States.

A major source of tension was the growth of Silair Almeida's megachurch in Pompano Beach. A number of Brazilian Baptist pastors point to CONJUBBRAN as a key factor in the growth of Almeida's megachurch and two things corroborate this observation: (1) a number of key leaders and pastors of PIB Florida were members of churches of the East Coast Lineage, especially First Brazilian Baptist Church of Greater Boston; and (2) the minutes of the East Coast Lineage churches show a number of members asking for letters of transfer from their communities to PIB Florida, especially in the years following PIB Florida's hosting of CONJUBBRAN. Almeida recognized the role of CONJUBBRAN in the growth of his community, and this dynamic created tensions among the leadership.[46] The impact of PIB Florida's growth on First Brazilian Baptist Church of Greater Boston was so great that between 1996 and 1999 the Boston church estimated that it lost fifty-one members to PIB Florida and around $12,000 in revenue in the first two years because of those losses.[47] Among the members who left Boston for Pompano Beach were eleven deacons, one vice president, and the treasurer. Almeida remembers that at times the tensions were so high that churches on the East Coast asked for him to send them part of the financial contributions of former members, a request he repeatedly denied.[48]

The connection between CONJUBBRAN and AIBBAN also played a role in the history of the congress. Although CONJUBBRAN was chronologically older than the AIBBAN, after the latter was created in the early 1990s, CONJUBBRAN was subordinated to its leadership. This arrangement created an intrinsic relationship between CONJUBBRAN and the AIBBAN. They became so strongly connected that their meetings took place as if they were one event. The two initiatives would either thrive together or fail together. Levy Penido, who hosted the first CONJUBBRAN when he pastored PIB Family Church in New York City, pointed out that "the two things [CONJUBBRAN and AIBBAN] needed to be separate" because denominational issues that concerned the AIBBAN were transferred to the CONJUBBRAN as a result of CONJUBBRAN's subordination to the association.[49] Francisco Izidoro, who succeed Penido at PIB Family Church, reflected that CONJUBBRAN was a vigorous movement but that it became too bureaucratic when

[46]   Almeida, interview.
[47]   *Atas da (Minutes of) Primeira Igreja Batista Brasileira da Grande Boston*, 1999, book 2, 40.
[48]   Almeida, interview.
[49]   Levy Penido, interview, October 29, 2015.

it came under the auspices of the AIBBAN. "For me," he said, "there was too much bureaucracy, too much politics, and because of the conflicts at the time, we did not have conditions to create a lighter structure that was more functional and less bureaucratic."[50]

Taken together, the conflicts generated by the internationalization of CONJUBBRAN, the bureaucratization of the event because of its subordination to the AIBBAN, and the discomfort caused by intrachurch migration that resulted from the gathering were responsible for its eventual demise. CONJUBBRAN's final meeting was in 2008. Since then, another initiative has emerged among Brazuca Baptist youth with the goal of uniting them nationally. Named "Alive," it is led by Lucas Izidoro, Francisco Izidoro's son. Based in PIB Family Church, where CONJUBBRAN first started, Alive is aimed at a different kind of youth, namely, Brazilians and Brazilian Americans who are comfortable communicating in English. The first Alive meeting was in 2014 at PIB Family Church. In 2015 it met in San Francisco, at the Brazuca church pastored by Ribamar Monteiro, followed by a 2016 meeting in Orlando at First Brazilian Baptist Church of Orlando.[51] Francisco Izidoro, Ribamar Monteiro, and Lécio Dornas have provided the pastoral impetus behind Alive.[52] Its objective is to involve the English-speaking youth that go to Brazuca Baptist churches and help these communities transition to a new generation that is less comfortable with Portuguese. The pastors who support the initiative, however, learned from the CONJUBBRAN experience and are careful not to commit the same mistakes. They want a youth-led, nonbureaucratic movement that will be effective in uniting the English-speaking Brazuca Baptists.[53] On the other hand, as Hélio Martins implied, focusing on English may doom the event, since there are so many other events already directed toward youth who are proficient in the language.[54] Perhaps an answer to that concern would be that culture transcends language, as it includes foods, habits, tastes, humor, political tendencies, and yes, even theological anxieties.

"Do You Really Think That Americans Will Listen to a Group of Immigrants?": AIBBAN

The AIBBAN was born out of Brazuca Baptist churches' perceived need to cooperate with each other beyond their previous national denominational affiliations. The CONJUBBRAN meetings gave Brazuca Baptist pastors the space and the opportunity to imagine an ethnic denominational cooperative

---

[50] Francisco Izidoro, interview, January 5, 2017.
[51] Ribamair Monteiro Jr., interview, March 13, 2016.
[52] Izidoro, interview.
[53] Monteiro Jr., interview.
[54] Martins, interview.

work that would be more geared to the needs of their immigrant communities. Yet the specific reasons for pastors who created the institution varied. Geriel de Oliveira, a former IMB officer, invited pastors to come to the Brazuca Baptist church he was pastoring in Silver Springs, Maryland, in 1995,[55] in order to give the initial impetus for the formation of the organization. He never imagined that the AIBBAN would develop into a potential competitor of the SBC in terms of the primary allegiance of Brazuca Baptist churches, as it did. His concern was born out of his experience in dealing with other ethnic Baptists in the United States as an officer of the IMB.

More specifically, Oliveira wanted an organization like the AIBBAN to help Brazuca Baptist communities keep the next generations in their churches more effectively than the Mexican Baptists did theirs. According to Oliveira:

> The AIBBAN began in our church. It began in the United Nations Baptist Church in Silver Springs, Maryland. I invited all the pastors there and gave them a place to stay the night. The church provided meals and I suggested we start the AIBBAN. I explained that the Mexican experience was that the churches were too concerned with the first generation and forgot about the second generation and, as a result, the second generation was lost and today we do not find Hispanics of the second and third generation in their churches. We could not do that. So, I suggested we start the AIBBAN, and the AIBBAN made the same mistake.[56]

Not unlike CONJUBBRAN, according to Oliveira the AIBBAN became an institution through which "a group of pastors wanted to make their names in Brazil"; these pastors "insisted" that their churches be affiliated with the Brazilian Convention."[57]

The strong connection between Brazuca Baptist pastors and the BBC was indeed an element of the imagination of pastors working in the United States. They wanted to work more closely with the BBC even if that meant distancing themselves from the SBC. Silair Almeida, who was elected executive secretary of the AIBBAN six times, celebrated the US government's official recognition of the association by writing to the *Jornal Batista* pointing out the

---

[55] Aloísio Campanha, a longtime leader in the Brazilian Baptist community in the United States, remembers that the first AIBBAN meeting happened in 1994. Damy Ferreira's article published by the *Jornal Batista*, however, suggests it started in 1995 (see Damy Ferreira, "Batistas Brasileiros nos Estados Unidos Realizam Assembléia," *Jornal Batista* XCV, no. 50 [1995]: 11). The minutes of All Nations Baptist Church corroborate Ferreira's observation (see *Atas da [Minutes of] Primeira Igreja Batista de Língua Portuguesa de Danbury*, 1995, book 2, 101).

[56] Oliveira, interview.

[57] Oliveira, interview.

potential benefits of such an institution. First, he said, the AIBBAN would create a direct transnational network allowing the denomination to keep members who migrated to the United States or returned to Brazil. This is a dynamic that holds special importance in the case of Brazilian immigrants, given that research shows that Brazilians in the United States in general have not seen themselves as immigrants but mostly as temporary workers who want to go back to their country, a phenomenon that has held for most of the history of Brazilian migration to the United States. This dynamic transcends issues of documentation and creates the impression that Brazilian migration includes both leaving the country and returning.[58] Focusing on the maintenance of returning members, therefore, was a reasonable and profitable strategy.[59]

Second, ethnic denominational cooperation would allow churches to grow faster and stronger in the United States. Furthermore, the AIBBAN signaled the globalization of the BBC, as it established a presence of the convention in the most powerful country in the world. For Almeida, the AIBBAN was "an integral part of the BBC and, for us, it is a joy being able to participate in this magnanimous assembly and communicate to all Brazilian Baptists that you are also present in the Land of Uncle Sam through the AIBBAN."[60] Jorge Bezerra, in another *Jornal Batista* article, was presented to the Brazilian audience as the leader of Brazilian Baptist work in the United States.[61]

Despite Almeida's rhetoric in the *Jornal Batista*, he knew that the bylaws of the BBC did not allow the AIBBAN to be an official arm of the BBC outside of Brazil unless it changed its constitution. Reflecting on his advocacy for the globalization of the BBC after the eventual dissolution of the AIBBAN, Almeida said:

> Look, nothing differentiates the Brazilian Baptists in America from the Brazilian Baptists in Brazil in terms of doctrine. We are absolutely the same. We believe the same things, preach the same things, the liturgy is the same, so I was trying to show during that time that we were an extension of the Baptist work in Brazil. Because, truly, I needed to change the bylaws of the BBC and they did not have vision at that time and, because of that, they lost a huge segment

[58] Ana Cristina Braga Martes, *New Immigrants, New Land: A Study of Brazilians in Massachusetts* (Gainesville: University Press of Florida, 2011), 4.

[59] Matt Reis found in his research that the new wave of Brazilian immigrants is wealthier and demonstrates less desire to return to Brazil than immigrants in previous waves. See Reis, "Brazilian Evangelicos in Diaspora in South Florida: Identity and Mission" (Ph.D. diss., University of Edinburgh, forthcoming 2021).

[60] Silair Almeida, "AIBBAN É Reconhecida Pelo Governo Americano," *Jornal Batista* XCIX, no. 10 (1999): 15.

[61] Silair Almeida, "Associação Das Igrejas Batistas Brasileiras Na América Do Norte: Brazilian Baptist Fellowship in North America," *Jornal Batista* XCIX, no. 1 (1999): 4.

of Baptists. The bylaws say, "all churches in the national territory may be a part of the BBC," and I had a very strong ally in the convention, and we wanted to change the bylaws to say, "national and international territory." It does not matter where you are in the world: if you are a Brazilian Baptist and have the same faith, the same creed, the same doctrinal declaration, let's expand. Today, if that had worked, the Brazilian Baptists would have more than one hundred churches in the United States connected to the BBC, contributing to national and international missions, and perhaps becoming stronger than a state like Sergipe and many other states that do not contribute much to the convention.[62]

He went on to say,

I wanted to change because when we got in Brazil for the Annual Meeting of the BBC we could not even register. . . . I am from Florida but I want to register, I want to be a part of the convention, I want to debate, I want to have a chair in the council and speak about the issues facing us in the United States, just like the Itamarati [the Brazilian Ministry of Foreign Relations] does. I represent the Itamarati today. I am a spokesperson for the Brazilian community in Florida with the Itamarati. They bring four hundred Brazilians who live around the world, every one of them has a chair around a table in order to discuss the issues of Brazilians abroad. This is vision! The Brazilians may have gone out of Brazil, but for the Itamarati they are still Brazilians. . . . But that was resisted [by the BBC] because of traditionalism, legalism, and lack of a globalized vision on the part of pastors and leaders. The same way they could not see that a missionary could be sent to the United States; that missionaries sent to the first world were there just to travel. A mediocre vision! . . . It was a lack of vision, and I believe that the BBC is diminishing little by little for the lack of an expansionist and globalizing vision.[63]

Almeida's insistence on becoming a full-fledged member of the BBC and having his and other Brazuca Baptist churches affiliated with the convention through the AIBBAN illustrates the feeling of denominational ambiguity among Brazuca Baptists. Many Brazuca Baptist have pastors who felt as if they belong first and foremost to the BBC, and to the SBC only because of historical appreciation and institutional technicalities.

Another pastor who had served as AIBBAN's executive secretary was of a similar mind to Almeida. In his view,

for the SBC, we were connected to their denominational structure. So creating an association or a convention here would be abnormal from their perspective because there is an entire denominational structure already in place.

---

[62] Almeida, interview.
[63] Almeida, interview.

So SBC officials always told us this: "For us, you are nothing but a fellowship. You are nothing more than eaters of cookies and drinkers of soda." I heard this several times. So Silair [Almeida] and I said "either we decide to create a Portuguese-speaking Baptist convention here in the United States that operates independently from the current Baptist structure in the country, or we will keep on hearing that we are nothing more than a fellowship. We will never go beyond this kind of talk." . . . There was [resistance from the SBC] and there will always be. Do you really think that Americans will listen to a group of immigrants? How will they manage their denomination here if we have a voice? This is foolishness.

Though the attempt to change the BBC's bylaws ultimately failed, Brazuca Baptist pastors sometimes returned to annual meetings of the convention as representatives of the Brazuca Baptist work during the years of the AIBBAN's operation.

Daniel Paixão was the first to go to Brazil as a representative of Brazuca Baptists in the United States. The church he then pastored, PIB New Jersey, sent him in 1995 to represent the group; it also sent messengers to the annual meeting of the BBC in 1996.[64] Jorge Bezerra went in 1999 in order to "deliver a report about the Brazilian Baptist churches [in the United States] on the first night [of the annual meeting of the BBC]."[65] Yet the continuous representation of Brazuca Baptists at the annual meetings of the BBC was only one aspect of the AIBBAN's presence in Brazuca Baptist churches. These latter also contributed financially to the AIBBAN and imagined the institution as one that had a level of doctrinal authority over affiliated churches.

Beginning in 1995, churches began to show financial contributions to the AIBBAN in their annual budgets. For example, the minutes of First Brazilian Baptist Church of Greater Boston for that year showed that "it was proposed and approved that a monthly percentage be sent to the AIBBAN in order to open a number of works."[66] At times, special offerings were taken up to benefit the association.[67] In 2004, All Nations Baptist Church contributed 12 percent of its budget to the AIBBAN with the express intention of these funds being invested in its mission initiatives.[68] Beyond administrative costs, the AIBBAN did indeed use its budget to help start new Brazuca churches and support foreign missions. Churches such as the ones in Danbury, Austin, and Tampa were

[64] See *Atas da (Minutes of) Primeira Igreja Batista de Língua Portuguesa de New Jersey*, 1995, book 1, 101, and 1996, book 1, 118.

[65] *Atas da (Minutes of) Primeira Igreja Batista (Boston)*, 1999, book 2, 39.

[66] *Atas da (Minutes of) Primeira Igreja Batista (Boston)*, 1995, book 1, 84–85.

[67] *Atas da (Minutes of) Primeira Igreja Batista (Boston)*, 1998, book 2, 6; 2002, book 2, 258; 2005, book 2, 397.

[68] *Atas da (Minutes of) Primeira Igreja Batista (Danbury)*, 2004, book 3, 57.

organized or formed with the association's help.[69] The financial commitment to the AIBBAN was so strong in some of these communities that the bylaws of PIB Family Church stated that in the case of dissolution, the church's New York City patrimony would go to the AIBBAN, not the SBC.[70]

In terms of doctrinal accountability and representational support, the AIBBAN was also strongly present in Brazuca Baptist churches across the nation. For instance, at PIB Family Church, the doctrinal standards were subordinated to the AIBBAN's, and at least once members who had complaints about the church's administration wrote to the association to express their concerns.[71] First Brazilian Baptist Church of Greater Boston sent the AIBBAN information regarding the firing of pastors, and when new leaders were hired, the AIBBAN sent them letters welcoming them to the community.[72] For all practical purposes, during the years in which the AIBBAN was in operation, Brazuca Baptist churches that were affiliated with the institution were doctrinally accountable to it for the purposes of their cooperation.

A controversy that was published in the *Jornal Batista* illustrates a number of key dynamics regarding the AIBBAN's place as an institution of doctrinal accountability and the conflicts that informed the eventual dissolution of the institution. When First Brazilian Baptist Church of Greater Boston had issues with its pastor, Jorge Bezerra, it asked the AIBBAN, not the SBC, to intervene. According to *Jornal Batista*, Silair Almeida, then executive secretary of the AIBBAN; Ophir de Barros; and Josias Bezerra were the AIBBAN officials directly involved in the intervention. The mutual accusations made by Almeida and Jorge Bezerra show the irreconcilable tensions between two of the most important leaders of the Brazuca Baptist community. Almeida accused Bezerra of financial irregularities, and Bezerra implied that Almeida used the AIBBAN to further his personal agenda. In addition, the report blamed Jorge Bezerra's presidency of the association for the unfriendly relationship between the AIBBAN and the New England Baptist Convention. By the end of the report, the AIBBAN recommended that Jorge Bezerra address his financial issues with his church and pledged to create mechanisms that would allow the institution to address similar issues more effectively in the future.[73]

The prominent place taken by the AIBBAN among Brazuca Baptist churches, however, should not lead one to believe that its place in Brazuca

[69] Almeida, interview.

[70] *Estatuto da (Bylaws of) Primeira Igreja Batista de Língua Portuguesa de New York*, 1995, 1.

[71] *Atas da (Minutes of) Primeira Igreja Batista (New York)*, 2004, book 2, 77, 85.

[72] *Atas da (Minutes of) Primeira Igreja Batista (Boston)*, 1998, book 2, 1998, 12; 1999, 129; 2000, 164.

[73] Mendes et al., "Parecer dos Líderes Que Estiveram em Boston," 9.

Baptist churches as well as the form of its operation developed uniformly among denominational leaders in the United States. Daniel Paixão, for instance, who ultimately resisted the effort to connect the AIBBAN with the BBC, represented the Brazuca Baptist work in the BBC's annual meeting. In 1995, when the BBC met in the city of Natal, Paixão spoke on behalf of Brazuca Baptists. He reported his experience to PIB New Jersey thus:

> I thank the vision of this church in allowing me, your pastor, the opportunity to represent it in front of the Brazilian Baptist Convention. After long hours of flying, we landed in the beautiful airport of the city of Natal. The meeting was already going on and the pastors' reunion had already happened. It was the largest pastors' reunion of the history of the denomination. I had the opportunity to be a part of the convention's official program. It was my responsibility to talk at the plenary at 10:30 a.m. on Tuesday, and there was much expectation from the public, who wanted to know about the Baptist work in North America. When I finished my talk, the audience, aware of what God is doing with the Brazilian Baptist churches in America, was so touched that it gave a standing ovation, giving glory to God. Following my talk there was a recommendation, support, and unanimous approval that we became messengers of honor and that the AIBBAN be recognized as the first association of Brazilian Baptists outside Brazil and that, at an opportune time, the AIBBAN would ask the executive council of the BBC for its official affiliation with the convention.[74]

Yet Paixão's apparent initial support for the internationalization of the BBC shifted, partly because of his conversations with Southern Baptist missionaries in Brazil. And despite his excitement about the success of the AIBBAN and its role among Brazuca Baptists, he later relinquished his support for the institution's internationalization. He said:

> The BBC does not have to opine on the Brazilian Churches in America because these churches are affiliated with local associations and state conventions. So this is not how things work; no way, it is not. We must follow the norms of the association and convention from where the churches are geographically located and, in general, of the SBC. There was a time in which I know that the [Brazilian] leaders here [in the United States] were in full agreement that their churches were affiliated with the BBC. As a matter of fact, when the recommendation was made [to the BBC]—there were many occasions on which we were there [in Brazil]. For example, in Bahia I was one of the keynote preachers. When we met in Natal I was also one of the preachers, and also in Belo Horizonte and in Vitória. As a matter of fact, during that time I was already an employee of the Florida Baptist Convention, and

---

[74] Daniel Paixão, "Convenção Batista Brasileira," *Folha da Primeira*, February 4, 1996, 1.

> I was in Brazil taking a group of Americans who wanted to partner with the BBC on a number of initiatives. I talked to a few [Southern Baptist] missionaries who were in Brazil about the issue of the affiliation of Brazilian Baptist churches in the United States with the BBC. They told me, "Look, Dr. Paixão, you as churches in America wanting to come under the wing of the BBC are completely out of order. Because the churches must be affiliated with the association and state convention from where they are located. Do not neglect all of this to affiliate with the BBC." This seemed 100 percent coherent to me.[75]

The issue that leaders such as Paixão and Oliveira had with the internationalization of the AIBBAN was informed by their own involvement in Southern Baptist institutional life. Before becoming pastors of Brazuca Baptist churches, both had served the SBC for decades and had a greater bond to SBC denominational structures than their peers whose careers had been defined by particular immigrant communities.

Not unlike Paixão, Oliveira ultimately resisted the internationalization of the AIBBAN on the basis of allegiance to local SBC structures. He said:

> I was one of those [pastors] who were opposed [to the AIBBAN's affiliation to the BBC]; me and Paixão also, because we wanted a denomination that was concerned with the United States and that had nothing to do with Brazil. But the executive secretary of the World Mission Board of the BBC wanted this to be possible because he wanted churches in America to contribute [more] to missions in Brazil. I was opposed for two reasons. First, I was an employee of the SBC, how can I support Baptist churches affiliated to the SBC to support the BBC? I could not do this; it would be against my own job. So I left. Same with Paixão. Paixão was also involved with the SBC and did the same thing; he could not promote this initiative.[76]

Oliveira did see a need for the SBC to work more closely with Brazilians, given that, according to him, Brazilian specific linguistic and cultural peculiarities made it particularly difficult to provide adequate attention to the group via the SBC's standard "Hispanic ministries" umbrella.[77] This realization encouraged an

[75] Paixão, interview.
[76] Oliveira, interview.
[77] Research shows that Brazilians, like many other immigrants from Latin America, do not generally self-identify pan-ethnically and tend to reject the term "Hispanic." Some Brazilians are more comfortable with the term "Latino," but they prefer to capitalize on the positive imagination that the dominant culture in the United States has of Brazilian culture. Brazilian Baptists in the United States are in harmony with the general scholarship on the topic. For more see Maxine L. Margolis, *An Invisible Minority: Brazilians in New York City* (Gainesville: University Press of Florida, 2009), 97–98; Beserra, *Brazilian Immigrants,* 57–58; Martes, *New Immigrants, New*

initiative on the part of the SBC in which the Home Mission Board would hire a Brazilian pastor to coordinate the Brazuca churches in the nation, giving them specific attention.[78] By the time this was tried, however, most Brazuca Baptist leaders were not in favor of such an arrangement.[79]

The opting out of important leaders such as Paixão and Oliveira—who also had allies in the BBC who were against the internationalization of the convention—regarding the appropriateness of Baptist churches in the United States affiliating with a convention in Brazil was an important aspect of the eventual failure of the AIBBAN. Yet the same issues that plagued CONJUBBRAN—territorial infighting and bureaucracy—had an even stronger role in the AIBBAN's failure. When asked, most of the past presidents of the institution use one word to explain it: *politicagem*. That is, too strong a focus on denominational politics, which involved power struggles between major leaders, such as Silair Almeida and Jorge Bezerra, who when their clashes began were pastoring the two strongest Brazuca Baptist churches. The last official meeting of the organization was in 2010; it stopped meeting altogether after that. Since then, the OBBPNA has replaced the AIBBAN in importance when it comes to ethnic denominational relations in the United States. Brazuca Baptist pastors still meet annually for the OBBPNA gathering and reinstated the AIBBAN officially at their 2017 meeting in San Francisco. The reorganization of the AIBBAN included the hiring of a pastor in partnership with the WMB in order to coordinate the Brazuca Baptist work, and regular AIBBAN meetings were resumed in 2018.[80] The pastor came from a traditional church in the city of Recife and has extensive denominational experience. Brazuca Baptists, then, may not yet have discovered the right recipe for ethnic denominational success—a feat that, in a Baptist setting, remains as complex as it may be unusual. They are, however, in a new phase of their ethnic denominationalism project and seem optimistic in regard to the possibilities that their form of transnational connectionalism brings.

Land, 223; Kara B. Cebulko, *Documented, Undocumented, and Something Else: The Incorporation of Children of Brazilian Immigrants* (El Paso, Tex.: LFB Scholarly Publishing, 2013), 20–24.

[78] The minutes of PIB New Jersey show that this missionary was José Calixto, who eventually stayed on as pastor of PIB New Jersey for some time. Calixto came in 2007 to be the AIBBAN's director of missions, but worked with the SBC's Home Mission Board. See *Atas da (Minutes of) Primeira Igreja Batista de Língua Portuguesa de New Jersey*, 2007, book 2, 136.

[79] Oliveira, interview.

[80] https://aibban.org/.

Conclusion

The history of Brazuca Baptist churches is marked by local and transnational allegiances. In terms of their local allegiances, Brazuca Baptists have been affiliated usually with the SBC through their local associations and state conventions. These official affiliations, however, are seen as neither ideal nor sufficient, and Brazuca Baptists have engaged in the development of a form of ethnic denominationalism. This phenomenon manifested itself strongly in the formation of the AIBBAN, an association of Brazuca Baptist churches that attempted to change the bylaws of the BBC so that churches in the United States could be affiliated with the BBC in Brazil. The creation of the AIBBAN, however, came in the wake of particular organizations, such as the CONJUBBRAN, and particular sentiments, such as a growing disappointment with aspects of the SBC. In other words, the AIBBAN and ethnic denominationalism among Brazuca Baptist churches were not a plan that pastors had originally but a response to contextual conditions.

Transnational networks that historically energized Brazuca Baptist ethnic denominationalism have been created and expanded by Brazuca Baptist pastors in a number of ways. These include reliance upon the *Jornal Batista* (which has documented developments in Brazuca Baptist churches), the presence of prominent figures in the Brazilian evangelical market in Brazuca Baptist churches, ads publicizing the services of Brazuca Baptist churches published in Brazil, and ritualized practices internal to Brazuca Baptist communities that have kept transnational relationships in evidence. In addition to these commonplace dynamics, an ethnic denominational youth congress, CONJUBBRAN, began in 1991 and was successful in uniting Brazilian Baptist churches around the country. CONJUBBRAN, in turn, paved the way for the AIBBAN, which eventually became responsible for Brazilian Baptist ethnic denominationalism and any event intentionally directed at building the unity of Brazuca Baptist churches.

In 2008 and 2010, respectively, both CONJUBBRAN and the AIBBAN were discontinued. Different transnational approaches regarding the proper pastoral response to undocumented immigration, different attitudes toward the internationalization of the BBC, and territorial infighting all contributed to their demise. The apparent failure of these initiatives, however, did not mean the end of Brazuca Baptist ethnic denominationalism. As mentioned, as of this writing a new initiative called Alive is trying to refocus the anxieties that CONJUBBRAN sought to address and direct them to a new generation of Brazilians and Brazilian Americans whose primary language is English. The

AIBBAN was also reinstated in 2017, in yet another official attempt to unite Brazuca Baptist churches around an ethnic denominational institution.

The difference of Brazuca Baptist denominational identity, however, is not fully encapsulated in the Brazuca Baptist attempts to form an ethnic denomination. As a matter of fact, ethnic denominationalism is an institutional manifestation of the anxieties of unbelonging raised by the complex migration dynamics that are part of the Brazuca Baptist quotidian. It is to the issue of how migration dynamics affect the congregational modus operandi and theological dispositions that we now turn.

5

WRESTLING

The Crisis of Undocumented Presence

Because if you're going to write a book about undocumented immigrants in America, the story, the full story, you have to be a little crazy. And you certainly can't be enamored by America, not still. That disqualifies you.

Karla Cornejo Villavicencio[1]

In the home of a church leader in the Florida Panhandle, during an interview with a Brazilian pastor whom the local Brazuca Baptist church wanted to call to be its senior minister, the head of the deacon board asked whether the pastor had any questions or concerns.[2] The pastor, who worked in a traditional church in Brazil and had never lived in the United States, said, "I was surprised to know that so many of the brothers and sisters in this church are illegals. I feel conflicted about the morality of pastoring illegals." Many deacons in the meeting were also undocumented, as were the individuals who contributed the most to the church, both in terms of finances and voluntary work. The worship leader, treasurer, and the individual serving as interim pastor were also undocumented—and although the church now met in the youth building of the First Baptist Church in their city, it had started in the living room of a business owner who was undocumented.

[1] Karla Cornejo Villavicencio, *The Undocumented Americans* (New York: One World, 2020), xv.
[2] This chapter is an extended and updated version of some arguments that appeared in João Chaves, "Migrating Theopolitics: The Effect of Undocumented Parishioners on the Pastoral Theology of Latin American Evangelicals in the United States," in *Migration and Public Discourse: Migrant Discourses and Narratives in World Christianity and World Religions*, ed. Afe Adogame, Raimundo Barreto, and Wanderley Rosa (Minneapolis: Fortress, 2019), 69–82.

By the time the final pastoral search committee interview took place, the church had already spent more than $10,000 on visa fees, roundtrip plane tickets for the pastor and his family, and lodging. Leaders in the community knew that if the pastor accepted the call, legal and immigration fees involved in acquiring a religious work visa for the pastor and visas for his family would be hefty—all expenses overwhelmingly covered by the financial contributions of the "illegals" about whom he felt so ambiguous. Yet the deacons were convinced he was the one God was calling to lead the church, and they eased the pastor's discomfort about pastoring undocumented parishioners. A few months later, the pastor and his family arrived in Florida, and the pastor embarked on the life-changing journey of wrestling with the existential, theological, and ecclesiological implications of pastoring undocumented bodies in a context in which "legality" and "morality" cannot be assumed to be closely connected.

This is scarcely an unusual story. In this chapter I begin uncovering characteristics of Brazuca Baptist churches that are particularly informative about the power that migration dynamics exert over religious identity and practice. These characteristics are the development of an ecclesiology of the undocumented (the particular focus of this chapter), the pentecostalization of Brazuca Baptist churches, and the role of women in leadership positions in these mostly Southern Baptist–affiliated churches. Although there is complexity and difference in the way in which these characteristics manifest themselves in Brazuca Baptist communities, I will show how they affect the way in which the migrant experiences and networks of parishioners guide the Brazuca Baptist presence across the United States. Similar to the above-described pastor hired to minister to the Brazuca church located in the Florida Panhandle, pastors of Brazuca Baptist churches are often challenged by the undocumented status of their parishioners. In part because pastors of Brazuca Baptist churches are trained in Southern Baptist–informed theological seminaries and are mostly documented, some of them initially find it difficult to navigate the issues related to immigration struggles. Ultimately, these pastors are challenged to address their conflicts with the undocumented status of many parishioners and to find ways to serve them to the best of their ability. If their official theology and ecclesiology have not prepared them to pastor invisible bodies marginalized by unjust laws, the daily struggles of their parishioners do.

Before I give a direct assessment of undocumented parishioners of Brazuca Baptist churches, however, a word about the complexities of immigration legislation is in order. As many leaders in the SBC—to which most Brazuca Baptist churches are affiliated—have explicitly and enthusiastically supported politicians and policies that punish undocumented immigrants, it is important to note that SBC missionaries to Brazil themselves were not always law-abiding immigrants. Conflicts regarding immigration papers are not present only among Global South migrants to the West. Rather, Southern Baptist missionaries themselves were often on the wrong side of the law on this issue. A few examples will suffice to illustrate this point. Swedish-born missionary Eric Nelson, known among Brazilian Baptists as the Apostle to the Amazon, registered himself and his family as American citizens when they arrived in Brazil despite the fact that their American naturalization was never finalized. His son, Gordon, found out he was Brazilian rather than American in Europe, when he was serving in the US Army. Nelson died in Brazil and was never able to stay in the United States after his retirement, despite several attempts, which included using different means to extend his visitor's visa.[3] When William Carrey Mein, the son of former South Brazil Baptist Theological Seminary director John Mein, came to the United States to study, he was threatened with deportation to Brazil because he had been sent to the United States as an immigrant. John Mein asked for the FMB's intervention in the matter several times, but William Carey had to go back to Brazil.[4] Finally, in order to circumvent immigration restrictions, the FMB contemplated sending missionaries to Brazil with tourist visas that they would intentionally overstay, much the same way that the majority of undocumented Brazilians enter the US labor market. In one of those instances, FMB secretary C. E. Maddry wrote to missionary Ben Oliver, saying that he was "sending six or eight new missionaries to Brazil on tourist visas with the understanding that, if they are excluded from Brazil finally, they will go to other Latin American countries and go to work."[5] In terms of immigration legislation, Southern Baptist missionaries were different from undocumented Brazuca Baptists proportionally but not necessarily in principle. The SBC was never a strict respecter of laws, and its attitude toward immigration law was no exception.

Undocumented Presence: The Effect of Undocumented Immigrants in Brazuca Baptist Churches

Undocumented immigrants have a central place in Brazuca Baptist churches. Although researchers have found a level of discrimination against undocumented members on the part of permanent resident and citizen members in

---

[3] John M. Landers, "Eric Alfred Nelson, the First Baptist Missionary on the Amazon, 1891–1939" (Ph.D. diss., Texas Christian University, 1982), 169–80.

[4] John Mein to C. E. Maddry, December 31, 1941, International Mission Board Archives, Richmond, Va.

[5] C. E. Maddry to Ben Oliver, October 6, 1941, International Mission Board Archives, Richmond, Va.

other Brazilian Protestant churches,[6] issues related to members' lack of immigration papers heavily inform the modus operandi of the Baptist communities. As one Brazuca Baptist pastor said:

> The church follows a parallel trajectory in which issues of documentation are irrelevant in terms of ascendancy to leadership positions. Testimony, character, and care with God's work are central, and the question of documentation is placed in a personal realm, and that has no role in the church's reality. If a person is documented, even with citizenship, but has a bad reputation, that person will never serve in the church. And another person without papers, if he is illegal and got saved here, can have a good reputation, a good testimony, and be a respected leader or deacon to whom people listen.

In Brazuca Baptist churches discrimination in terms of eligibility for participation in the church based on immigration status only appears in a few communities' handling of positions that may entail legal representation before governmental agencies.[7]

The presence of undocumented immigrants in some Brazuca Baptist churches is so significant that it amounts to the reason for their existence. The number of undocumented parishioners is or has been overwhelming in most Brazuca communities of faith. It is no exaggeration to say that the success of Brazuca Baptists as a whole is inseparable from the financial and vocational investment made by their undocumented members. A few pastors of established Brazuca Baptist churches have estimated that the vast majority of their communities at some point comprised mostly undocumented Brazilian migrants. To this day, some communities include only a very few permanent residents and United States citizens as members. The account of a longtime pastor of Brazuca Baptist churches illustrates this common phenomenon:

---

[6] Bernadette Beserra, *Brazilian Immigrants in the United States: Cultural Imperialism and Social Class* (New York: LFB Scholarly Publishing, 2006), 105. Beserra noticed a level of discrimination against "illegals" in the Brazilian Adventist church that she analyzed. In Brazuca Baptist churches, institutional discrimination is limited to a member's eligibility for leadership roles that may entail legal representation of the church. Explicit discrimination between members on the basis of immigration status does not seem to be a major issue in Brazuca Baptist churches.

[7] A controversy involving the office of treasurer in an East Coast community illustrates this point. The church went through a considerable crisis because the treasurer was the pastor's son, something with which most members were not comfortable. The church's position, however, was that the treasurer had to be documented—presumably because he or she would need a Social Security card for financial transactions—and they could not get a member to fill the position. In October 1995, at the peak of the controversy, a leader of the community stated that "we have to follow the Bible but also the laws of the country. I am praying to God that you, brothers and sisters, may have your Green Card so that you are free to take up certain offices in the church." Eventually the position was filled by a recently documented member.

"When we started the work here, fifteen years ago, there were three documented members in the church: me, my wife, and my son. Today we have approximately 35 percent of the church with their papers and about 15 percent involved in legalization processes." Many churches have far more undocumented members.

Maxine Margolis found in her research among Brazilian immigrants in New York City that whereas 50 percent of Brazilian immigrants in the city in the 1990s were undocumented, the percentage increased in the 2000s to 70 percent.[8] In addition, reports Margolis, the Department of Homeland Security estimated a 70 percent rise in the number of Brazilian undocumented workers between 2000 and 2005, although she argues that DHS grossly underestimated the number of undocumented Brazilians in New York City as being in the low thirty thousands.[9] Despite the fact that no reliable national estimate is available, the overwhelming presence of undocumented parishioners in Brazuca Baptist churches suggests that their numbers are proportional to the number of Brazilian undocumented immigrants in general.

The moral issues raised by the overwhelming presence of undocumented parishioners represent a tension. Whereas Paul Freston noted this in relation to Brazilian Protestants in the United States in general, his comments are particularly applicable to Brazuca Baptists. In their churches, the moralism that typifies Brazilian Protestantism is forced to adapt to cope with so many of members being outside of the law.[10] As Kara Cebulko argued, undocumented status changes the role of the church in immigrant life,[11] given that the church often becomes a place that gives people a measure of protection from the struggles of undocumented living. Church life, however, is also changed in the process, as legal pastors arrive to pastor these churches armed with religious visas and legalistic mentalities, only to confront the reality that the churches are backed by undocumented money and that they cannot ignore their members' narratives of migrant experiences.[12]

---

[8] Maxine Margolis, *An Invisible Minority: Brazilians in New York City* (Gainesville: University Press of Florida, 2009), ix.

[9] Margolis, *Invisible Minority*, 7–8.

[10] Paul Freston, "The Religious Field among Brazilians in the United States," in *Becoming Brazuca: Brazilian Immigration to the United States*, ed. Clémence Jouët-Pastré and Leticia J. Braga (Cambridge, Mass.: David Rockefeller Center for Latin American Studies, 2008), 264.

[11] Kara B. Cebulko, *Documented, Undocumented, and Something Else: The Incorporation of Children of Brazilian Immigrants* (El Paso, Tex.: LFB Scholarly Publishing, 2013), 8.

[12] A small number of Brazuca Baptist pastors are themselves undocumented.

Though the adaptation of Brazuca Baptist pastors' moralistic tendencies to the reality of undocumented immigration is by no means seamless or automatic, the existential, ministerial, and financial price of nonadaptation is too great for them to bear. The testimonies of influential Brazuca Baptist pastors in regard to this crisis reveal the tension created by the moralistic tendency pointed out by Freston and the reality of US immigration dynamics. Two long-time pastors in the United States tell similar stories that include their experience of seeking the opinion of immigration agents to cope with the existential conflict connected to their harboring of immigrants on the wrong side of the law. A pastor in the southern United States said:

> I was once in crisis in relation to the immigration status of undocumented people in the church and I asked an immigration officer: "How should a pastor act in this situation?" And he told me this: "What is written on your church's sign?" I told him [the name of my church]. He said: "So it is not an immigration agency; it is a church. You cannot pay attention to the kind of people that are coming and ask them about their immigration status." After this I became convinced of something. I am not interested in who comes to the services to worship God. If they are here with an overstayed visa—I don't call them illegals but undocumented—or if they are without proper papers or not.

A retired pastor whose career pastoring Brazuca Baptist churches developed on the East Coast reported that

> [another Brazilian Pastor on the East Coast], when he got here, was so impressed by [the number of undocumented members] that he decided to call immigration. And he called the immigration to talk to them, and the immigration agent told him: "What are you?" He said, "I am a pastor." The agent then responded: "Then take care of your sheep and let us take care of immigration issues."

These two cases illustrate that the conflictive nature of pastoring undocumented parishioners is considerable and that at least in some instances Brazuca Baptist pastors have received pastoral lessons from US immigration officials.

Given the importance of undocumented members in immigrant churches, it is not surprising that most of these faith communities legitimize the presence of undocumented immigrants either directly or indirectly through practices that include prayers for people crossing the border, testimonies of successful border crossing or successful obtainment of tourist visas (that will be overstayed), setting up living and employment arrangements for incoming migrants, and establishing programs that help parishioners navigate their new country more effectively.[13] Religion also informs who migrates and where migrants travel to, especially when, as in the case of Brazilian immigrants, the migration event involves crossing more than a land border. This is because immigrants will consider their connections to social networks before migrating when the cost of migration is high.[14] In terms of influences that do not involve direct advertisement in denominational publications, ritual or networking dynamics provide indirect legitimation of immigration. A pastor provided an example that illustrates this form of influence: "If someone calls saying 'I want to go to the United States' there is no discouragement. Most leaders would say: 'Here is good. You will be illegal but almost everyone here is illegal anyway. Come and join us.'" Another pastor said:

> This is a problem for us. For instance, let's say there is a member of the church who comes to you and says, "Pastor, I will bring my sister," and the pastor responds, "Oh, God bless you." So there is a lot of support that we Brazilian Baptist pastors in America give to illegal immigration. This is a very debatable opinion, but I think that this is like Abraham did, right? Because it is beneficial to the church. When someone says, "Hey, I will bring my uncle and he is a Baptist," the pastor rejoices. But I don't think pastors go to Brazilian churches in Brazil and call people to come here. This may have happened only sporadically. I am, for instance, approached by people who are in Brazil and reach out to me so that I can support their trip to America. And worst of all is when in a prayer meeting a sister stands up and asks for prayer for someone crossing the border. This is the worst.

There are Brazuca Baptist pastors who state that their churches are neutral in regard to their role in the decision of immigrants to migrate. They do, however, also engage in the same legitimizing practices that characterize Brazuca Baptist churches in general.

In terms of programs of immigrant assistance, Brazuca Baptist churches engage in initiatives that create a safety net that transcends common avenues of socioeconomic relief. Sometimes these initiatives manifest themselves transnationally in ways that ensure an easier migration experience. The testimony of a pastor who led denominational institutions in Brazil and the United States illustrates this dynamic:

---

[13] Annie McNeil Gibson, *Post-Katrina Brazucas: Brazilian Immigrants in New Orleans* (New Orleans, La.: University of New Orleans Press, 2012), 224. Gibson also noticed this dynamic in Brazilian Pentecostal churches in New Orleans. She argued that not only do churches justify illegal migration, going to church functions is an additional practice that legitimizes the migration experience.

[14] Phillip Connor, *Immigrant Faith: Patterns of Immigrant Religion in the United States, Canada, and Western Europe* (New York: New York University Press, 2014), 23–25.

We have a ministry of support to the Brazilians who are coming. So the idea is to connect to the immigrant before he comes, so that the immigrant can receive some orientation that can minimize his suffering when he arrives. And when he gets here he will have support. There are cases in which families get here and they already have a rented apartment, because there was a previous connection with the church's ministry and we put them in contact with people, they chose where they would live and all. Today we do this, and I think it is a very important thing. We do this because the six first months of those who migrate here, especially those who migrate without having much knowledge of the American reality, are very difficult if there is no support.

Brazuca Baptist churches have learned that helping new arrivals is not only a good way of meeting the needs of people but also helps the growth of local congregations. Social initiatives, then, have had a multilayered function that helps immigrants, the local church, and the broader community in which Brazuca churches are located. One pastor shared a sentiment that illustrates this dynamic:

Our church adopted as a main strategy giving support, shelter, and embrace to those who arrived. Churches that lead the embracing [of immigrants] grew. Those [churches] that focused on the pulpit, on preaching, did not grow, because people wanted something more. People came [to the United States] in search of bread; then, in their search of bread, they found Christ. We maintained, I would say, very strong social initiatives.

Social initiatives that help individuals and families in need are not aimed only at undocumented immigrants; rather, churches do not discriminate on the basis of immigration status or form of migration.

Church leaders also are invested in helping their parishioners with legal issues when they arise. One church, for example, has a lawyer whom it hires specifically for cases related to arrests of undocumented members. Talking about his church's stance in cases of immigration arrest, the pastor shared:

Today we have one man who is arrested. Every week someone is arrested. What is our protocol? Our church has a lawyer. She is Brazilian. Any immigration case in which the church involves its lawyer, the lawyer enters the field [a soccer analogy]. She is a Brazilian woman from Belo Horizonte, and she enters the field and solves it for the church.

The pastor shared that if the family has the financial means to pay the church back—which happens in the majority of the cases—then the church is reimbursed. However, the church is ready to assume financial responsibility when necessary. Not all issues, however, are free of unsettling complexities. The hiring of lawyers to look into a parishioner's case can also help churches decide which cases are worth pursuing. The pastor continued:

> I got involved some time ago, asking the Brazilian ambassador to release a Brazilian pastor who was arrested, he was from Fort Myers. I told him, "He is a good guy." But soon afterward the ambassador called me and said, "This guy sold some immigration processes, some religious visa possibilities in Fort Myers. Are you sure you want to continue defending him?" I told him, "Never mind, I am sorry." So today I ask our lawyer to filter different cases, because I can't know when immigration is being unjust. I don't know if they have a deportation order from ten years ago, twenty years ago, I don't know if they committed a crime, so we have this protocol. For every one of our cases.

The pastor's distinction between just and unjust immigration arrests illustrates the complexity with which Brazuca Baptist leaders approach immigration legislation.

Churches have also developed programs to proactively address the lack of immigration papers, sponsoring clinics and seminars about immigration laws, applying for religious visas for leaders of the church whom the community wants to hire officially, or partnering with businesses and educational institutions that could help immigrant members change their visa status. The example of a pastor in California illustrates this point. According to this longtime pastor, who originally came to the United States as a migrant worker who overstayed his visa:

> Today my church is no longer letting those who are arriving stay here illegally. So what we are doing here is a school program that we have. We have a school that we don't really have an official partnership with but we have people in there who already help us enroll the Brazilians that arrive in this school to study and become legal here in the United States. Because illegality was an issue in a time when we did not have much information. But there were before, as there are today, programs in this area of education that can give the person, even further into the future, the possibility of a profession or even legality. So I am working with this here. So the person arrives and I interview him or her right away. I interview people, and we send them to an immigrant class so that they can know what it means to be an immigrant. We give information about everything they need to do. So there is this class, and from this class we already talk about the possibility of them staying here in a legal way, not illegally.

The issue of undocumented status, then, has prompted such churches to facilitate a transition to legal immigration status whenever possible.

In addition, the role possibly played by religious communities in influencing the migration of Brazilians who cross the US–Mexico border or who plan to overstay their visas once in the country exacerbates the tensions between pastors' moralistic tendencies and the challenge presented by undocumented bodies. Brazuca Baptist pastors are aware of this phenomenon and have developed diverse ways of rationalizing their potential role in migration dynamics or admitting to and coping with the situation. A pastor who advertises his Brazuca church in Brazil mentioned that

> coming from Brazil there are at least five different scenarios for coming undocumented. A person can come with an EB-5 [investor's visa], with an L-1 [visas for multinational employees], with a student visa [and presumably a tourist visa or crossing the Mexican border]. So when I advertise my church in Brazil, I am indeed attracting migrants, but I am not saying: "Come as an undocumented immigrant" . . . because it is very hard for an undocumented person to live in this country without a driver's license—especially in my state, which does not give drivers' licenses to undocumented immigrants—but people come anyway. And now, the number of people coming from Brazil is as large as it was during the peak of Brazilian migration between 2000 and 2003. . . . I believe in that [Bible] verse that says, "The earth is the Lord's, and everything in it, and all who live in it." I do not believe in borders. I believe that God puts us in places and opens the doors for us to live in them.

The migration dynamics in which this pastor is involved have informed the development of a theology of borderlessness that allows him not only to legitimize his potential role in the decisions of people who migrate but also to sanctify it.

Readers of the *Jornal Batista* have not been oblivious to the complexities involved in pastoring Brazilian immigrants in the United States in terms of the diversity of immigrant stories. Indeed, at times the pastoral crisis created by the presence of undocumented parishioners has been made public in the flagship denominational publication in Brazil. As early as 1985, Humberto Viegas Fernandes let his Brazilian audience know, through the *Jornal Batista*, about the struggles of undocumented Brazilian immigrants to the United States. Talking about the challenges his undocumented parishioners faced, Fernandes wrote, "Some of our members went through vexing situations, in terms of employment, living, and legalization. We must say that a great number of church members do not yet enjoy a stable situation here in the United States. Many are still desperately fighting for their legalization and permanence, which is not easy."[15] Fernandes' church, however, was not the only one to benefit from undocumented money. The host church in whose buildings

[15] Fernandes, "Cartas de New York: Lutas e Vitórias do Segundo Ano," *Jornal Batista* LXXXV, no. 5 (1985): 11–12.

the Brazilian Baptist church met borrowed $13,000 from the Brazuca Baptist church in New York City in the 1980s.[16]

The instances of the benefits given by immigrant churches that count on the support of undocumented money are too many to list. To cite a few examples, a Brazuca Baptist church in Florida bought its multimillion-dollar campus from a dying Anglo-American Southern Baptist church and then hired some Anglo-American pastors from the English-speaking church who would otherwise be unemployed. A Brazuca Baptist church in New Jersey partnered with the city to promote events for the wider community. All across the country, Brazuca Baptist churches run food pantries for immigrants and locals alike, childcare for their surrounding communities, counseling sessions in English, and a number of other social services. These services are financed by the contributions of Brazilian Baptist immigrant multinational owners, Silicon Valley engineers, Harvard professors, diplomats, and medical doctors, but also by undocumented nannies, construction workers, business owners, house cleaners, cooks, waiters, and drivers, who may not be considered people by a state that insists on keeping them in the shadows but who nevertheless contribute to the betterment of their communities.

Edvar Oliveira, who pastored a church in Florida, likewise shared his experiences of trying to cope with his role in legitimizing, and being supported by, undocumented migrants. Oliveira had a column in the *Jornal Batista*, in which he used to write about various ethical and theological subjects. When he left Brazil to pastor a church in South Florida, he continued to contribute to the publication. In 2003, the year Oliveira arrived in Florida, the *Jornal Batista* published three pieces that documented the progression of his thought on the morality of undocumented immigration and his pastoral position in regard to undocumented immigrants. The first time he wrote about the issue, Oliveira provided objective observations about undocumented immigrants, saying they were hard workers who lived well financially but whose insecurity in terms of immigration papers caused great anxiety, mostly because they could not visit family members in Brazil.[17]

After he had spent more time pastoring a community that served many undocumented immigrants, Oliveira's account—written before the Obama administration implemented the DACA program that opened opportunities for a significant number of undocumented people—was much more personal:

> It hurts me every time I listen to the cries of the sons and daughters of undocumented immigrants, who came to the United States when they were still

[16] Fernandes, "Cartas de New York," 11–12.
[17] Edvar Gimenes de Oliveira, "Welcome to America: Sem Documentos," *Jornal Batista* CIII, no. 34 (2003): 11.

very little, without knowing what awaited them. They studied until they finished high school and then, even though they were exemplary students and are totally integrated into North American life, must endure the profound sadness of being denied access to the university for not being recognized as citizens. Waiting for the North American government to act altruistically, looking to benefit the immigrants or the poor in the planet, is naïve because the ethic that rules the world is the ethic of convenience, even when those who occupy positions of leadership, such as President Bush, advertise themselves as practicing Christians.[18]

Later, Oliveira extended his solidarity to include undocumented immigrants in general, going beyond undocumented children. Oliveira told the Brazilian audience of his meditations, during his walks in Florida streets. He said that on a hot morning, he passed by a street made with interlocking brick pavers—a work very commonly done in Florida by Brazilian undocumented immigrants—and that this street reminded him of an undocumented leader in his church who worked under harsh conditions. Oliveira reflected, "I was then reminded that, as pastor, I live from the tithes and offerings dedicated to God that are given by people who, like this leader, work hard."[19] The title of the *Jornal Batista* column in which Oliveira tells this story is suggestive: "Solitary Walk and Paradigm Shift." It was then, it seems, that Oliveira realized the full implications of the fact that for Brazuca Baptists it is impossible to separate the idea of a calling to minister to Brazilian immigrants from the reality that such a calling is inevitably an invitation to side with undocumented bodies in their daily struggles. Another pastor in Florida shared an analogous sentiment:

> I have been solving this kind of problems for twenty-five years. Twenty-five years seeing these immigration issues coming up, separation of families. The father is deported, the mother stays with the children, and then the family can't stay and have to go back to Brazil, but the kids are American citizens. And then when they turn eighteen they want to come back to live here, we open the doors for them to return. So, there is a whole cycle and story of immigration.

Some Brazuca Baptist leaders are now pastoring the returning US citizen sons and daughters of their deported parishioners—now young adults trying to reckon with the material effects of a pernicious immigration system.

---

[18] Edvar Gimenes de Oliveira, "Dores de um Brasileiro," *Jornal Batista* CIII, no. 42 (2003): 11.
[19] Edvar Gimenes de Oliveira, "Caminhada Solitária e Mudança de Paradigmas," *Jornal Batista* CIII, no. 44 (2003): 11.

The challenging call to side with undocumented bodies causes difficulties for Brazuca pastors who usually have only theoretical knowledge of the struggles involved in undocumented living but who do not themselves feel the anxieties and limitations that the condition creates. Once most Brazuca Baptist pastors arrive in the United States with their papers, their level of identification with undocumented parishioners is limited at best. Elements of condescension toward the undocumented, commonly present in pastoral language and practice, are manifestations of the contextual gap that exists between documented and undocumented immigrants—a gap that cannot always be fully bridged by ethnic solidarity. Nevertheless, pastors often attempt to minister to their flock as if full identification were possible.

The line between legality and illegality, however, is not insurmountable, and sometimes pastors who were once undocumented have been able to become legal residents and even citizens of the United States. In those exceptional instances, closer identification between the pastor and the undocumented parishioner is indeed possible, if not always successful. One pastor who had been an undocumented immigrant, for instance, used his previous experiences to create a form of incarnational pastoral practice. He said that

> the form that I have found to deal with . . . [the struggles of undocumented members]—and this has eased my relationship with undocumented immigrants and gave me better position in relation to this reality—is to live with them as if I was not legal myself, to feel their pain, to share their struggles, to fight their fight. So when I do this I diminish the suffering they feel, I feel they feel loved, that there is someone who worries about them and wants their best. When I get close to them they see that the people, if they have patience and perseverance, have opportunity. So this is the form that I have found to minimize this issue here.

It is unclear what this pastor meant by living "as if I was not legal myself." Does he not hand over his driver's license to a police officer at a traffic stop or his immigration-related paperwork during an ICE raid? How about the existential insecurity so commonly felt by undocumented immigrants living under an antagonistic empire? Whatever the specifics, the point here is that pastors at times have been so involved in their relationship with their undocumented members that they have regarded their condition as something they should imitate to be able to offer more appropriate pastoral care.

Pastor Josias Bezerra, who had formal training in theology and psychology, often pondered the effects of undocumented living in his pastoral texts—printed in the church's bulletin—directed to the membership of the church he pastored in Elizabeth, New Jersey. In March 2000 Bezerra wrote down his reflections in a pastoral letter entitled "The Immigrant's Emotional Health" (A Saúde Emocional do Imigrante), in which he said:

> Self-esteem seems to be the great source of immigrants' emotional problems. Although all work is dignified, in general the immigrant works in areas where those who belong to the land do not want to work, such as cleaning, construction, and other related activities. Some people can work for years in these areas without apparent issues. Most, however, stay because they have no other option. They lack language skills, documents of legal residence, or even courage to begin to study. As a result, dissatisfaction begins to take over the heart. The feeling could not be different from one that takes the color out of life. For those who have a healthy space for social living, things are better. In the last decade Brazilian immigrants formed churches. They have a very important role in the preservation of the culture and in the maintenance of the Brazilian identity. The less charged with prejudices and more open to laughter and community life—without leaving the Bible aside—the more important for the emotional health of its members a church becomes. The church, because of the opportunity it gives for individuals to take up roles and feel useful, acts in the strengthening of their self-esteem, a function that, in and of itself, is already a great service to the community.[20]

Bezerra understands the church as helping undocumented immigrants endure the daily struggles of their lives in the United States by providing a space for meaningful activity. In a piece for the *Jornal Batista* he argued that in an immigrant context it is more important to have churches that function as "therapeutic communities" than those that focus strongly on abstract doctrinal matters.[21]

Bezerra's approach to the conundrum presented by undocumented bodies, however, went beyond concerns about emotional health. His migration experience, like that of other Brazuca Baptist leaders, opened his eyes to broader migrant motifs in the Bible. In his *Jornal Batista* article entitled "Abraham: An Immigrant Who Succeeded" (Abraão: Um Imigrante Que Deu Certo), Bezerra wrote, "I want to highlight aspects of Abraham the immigrant, bringing them into harmony with situations experienced by other immigrants, particularly us, Brazilians living in other lands." He went on to say that Abraham, not unlike most Brazilian Baptist immigrants, left his own land, had problems with Egyptian "immigration," and had to work very hard in a strange land.[22]

---

[20] Josias Bezerra, "A Saúde Emocional do Imigrante," *Folha da Primeira*, December 3, 2000, 1, 3.

[21] Josias Bezerra, "Opressão num Contexto de Imigrantes," *Jornal Batista* XCX, no. 48 (2000): 11.

[22] Josias Bezerra, "Abraão: Um Imigrante Que Deu Certo," *Jornal Batista* XCX, no. 26 (2000): 13.

After Bezerra read an article written by famous liberation theologian Gustavo Gutierrez—an author not commonly appreciated among average Brazilian Baptists—he began to apply liberationist insights to his pastoral anxieties. He wrote:

> Yesterday I was reading an article written by Gustavo Gutierrez about liberation theology in which he analyzed the trajectory of the movement since its inception. Among a number of challenging things, the text calls us to act in a liberative fashion in all occasions of our walk in the world. This means that Christian practice must always come with the most absolute respect for the human being, and must compel us to act with the intention of liberating humans from any form of oppression to which they may be subjugated. . . . In the church, acting in a liberative way is, among other things, fostering a (collective) conscience of dignity and value in the members of the community—practicing tolerance toward the deviants and avoiding any moves, in gestures or verbally, that diminish the other.[23]

Furthermore, the issue of undocumented workers fit Bezerra's broad application of Dietrich Bonhoeffer's ethics, in which, according to his interpretation of the German theologian, issues of right and wrong—and consequently legality and illegality—had to be measured according to specific contextual dynamics. For Bezerra,

> No one should expect, therefore, that God's will is readily systematized in a body of rules that comes to us from the top down or the inside out. No! God's will is born out of relationship with Christ, out of hearing him in intimacy, and it manifests itself as an answer, given in Jesus, to the stimulus of a specific situation.[24]

Thus, Bezerra applied the insights of famous theologians such as Gustavo Gutierrez and Dietrich Bonhoeffer to help him cope with the tension caused by undocumented parishioners. Although his language and choice of theological dialogue partners may be idiosyncratic, his anxieties ably encapsulate the much broader general spirit of Brazuca Baptist leadership.

The centrality of the anxieties of unbelonging named in Bezerra's observations also appeared in the perspective of other Brazuca Baptist pastors. These anxieties are common among Latinx immigrants in general, but Brazuca pastors indicate that they are exacerbated by undocumented status. A pastor of a

---

[23] Josias Bezerra, "Ecos de Libertação," *Folha da Primeira*, April 3, 2000, 1. Bezerra reprinted the same article in the *Folha da Primeira* issue of July 9, 2002.

[24] Josias Bezerra, "A Vontade de Deus na Ética Cristã de Bomhoeffer," *Folha da Primeira*, July 2, 2002, 1.

large church in the southern United States shared, "It is the issue of belonging; belonging is a very strong thing. We explore [this issue] in our small groups; we have fifty-one very strong small groups today. They have strong leaders and [the focus] is this idea of belonging." Another pastor, who worked with Brazilian immigrants in the East Coast and the southern states for over three decades mentioned that

> the church has a dual function. At the same time that it preaches the gospel, it has to be a social center, a meeting place. And the church here does that, in the sense of mediating and giving linguistic support, emotional support for those who are arriving. The church functions in this manner. It promotes these social encounters, and, through this, many hear the gospel and convert to the gospel. Because one of the things that happens is that Brazilians leave behind their cultural environment, linguistic, emotional, leaving friends, etc. And they need to find a place of support here. And it is where the church can take advantage of this moment and enter into people's lives.

Displacement itself causes a number of issues related to Latinx unbelonging. The problem of immigration documentation, however, so magnifies the sense of immigrant unbelonging that Brazuca Baptist churches have incorporated in their own self-understanding the need to be a place for belonging irrespective of one's place in broader society.

When it comes to the presence of undocumented pastors, however, most Brazuca Baptist leaders tend to be against permitting them to pastor without legal immigration papers. Although the overwhelming majority of Brazuca Baptist pastors are permanent residents or United States citizens, some have lived or still live in the country without legal status. Yet those pastors who are against this phenomenon find their own views complicated at times by their own migration experiences. The business meeting of a Brazuca Baptist church in New England reveals such complexity. In a crisis created by the issue of undocumented preaching, the church minutes registered a heated exchange between the pastor and the members:

> The pastor also talked about his position about an illegal pastor, questioning the ability of such an individual to go up to the pulpit to preach. The pastor said that during the week two people approached him questioning him and saying: "you were also an illegal and you were deported!" The pastor then explained that he came with a student visa (he had a visa) and he was deported because he changed universities without communicating, but only because he did not know that when moving from one university to another he would have to communicate [this to] the immigration office. Also, he said he was not yet a pastor when this happened, affirming once again that he is

still adamant in his position, thinking that it is wrong for a pastor to minister if he is undocumented.

Interestingly in that same church the conversation about the documentation of ministers did not extend to the legitimation of the immigration status of members in general. The minutes of the meeting show an interaction between an undocumented member and the same pastor who was adamantly against undocumented ministers. It reads, "Brother José questions the pastor about the illegality of members: 'What would be the right thing to do? Getting in the plane and leaving?' The pastor responded justifying that the brothers escape from Brazil 'because of the economy, and escaping is normal.'"

As this example illustrates, even the condemnation of the illegality of the very small number of Brazuca Baptist pastors experiencing this condition often comes with the accompanying legitimation of the illegality of everyone else. Another East Coast pastor (now retired) made this dynamic even more explicit. In his church, he said, "[being undocumented] did not change anything, nothing. I did not pay attention to this; I did not ask who was documented or not. I was against undocumented pastors, this I was against. But any other person was not a problem for me."

The implications of the moral, theological, and practical negotiations experienced by Brazuca Baptist churches because of the presence of undocumented parishioners are manifold. First, the sheer numbers of undocumented immigrants in most of these church communities accounts for their financial feasibility. Second, the moralism generally associated with the theology of Brazuca Baptist pastors—who were educated in Brazilian Baptist seminaries that taught a translated form of Southern Baptist theology, which in the United States has been generally outspokenly against illegal immigration—is negotiated in the US context because of this reality. Third, Brazuca Baptist churches legitimize undocumented living in a number of ways, such as through prayer, testimonies, church advertisement, and pastoral practice, and they use those same practices to encourage migration. Finally, the presence of undocumented bodies has shaped the social initiatives of Brazuca Baptist churches, prompting them to direct their attention and resources toward various activities that aim to help immigrants adjust and to protect them as much as possible.

There is no theological system that articulates the theological reasoning that legitimizes Brazuca Baptist beliefs and practices regarding the presence of undocumented parishioners. From the representative examples already mentioned, however, one can attempt to account for the fundamental anxieties behind the rudimentary theological dispositions of Brazuca Baptists who are pushed to make theological concessions to their otherwise moralistic leanings. Freston already helped in this regard, pointing out that a rudimentary theology of the undocumented includes arguments such as God created a world without borders, Jesus was an illegal immigrant in Egypt, Jews are ordered to treat the aliens well, and the United States is a land of immigrants.[25] But behind these explicit theological apologies, there is a more fundamental and more practical feeling: that there is something within the law itself that is deeply immoral and that US immigration law is fundamentally unjust. In a practical and particular fashion, Brazuca Baptists in general manifest a disposition encapsulated by Jacques Derrida:

> The law, as such, can be deconstructed and has to be deconstructed. That is the condition of historicity, revolution, morals, ethics, and progress. But justice is not the law. Justice is what gives us the impulse, the drive, or the movement to improve the law, that is, to deconstruct the law. Without a call for justice we would not have any interest in deconstructing the law.[26]

The unlikely overlap between Brazilian migrants and the Algerian philosopher is that, in the context of churches whose membership largely comprises undocumented immigrants, an incarnational theology and practice that claims to love the human being and God simultaneously must inevitably understand as antagonistic the relationship between justice and current US immigration law. Not only is this disposition consistent with Christian theology—it also allows Brazuca Baptist communities to embrace the deviants without guilt.

The Brazuca Baptist support of their undocumented members, however, should not be taken as an indication that these churches are antagonistic to other parameters of legality. In terms of moral behaviors and ideologies beyond immigration issues, Brazuca Baptist churches still align closely with their Southern Baptist heritage and, as such, are disseminators of a message of strict moral conduct that discourages any form of illegal activity or disruptive behavior. What happens with undocumented members of Brazuca Baptist churches, as Teresa Sales has pointed out in relation to Brazilian undocumented immigrants in general, is that "they are in a situation of illegality, but not illegitimacy."[27] Indeed, the undocumented condition even encourages behavior that is respectful of all other US laws, whether due to fear of deportation or hope of legalization.

[25] Freston, "Religious Field," 265.
[26] John D. Caputo, ed., *Deconstruction in a Nutshell: A Conversation with Jacques Derrida* (New York: Fordham University Press, 1996), 16.
[27] Teresa Sales, *Brasileiros Longe de Casa* (São Paulo: Cortez, 1999), 147.

Collateral Effects of Immigrant Instability

The moral issues generated by the presence of undocumented parishioners and support for migration generally do not exhaust the contextual challenges of Brazuca Baptist churches in terms of the complexities imposed by migration dynamics. Most Brazilian immigrants to the United States, and undocumented migrants in particular, are in the country mostly for one reason: dollars. For much of the history of Brazilian migration to North America, Brazilian immigrants have had their bodies in the United States but their heads in Brazil. That is, unlike some other migrant groups, Brazilian immigrants as a group do not seem themselves as immigrants per se but as temporary workers and target earners who will go back home as soon as they can. Although this dynamic may be changing, as of this writing it certainly has affected Brazuca Baptist churches.[28]

The common mentality of return that characterizes Brazilian migration deeply affects church life in two major ways: membership fluctuation and parishioner commitment. In 1984, Humberto Viegas Fernandes already noticed this phenomenon in the oldest Brazuca Baptist church:

> If it wasn't for the fluctuation of members, once many come back to Brazil or move to other states (we lost eleven members, in this first year, because four returned to Brazil, one went to heaven, five moved to Florida, and one was excluded), we would have doubled our membership during this period.[29]

---

[28] There is no consensus regarding what Soraya Fleischer has referred to as "the myth of return," which is the narrative widely disseminated by Brazilian immigrants that they will stay in the United States for a limited amount of time and then return to Brazil. Paul Freston argues that members of Brazilian immigrant religious communities have a temporary mentality that affirms that they are not traditional immigrants and will return (see Freston, "Religious Field," 258–59). Fleischer points out the inconsistency of these narratives, saying that even Brazilians who stay in the United States for a long time perpetuate the myth of return (see Fleischer, *Passando a América a Limpo: O Trabalho de Housecleaners Brasileiras em Boston* [São Paulo: Annablume Editora, 2002], 27). More recently, Ana Cristina Braga Martes has agreed with Freston's position (see Martes, *New Immigrants, New Land: A Study of Brazilians in Massachusetts* [Gainesville: University Press of Florida, 2011], 4). Catarina Fritz, Clemence Jouët-Pastré, and Leticia Braga argue that this particular characteristic of Brazilian immigrants no longer holds true (see Catarina Fritz, *Brazilian Immigration and the Quest for Identity* [El Paso, Tex.: LFB Scholarly Publishing, 2010], 1–2; and Jouët-Pastré and Braga, "Introduction: Interdisciplinary Perspectives on Becoming Brazucas," in *Becoming Brazuca*, 3). Among US Brazilian Baptist churches themselves, the myth of return is a rather prominent motif.

[29] Humberto Viegas Fernandes, "Cartas de Nova Iorque: Bênçãos do Primeiro Ano—II," *Jornal Batista* LXXXIV, no. 9 (1984): 11–12.

In the following two years, until his return to Brazil, Fernandes would complain about the fluctuation in numbers and the attendant instability.[30] Paulo Moraes, assessing a similar situation in the First Brazilian Baptist Church of Greater Boston, used a term that aptly describes the issue, noting that in the Boston church there was a great "transient syndrome" that was an obstacle for church work.[31]

The transient syndrome in Brazuca Baptist churches became so significant that a few churches created a special kind of member, sometimes called "congregated member," in order to better categorize immigrants who expected to return to their country of origin soon.[32] After pastor Nivado Nassif took over the role of senior pastor in the Boston church, he discovered that seventy people who were still on the church rolls as active members were actually either back in Brazil or in another state.[33] At PIB New Jersey, the same happened when Pastor José Calixto led the community. In 2005 he asked for an investigation into the number of "disappeared members" and discovered that many were already back in Brazil.[34]

The Brazuca Baptist transient syndrome is characterized by a focus on quick financial gain that will allegedly make a timely return to Brazil possible. A 1992 entry in the minutes of All Nations Baptist Church in Danbury further illustrates how this issue affects church life: "It continues to be a problem that people accept Christ and are not baptized, add to that the issue that the dollar is the great objective of everyone, and that makes it hard to even set up a new converts class."[35] A pastor on the East Coast said that, according to his experience, "about 80 percent (of Brazilian immigrants) came to make money and go back. Ten percent came to stay, and 10 percent came to study."

The mentality of target earning for returning to Brazil, together with its corollary focus on quick monetary gain, affects the time investment and intensity of commitment of Brazuca Baptist immigrants to their church. A Florida pastor—one of many Brazuca Baptist pastors with formal training in psychology—described this dynamic well:

> I have been analyzing this very well from the psychological point of view too. This is the deal: the Brazilian does not immigrate; the Brazilian comes

[30] Humberto Viegas Fernandes, "Cartas de New York: Lutas e Vitórias do Segundo Ano," *Jornal Batista* LXXXV, no. 5 (1985): 11–12; Fernandes, "Cartas de Nova Iorque: Bençãos do Terceiro Ano," *Jornal Batista* LXXXVI, no. 8 (1986): 12.

[31] Paulo Moraes, "Igreja Brasileira em Boston É Luz numa Cidade em Trevas," *Jornal Batista* XCV, no. 42 (1996): 13.

[32] *Atas da (Minutes of) Primeira Igreja Batista Brasileira da Grande Boston*, 1991, book 1, 20.

[33] *Atas da (Minutes of) Primeira Igreja Batista (Boston)*, 2003, book 2, 281.

[34] *Atas da (Minutes of) Primeira Igreja Batista de Língua Portuguesa de New Jersey*, 2005, book 1, 111.

[35] *Atas da (Minutes of) Primeira Igreja Batista de Língua Portuguesa de Danbury*, 1992, book 1, 25.

to the United States. He does not immigrate. This is different, for example, from the Hispanics because the Hispanics immigrate to the United States, so here will be their place today, tomorrow, after, and forever. So they are willing to invest here. They invest emotionally, culturally; for example here in the Hispanic church I have a number of boys who are studying with a full scholarship at Columbia University, at Harvard University, and in the Brazilian [church] there is no one [attending college]. So this is the deal: the Brazilian girls and boys finish high school and very few go to the university, it is a very small group. Because when they finish high school they want to work so they can get a car and that's it. So the vision of the Brazilian is just "dollars." Got it? The only thing that interests the Brazilian immigrant is the dollar. So, as I was saying, he comes to the United States, he does not immigrate to the United States. So he comes here to make some money. So what happens? You have a group that is very nomad[ic] and they are here today and in New York tomorrow and in Boston the day after. Wherever they [get paid] more, this is where they go. So the people come [to the United States] but do not unpack their luggage, and their sole interest is having dollars. And many, when they get the dollar, they go back [to Brazil]. So they make no investments here.

This dynamic presents a completely different pastoral challenge from the challenges of Baptist churches in Brazil. According to an East Coast pastor:

It is completely different to pastor a church in Brazil, where people are in their own land, their own ground, and their own culture. They come here, the people who came here when I came, they really came here due to financial needs because they did not have the ability to support themselves in Brazil. So they came desperate, and in this desperation they crossed the Mexican border and did everything you can imagine coming here and chasing their dream. So pastoring groups like this, which are truly more interested in solving their personal problems and don't worry about their church life [is difficult]. So the church was a safe harbor for those who came insofar as it was a point of "Brazilianness." But the person arrived, and we would do things for them that normally would not have been done in Brazil. We did literally everything because the person is excluded from everything here, right? No friends, no papers, excluded in all aspects. You'd have to find work, find living accommodations, transportation, until the person was able to take care of himself. Many left family in Brazil, so it was not easy, it is not easy today pastoring these kind[s] of people because they are not people who came as immigrants to stay; they came to make money and go back.

The insights of a pastor in Texas reinforce this point:

People here do not have the same availability of time as people in Brazil. People in Brazil work one shift and then go home just like the Americans do here. But the Brazilian immigrant is different; he leaves one job to go to the next and sometimes even a third one. So the focus of the people here is making money to save some money. The financial question here is the preponderant one for all Brazilians. So the way in which people get involved with the church is very different.

Pastors interviewed for this book were, in general, concerned about this dynamic because it affects the stability of their communities in several ways, but especially in terms of allowing them to implement a long-term budget and the ministries it allows. The transient syndrome of Brazilian immigrants has forced Brazuca Baptist churches—even those that have transitioned to a more stable situation in terms of the number of documented members—to develop in an environment that does not allow for ministry stability.

Pastor Josias Bezerra touched on the perceived relationship between biblical stories and immigrant narratives in an address to his PIB New Jersey community. In a text entitled "On Being More in the Land of Having More" (Ser Mais na Terra do Ter Mais), in which he included a quotation from a famous Brazilian poem by Gonçalves Dias written when Dias was an immigrant in Portugal, Bezerra wrote:

> The prophet Jeremiah was accused by some leaders of the people of Israel, who were in the Babylonian exile, of being a traitor without patriotism, because he defended the necessity of the people to fight for the peace of the city, which meant, in the mind of the Man of God, the peace of his people. He said that those exiled should strengthen their roots in the country where they lived, buying houses, creating businesses, getting married, dreaming, that is, living their lives. He knew that the exile would not end soon and that living in melancholy would be foolishness. Just like in that context, most Brazilian immigrants have no chances of returning to Brazil. And some do not even dream of this anymore, because they do not want to return, or due to resignation: "Go back and do what?" What cannot be done is to live here with the head entirely there. This position ends up weakening one's ability to fight for a more defined place under the American sun and also diminishes the quality of life, because the money that is gained is saved for the day of return. So, the years go by without a life well lived here and now. Not that I am against those who want to return. Actually, I think the opposite. If there are conditions for return, even if risks are involved, I encourage anyone who wants to make the way back. As a matter of fact, my prayer has been that the Brazilian economy gets better so that those who are there do not need to come here and those who are here have better chances in the case of an eventual return.

After all, "our land has palm trees where the thrush sings, and the birds that sing here, do not sing as they do there."[36]

Like many other Brazuca Baptist leaders, Bezerra was concerned not only with the strategically relevant issues raised by the transient syndrome but also with the existential anxieties that such a condition causes.

The challenges of Brazuca Baptist churches, therefore, go far beyond the already difficult need to pastor undocumented members vis-à-vis the legal and moral conundrums that such activity may entail. This is so because the transient syndrome, which is connected to the form of Brazilian labor migration to the United States, poses a constant threat of instability—mostly in numeric and financial terms but also in terms of well-trained lay leadership. The tendency of Brazilian immigrants to imagine an eventual move back to Brazil and their flexibility in moving from one state to another chasing short-term financial benefits together affect the daily lives of many Brazuca Baptist churches to an extent that is not true of Baptist churches in Brazil. The paradox created by this situation is that the churches that were originally founded to serve people who had the courage to cross borders for money find a potential threat to their stability in this very border-crossing disposition.

Brazilian Baptists, Race, and Ethnicity

The dynamics created by the high numbers of undocumented Brazuca Baptist parishioners, which include moral and logistical matters, are also problematized by the issue of Brazuca ethnic identity. Brazilian immigrants generally do not feel a sense of belonging among other immigrants from Latin America or of Latinx heritage. This peculiarity sometimes makes Brazilian immigrants feel that they are not included in movements and initiatives of Latinx social justice. What Teresa Sales said in 1999 remains true today: "Brazilian immigrants form a group in process of constructing an ethnic identity."[37] The fact that Brazilians speak Portuguese, that the first wave of Brazilian mass migration is less than four decades old, that Brazilians often see themselves as target earners who will return to their home country, and the lack of a significant presence of a second and third generation that can be studied in terms of their racial and ethnic identity are all examples of how Brazilians resist pan-ethnic labels.[38] Furthermore, in order to understand the intentional dynamics of

---

[36] Josias Bezerra, "Ser Mais na Terra Do Ser Mais," *Folha da Primeira*, November 12, 2000, 1.

[37] Sales, *Brasileiros Longe de Casa*, 129.

[38] My data collection did not include a robust sample of second-generation Brazilian immigrants (i.e., Brazilian Americans). Given the recent nature of Brazilian

Brazuca Baptist churches, one must consider the fact that they are led almost exclusively by first-generation ministers and lay leaders. Although the second generation is a source of great concern for a leadership trying to devise ways to keep them in Brazilian ethnic churches, the decisions and representation are in the hands of Brazilian-born immigrants.[39] These latter, in turn, import racial categories and ethnic characteristics that are constantly contested by local imaginations of otherness. In sum, terms such as "Hispanic" and "Latinx" are ideal pan-ethnic descriptors of Brazilian immigrants in the United States and Brazilian Americans. However, Brazilians often resist moving away from their attachment to their national identity—and thus sometimes distance themselves from pan-ethnic terms.

When it comes to race, it should be emphasized that Brazilian racial taxonomies emphasize phenotypes rather than ancestry and that many Brazilians in Brazil who self-identify as white have African ancestry.[40] In addition, factors such as the influence of anthropologist Gilberto Freyre's understanding of Brazil as a racial democracy and subsequent legal and political resistance to emphasizing racial difference in Brazil are significant. They provided an environment in which Brazilians—until very recently—did not develop a robust notion of race capable of moving past racial democracy ideology and its colorblind rhetoric, which contains deeply racist undertones.[41] A 2012

---

mass migration to the United States, only a few works within the already scant literature on Brazilian migration stand out as having a strong focus on the second generation. For examples, see Gustavo Hamilton Menezes, "Filhos da Imigração: A Segunda Geração de Brasileiros em Connecticut," in *Fronteiras Cruzadas: Etnicidade, Gênero e Redes Sociais*, ed. Ana Cristina Braga Martes and Soraya Fleischer (São Paulo: Paz e Terra, 2003), 157–74; Fritz, *Brazilian Immigration and the Quest for Identity*; Cebulko, *Documented, Undocumented*; Catarina Fritz, "Redefining Racial Categories: The Dynamics of Identity among Brazilian-Americans," *Immigrants & Minorities* 33, no. 1 (2015): 45–65.

[39] Rodrigo Serrão and James Cavendish found that the Brazilian churches in Texas they studied did not "seem to worry about transitioning to the second generation." My claim is that Brazuca Baptist churches are generally concerned about the second generation even if not aggressively active in incorporating it in evident ways. See Rodrigo Serrão and James Cavendish, "The Social Functions and Dysfunctions of Brazilian Immigrant Congregations in 'Terra Incognita'," *Review of Religious Research* 60, no. 3 (2018): 367–88.

[40] Edward E. Telles, *Race in Another America: The Significance of Skin Color in Brazil* (Princeton, N.J.: Princeton University Press, 2014), 1–2.

[41] Originally published in 1933, Freyre's *The Masters and the Slaves* was the strongest factor in the intellectual dissemination of the idea of Brazil as a racial democracy. For a version in English see Gilberto Freyre, *The Masters and the Slaves (Casa-Grande & Senzala): A Study in the Development of Brazilian Civilization* (Berkeley: University of California Press, 1987). For good overviews of the legal and political discouragement of using racial categories to diagnose social problems in Brazil, see Graziella Moraes Silva and Marcelo Paixão, "Mixed and Unequal: New Perspectives on Brazilian

article by Mara Loveman, Jeronimo Muniz, and Stanley Bailey, who have in-depth knowledge of both US and Brazilian racial taxonomies, illustrates the complex differences between these two contexts. A central question asked by Loveman et al. was, if the "mixed-race" category, so prevalent in the Brazilian racial taxonomy, were eliminated, would Brazil look darker or lighter?[42] What they found was that if a "white/nonwhite" binary was enforced in Brazil, close to half of the Black and Brown population would choose to be white. That is, using a white/nonwhite paradigm in Brazil would result in the swelling of the white population.[43] Yet, if the Brazilian population were categorized according to US racial categories, at least 60 percent of the country would be Black.[44] In recent years, however, more people in Brazil have begun to self-identify as Black and Brown for a variety of reasons, including policies created to remedy historical injustices, such as affirmative action.

Scholars have pointed out that it was only during the last term of President Fernando Henrique Cardoso (1999–2002) that the Brazilian government began to abandon policies that silenced official diagnoses of national racial problems and instead began to acknowledge racial discrimination openly.[45] The long history of the ideology of racial democracy, however, still guides the racial imagination of most Brazilians and may function as a tool to legitimize racial inequalities in the country.[46] For the purposes of studying Brazilian immigrants to the United States, this factor is central; among Brazilians in Brazil and abroad, it informs a generalized disregard for antiracist strategies or even a lack of sense of racial solidarity.[47] That is, in terms of racial justice issues in the United States, Brazilian immigrants, in general—despite significant numbers being considered Latinx, Black, or Afro-Latinx in the United States—either lack the imagination to see themselves as fitting into that category or utterly resist what they see as a foreign taxonomy.

Ethnoracial Relations," in *Pigmentocracies: Ethnicity, Race, and Color in Latin America*, ed. Edward Telles (Chapel Hill: University of North Carolina Press, 2014); and Micol Seigel, *Uneven Encounters: Making Race and Nation in Brazil and the United States* (Durham, N.C.: Duke University Press, 2009).

[42] Mara Loveman, Jeronimo O. Muniz, and Stanley R. Bailey, "Brazil in Black and White? Race Categories, the Census, and the Study of Inequality," *Ethnic & Racial Studies* 35, no. 8 (2012): 1468.

[43] Loveman, Muniz, and Bailey, "Brazil in Black and White?" 1476–80.

[44] Stanley R. Bailey, Mara Loveman, and Jeronimo O. Muniz, "Measures of 'Race' and the Analysis of Racial Inequality in Brazil," *Social Science Research* 42, no. 1 (2013): 111.

[45] Silva and Paixão, "Mixed and Unequal," 181–83; Stanley R. Bailey, "Group Dominance and the Myth of Racial Democracy: Antiracism Attitudes in Brazil," *American Sociological Review* 69, no. 5 (2004): 730.

[46] Bailey, "Group Dominance," 728.

[47] Bailey, "Group Dominance," 732.

Noticing the gap between the self-perception of many Brazilian immigrants in the United States and the way in which they are socialized by Anglo-Americans, the Brazilian Embassy asked Brazilians to self-identify as Hispanic or Latino in the 2020 census. The embassy engaged in a social media campaign to encourage Brazilians to select the "Hispanic, Latino, or Spanish origin" category and then write "Brazilian" in the box. In previous years, Brazilians mainly selected "Other" and included their nationality. Although Brazilian immigrants may resist using the "Hispanic" or "Latinx" labels, scholars have argued that while such a stance may work for light-skinned individuals, the group as a whole is often included under the Hispanic label.[48] Several institutions and denominations—including the SBC—approach Brazilians via their Hispanic ministries. Since the 1960s, many Brazilian Baptists pastored Spanish-speaking churches and led denominational positions that assumed they were Hispanic. In the broader landscape of theological and religious education, universities and seminaries extend scholarship opportunities for Hispanic students to Brazilians. Institutions such as the Hispanic Theological Initiative formed and continue to serve a significant number of Brazilian leaders working in the United States and abroad. These realities, however, do not always square with the self-perception of newly arrived immigrants from Brazil—who often fall into the temptation of distancing themselves from the ethnic group in which they should be included.

When talking about their own racial self-understanding, a great many Brazuca Baptist leaders lack the language to define their category according to the US taxonomy. For instance, according to a longtime pastor, in his church there are no racial differences: "The Brazilian race is almost homogeneous in its majority. They are Mestizos and there is no white or black purity, so to speak." Another one said, "I am a son of Italians, Portuguese, and Indians [Native Brazilians]. I am a Mestizo. That is the same as Brazilian, right?" Perhaps the most powerful example of this complexity, however, comes from an informal conversation I had with a recognizably Black Brazilian woman—by US standards—who had migrated to the United States in the early sixties. When I asked whether she was here during legal segregation, thinking that I would hear her stories of struggling with the system, she answered that it was bad, "but only for Blacks," not for her.

Brazuca Baptists then, reflect the findings of a number of researchers who have performed localized works on the racial identity of Brazilian immigrants. For the latter, national identity is tied to racial identity as a response to the different racial imaginations of the two countries. The

---

[48] Gibson, *Post-Katrina Brazucas*, 18.

second generation, although still understudied, seems to be copying their parents in this regard.[49] The lack of solidarity on the part of Brazuca Baptist churches with issues of race is also informed both by the lack of emphasis on racial justice in Brazilian theological training and church practice and by the resistance of Brazilian immigrants to being defined according to the racial categories of the United States. A similar dynamic is observable in regard to the application of pan-ethnic terms such as Hispanic or Latinx to Brazilian immigrants.

If these complexities are already significant, the ethnic identification of Brazilians is by no means simple. Although Brazilian intellectuals recognize the accuracy, inevitability, and advantages of adopting the "Hispanic" and/or "Latinx" labels, at the core of Brazilian ethnic self-understanding there is a fundamental element: the need to differentiate themselves from other groups of Latin American origin and resist the term Hispanic. The construction of ethnic identities in general passes through the process of differentiation from the "Other," and for Brazilians this process is oftentimes determined by the white American racist framing of Hispanics—the category into which Brazilian immigrants are most commonly socialized in the United States. This happens because Brazilian immigrants want to take advantage of a commonly romanticized version of their culture. Because US whites often romanticize Brazilian culture and espouse negative understandings of Hispanic cultures, Brazilians tend to want to distance themselves from the Hispanic label.[50] This represents the appropriation of preexisting stereotypes in US society regarding both Brazilian culture and Hispanics. In this sense, it is socially advantageous for Brazilians to resist both racial and ethnic US understandings of their ideal categorization. As Ana Martes states, "Brazilian identity is of the contrasting

---

[49] Ana Cristina Braga Martes, "Raça e Etnicidade: Opções e Constrangimentos," in *Fronteiras Cruzadas: Etnicidade, Gênero e Redes Sociais*, ed. Ana Cristina Braga Martes and Soraya Fleischer (São Paulo: Paz e Terra, 2003), 76; Judith McDonnell and Cileine de Lourenço, "Brazilian Immigrant Women: Race, Ethnicity, Gender, and Transnationalism," in Jouët-Pastré and Braga, *Becoming Brazuca*, 165–67; Ana Ramos-Zayas, "Between 'Cultural Excess' and 'Racial Invisibility': Brazilians and the Commercialization of Culture in Newark," in *Becoming Brazuca*, 271; Fritz, *Brazilian Immigration and the Quest for Identity*, 37; Martes, *New Immigrants, New Land*, 223.

[50] Ramos-Zayas, "Between 'Cultural Excess' and 'Racial Invisibility,'" 271–81; Teresa Sales, "Identidade Étnica entre Imigrantes Brasileiros na Região de Boston, EUA," in *Cenas do Brasil Migrante*, ed. Rossana Rocha Reis and Teresa Sales (São Paulo, Brazil: Boitempo Editorial, 1999), 41; Maxine Margolis, "Na Virada do Milênio: A Emigração Brasileira para os Estados Unidos," in *Fronteiras Cruzadas: Etnicidade, Gênero e Redes Sociais*, ed. Ana Cristina Braga Martes and Soraya Fleischer (São Paulo: Paz e Terra, 2003), 61–62; Beserra, *Brazilian Immigrants*, 57–58.

type, constructing itself by establishing friction with the Hispanic identity."[51] In other words, Brazilian immigrants are prone to have internalized not only the racial imagination of Brazilian society but also to incorporate the US white racial frame into their self-understanding. Their imagination is often captured by intersecting white supremacist societies.

Bernadete Beserra's work on Brazilian ethnic identity in Chicago summarizes well the scholarly debates surrounding this issue:

> The study of cooperation within the Brazilian immigrant population as well as between it and other immigrant groups or U.S. minorities has been neglected in favor of a focus on Brazilian disunity and their objection to being called "Hispanics" and/or "Latinos." I have questioned both concerns, pointing out that the acknowledged disunity among Brazilian immigrants is better explained as a strategy to which all individuals resort in their attempts at integration than as a feature confined to Brazilians and that Brazilians' rejection of the terms "Hispanic" and "Latino" has to do with their association with being poor, working-class, undereducated, lazy, and illegal. While Brazilians are not the only Latinos to reject these labels for their negative connotations, they are the ones who can most easily demonstrate their distinction in terms of colonial rule by Portugal instead of Spain, language, geopolitical position in Latin America, and Carnival.[52]

Brazuca ethnic construction—with its deeply problematic appropriation of white US prejudice—affects churches precisely as these communities try to negotiate attempts to walk alongside Latinx peoples of different origins.

The dynamic of ethnic identity plays out in Brazuca Baptist churches in a peculiar way. In many churches, pastors know that it would be beneficial for the growth of the community to be more open to working alongside other Hispanics. Still, first-generation members often resist such an arrangement. A Brazilian pastor whose church is on the East Coast and who had just recently arrived in the United States offered an illustration of his particular conundrum while criticizing his parishioners' ethnocentrism. I quoted part of this pastor's comment above. An extended quotation of his opinion regarding Brazilians and other Hispanics, however, also illustrates this particular issue well:

> I saw a strong ethnocentricity among Brazilian Baptists here. We talk about multiethnic churches, but they do not work in practice. For example, we have a church that is [mostly] formed of Brazilian immigrants, but we know that

[51] Ana Cristina Braga Martes, "Neither Hispanic, nor Black: We're Brazilian," in *The Other Latinos*, ed. José Luis Falconi and José Antônio Mazzotti (Cambridge, Mass.: David Rockefeller Center for Latin American Studies, 2008), 240.

[52] Bernadete Beserra, "Samba in Chicago: Escaping Hegemonic Multiculturalist Boundaries," *Latin American Perspectives* 39, no. 3 (2012): 107.

we have a Hispanic community and if we begin to open a work that serves the Hispanic community, that is, if we open the church to a vision that is more missionary, deep inside the Brazilians [will] always want to be in control of everything. They do not want to relinquish power and do not want to share leadership in a multiethnic church. So we perceive this strong ethnocentrism among Brazilians. They say, "No! We want to be Brazilian and we want to live like Brazilians," and this closes doors to an openness for an heterogeneous church and we live in a homogeneous church, and a homogeneous church in the world in which we live, as immigrants, has many difficulties of growth and development. Why? Because this vision comes with the members; it is in the first generation's head. And if you want to change this, you will have to have a lot of patience and be really careful to avoid divisions, splits, and discomfort. Why? Because it is the first generation that supports the church today. . . . Brazilians, when they look at other Latinos, think they are superior, and this influences how they relate to these groups in the church, unfortunately.

Reflecting on the failed attempt to have a ministry that is more inclusive of other Hispanics in his church, another pastor said, insidiously maintaining a distinction between Brazilians and other Hispanics, "The Brazilians and Hispanics in our church split because the Brazilians did not treat the Hispanics as if they were members. There was a Brazilian racism against the Hispanics, which exists. We, Brazilians, deplore Hispanics in America." A West Coast pastor confirmed that there are tensions between Brazilians and other Hispanics but offered an explanation that emphasized an alleged Hispanic shyness as a reason for the difference between the two groups:

I think that this [Brazilian feeling of superiority toward Hispanics] comes mostly from the Hispanics. But if you make any church with people from different places, it is difficult to walk together. But we see that they are shyer than we are. They are more reserved. They think they are less.

This pastor's opinion suggests that the issue is not Brazilian internalized racism and illusion of superiority but a Hispanic sense of inferiority—a position that itself reflects the problematic issue of the distorted Brazilian self-understanding in the US context. Whenever Brazilian immigrants to the United States resist adopting the term "Hispanic," they are internalizing precisely the discriminatory culture that helps create barriers to their appropriate incorporation into US society.[53] Also, there is no evidence to suggest that such resistance keeps the dominant culture from categorizing Brazilians as

---

[53] For an excellent study on the construction of racial categories among second-generation Brazilian American Evangelicals, see Rodrigo Serrão, "Winning America for Jesus? Second-Generation, Racial Ideology, and the Future of the Brazilian Evangelical Church in the U.S." (Ph.D. diss., University of South Florida, 2020.)

Hispanics and/or Latinxs, even if Brazilian culture may be romanticized by white Americans. Ultimately, such a strategy of ethnic construction seems to be both ineffective and counterproductive.

The antagonism between Brazilian immigrants and those they label Hispanic is nevertheless notable, and the Brazuca Baptist track record of importing the widespread "us against them" mentality of Brazilian ethnic construction into their faith communities is significant. Cases in which Brazuca Baptist churches are successful in implementing long-term relationships with ministries to and with other Hispanics in their churches are rare. Also, leaders' perception that Brazuca Baptist parishioners share with Brazilian immigrants more broadly a resistance to Hispanic identity markers and social organizations is notable. Yet, for most of its history, the SBC—naturally following the patterns of broader US culture—has included Brazuca churches under their "Hispanic ministries" umbrella. Such an approach is part of the reason for the lack of success on the part of the SBC in imparting a strong sense of denominational participation to a group whose leaders have been trained into appreciating all things Southern Baptist. More broadly, Brazuca Baptist churches lack a history of robust participation in or support for social and political issues that affect the Hispanic community. With the exception of issues relating to immigration, Brazuca Baptist churches often do not demonstrate a sense of solidarity with other Hispanic initiatives or organizations despite the fact that Anglo-Americans often characterize Brazilian immigrants as Hispanics and/or Latinxs. According to most Brazuca Baptist leaders, however, this trend is ultimately neither a beneficial nor an accurate approach to Brazuca ethnic and pan-ethnic identification and the Brazilian government also began encouraging Brazilians in the US to adopt "Hispanic" and/or "Latinx" pan-ethnic labels.

Conclusion

Brazuca Baptist churches differ from the communities of Brazilian Baptists and Baptists in the United States for several reasons, most of which are connected to migration dynamics. There is of course diversity among Brazuca Baptists, and their differentiating characteristics do not manifest themselves in the same way or with the same intensity. Yet the presence of undocumented parishioners is part of the core identity and practice of these churches. The stance of Brazuca Baptist churches on this issue puts these communities at odds with both Brazilian Baptists and the United States denominations with which they are affiliated—most significantly the SBC.

The differences between Brazuca and Brazilian Baptists are already illustrated in the moral conundrum presented to pastors who migrate in order to lead communities that are characterized by the presence of undocumented members and congregants. Coming mostly from a Southern Baptist–inspired theological education, Brazuca Baptist pastors have made the journey from crisis, to discomfort, to acceptance, and finally to defense of undocumented members, as their publications, recollections, church activities, and practices show. The pastoral stance toward the deviant immigrant has become so important that the rare instances of Brazuca pastoral ordination in the United States are accompanied by questions about the candidate's stance on undocumented churchgoers—presumably implying that a favorable stance is a condition sine qua non for ordination.[54] In addition, a number of pastors who were ordained in the United States were themselves once undocumented, which illustrates further the legitimation of the undocumented condition among Brazuca Baptists.

The racial and ethnic confusion among Brazuca Baptists also shows how this group manifests the general tendency among Brazilian immigrants of resisting racial and ethnic categories imposed on them by the dominant culture. Brazilian immigrants in general and Brazuca Baptists in particular want to distance themselves from the racial and ethnic taxonomy of the United States, in part because they view an emphasis on nationality as socially beneficial. Although Latin American immigrants in general prefer national to pan-ethnic identification (e.g., Hispanic or Latino), Brazilians see terms such as "Hispanic" not only as imperfect descriptors of their heritage but as terms that are actively antagonistic to their national identity. Like other immigrant groups, Brazucas avoid self-identifying in pan-ethnic terms in general, despite their particular reasons to do so. In short, Brazucas want to be identified as Brazilian, and although the desirability of national identification is true to some extent of other immigrant groups as well, it is vehemently true of Brazucas. The result of this dynamic is that there is little Brazuca solidarity with Hispanic and Latinx initiatives and projects. In addition, denominational efforts to give support to Brazuca Baptist churches in a way that includes them under the Hispanic umbrella have failed to implement a sense of denominational belonging in these churches. Brazuca Baptist communities are not comfortable with their affiliations to US denominational bodies—sometimes because of the ethnocentrism of Anglo-US denominations, sometimes because of the ethnocentrism of Brazilians and Brazilian Americans themselves.

[54] The minutes of PIB Family Church, for example, show that a candidate for a pastoral post was questioned about his position regarding the undocumented in Brazuca churches; in response, the candidate said that he had no issue with their situation, and that he would pray and care for them.

6
MORPHING

Pentecostalization and Women's Leadership

Pentecostalism and Charismatic Christianity transformed the religious landscape of Latin America in the period between 1970 and 2000. Contemporary praise songs, "spiritual warfare," speaking in tongues, prophecy, and supernatural healing became common features of churches across the region. Despite the disdain with which the intelligentsia treated them, Pentecostals and Catholic Charismatics were not the fringe but rather two heavyweights fighting for the title of most influential religious movement in Latin America.

Todd Hatch[1]

The internal registry of the OBBPNA exemplifies the multilayered activities of Brazuca Baptist leaders in the United States. A recent version of the registry, which is only circulated among affiliated pastors, reveals the multilingual, multiracial, multinational, and transdenominational aspects of the Brazuca Baptist network. The registry is made up mostly of Brazuca Baptist leaders, but not exclusively. Connected to the OBBPNA, and present in this internal registry, are the past and current presidents of the BBC (both of whom lived in the United States for extended periods of time), a vice president of the Baptist World Alliance, Brazilian missionaries in Haiti and Africa, Brazilian members of pastoral teams of predominantly white Southern Baptist churches, presidents of nondenominational ministries, senior pastors of Spanish-speaking churches, executives of the WMB, pastors of Brazuca

[1] Todd Hartch, *The Rebirth of Latin American Christianity* (Oxford: Oxford University Press, 2014), 91.

churches located in several Canadian cities, pastors of large churches in Brazil, an Angolan pastor who was naturalized as a Brazilian citizen and now pastors in the United States, one Brazilian who worked for Texas Baptists, white Americans who pastor Brazuca groups in the United States, several Brazilian immigrants to that country who work for their respective Baptist state conventions (SBC), US missionaries working in Brazil, leaders in theological education among Brazilian immigrants, and dozens of pastors of Brazuca Baptist churches who lead immigrant faith communities in over twenty-two US states.

The multilayered representation of Brazuca Baptist diversity contained in the OPBBAN internal registry shows the complexity and reach of Brazuca religious communities in particular and of immigrant churches in general. Brazuca leaders and their transnational network include theological educators, denominational leaders in Brazil and the United States, megachurch pastors, Brazilian and American missionaries, pastors in dozens of US and Canadian cities, and more. The tensions present among them, however, manifest themselves most obviously in the daily lives of immigrant communities, which are deeply affected by migration dynamics. The case of Brazuca Baptist communities, which serve as a representative example of broader dynamics in immigrant religious practice, reveals central ambiguities of immigrant church life—especially in the case of denominationally connected groups. In addition to the interconnected challenges of the aforementioned presence of undocumented and transient members, the migration dynamics of Brazilians to the United States also generate tension in Brazuca church communities due to the immigrants' multidenominational makeup. The fact that immigrant churches often attract parishioners more because of a sense of ethnic solidarity than because of a shared denominational background forces Brazuca Baptist churches to negotiate their commitment to beliefs and practices often taken for granted as bona fide Baptist elements, such as an emphasis on baptism by immersion and the discouragement of practices generally associated with Pentecostalism (e.g., speaking in tongues, divine healing, and prophesying).[2]

Brazuca Baptist churches not only have a history of serving a considerable number of undocumented or formerly undocumented members; they have also served many individuals who were Protestants in Brazil but of non-Baptist

---

[2] For more on how Brazuca Baptists negotiate the practice of baptism by immersion, see João B. Chaves, "Disrespecting Borders for Jesus, Power, and Cash: Southern Baptist Missions, the New Immigration, and the Churches of the Brazilian Diaspora" (Ph.D. diss., Baylor University, 2017).

and mostly Pentecostal backgrounds—and even, to a lesser extent, of Roman Catholic affiliation.[3] This particular form of migrant multidenominationalism presents a pastoral issue that calls for creativity and inclusivity radically different from the challenges present in the Brazilian context. Erika Helgen correctly points out in her history of religious conflict in twentieth-century Brazil that "the allure of fundamentalism, religious nationalism, and violent religious intolerance would never fully disappear from Brazilian social or political discourse, and ecumenical projects would be plagued by memories and traditions of religious conflict and competition."[4] Brazilians in the United States, however, are often pushed to transcend the animosity that characterized the forms of religious intolerance they knew in Brazil.

The negotiations that happen within Brazuca Baptist churches owing to the diverse religious backgrounds of their members, therefore, challenge the tendency of Brazilian Baptist leaders affiliated with the BBC to resist non-Baptist doctrines and practices, especially Pentecostal ones. The anti-Pentecostal disposition present in traditional Baptist life in Brazil stems from a specific history that involved the emergence of Pentecostalism in Brazil, the activity of Southern Baptist missions, and the schism within the BBC that gave rise to the smaller but influential National Baptist Convention (NBC).

Another issue central to the way in which Brazuca Baptists differ both from their Brazilian Baptist context and the SBC is the question of the ordination of women. There has been no extensive scholarly work done on the development of women's ordination in the BBC. However, according to research conducted by Rev. Silvia Nogueira, the first woman to be ordained in a BBC church and recognized by the Order of Baptist Pastors of Brazil (OBPB), there are eighty-eight woman Baptist pastors who are both ordained and recognized by the order (and hundreds more who are not yet recognized by their respective state chapters)—in a universe of thirteen thousand Brazilian Baptist pastors affiliated with the BBC.[5]

Despite the many challenges that remain for the full acceptance of women pastors among Baptists in every state of Brazil, the fact that the BBC does not aggressively resist their ordination reflects a sharp difference between Brazilian

---

[3]   See Matt Reis, "Brazilian Evangelicos in Diaspora in South Florida: Identity and Mission" (Ph.D. diss., University of Edinburgh, forthcoming 2021).

[4]   Erica Helgen, *Religious Conflict in Brazil: Protestants, Catholics, and the Rise of Religious Pluralism in the Early Twentieth Century* (New Haven: Yale University Press, 2020), 18.

[5]   *Mulheres Também São*, 2020, YouTube video, https://www.youtube.com/watch?time_continue=23&v=y0BA7nam614&feature=emb_logo.

Baptists and Southern Baptists.[6] The openness to the ordination of women within Brazilian ranks can also be understood as a development facilitated by the country's pentecostalization. Given that many Pentecostal denominations in Brazil ordain women and that the presence of prominent women pastors has been normalized in some religious and cultural circles, Brazilian Baptists are pressured by a context dominated by Pentecostals to modify their position on the issue. Furthermore, because both Pentecostalism and the socioeconomic power of women are greater in Brazuca Baptist churches than they are in Baptist churches in Brazil, these communities are more open to the ordination of women than Baptists in either the BBC or the SBC. Notably, this openness puts Brazuca Baptist churches at odds with the SBC, an issue of which Brazuca Baptist pastors are fully aware.

In order to contextualize the shift within Brazuca Baptist churches toward a pentecostalized reality, in this chapter I tell the general story of Pentecostal growth in Brazil and of the charismatic schism among Brazilian Baptists. In doing so I set the stage for how Brazuca Baptists differ from their counterparts in the BBC. Indeed, the growth of Pentecostalism in Brazil that was partially responsible for the schism within the Baptist denomination ensured that traditional Brazilian Baptist leaders became resistant to Pentecostal beliefs and practices. In many ways, the stronger the Pentecostal movement became in Brazil—which is the largest Pentecostal country in the world—the more traditional Baptist leaders asserted how non-Pentecostal they were. While the pentecostalization of Brazilian Christianity as a whole has affected traditional Baptist practice in general, Brazuca Baptists specifically have been pushed toward pentecostalization (and the correlated issue of the ordination of women) for reasons mostly related to migration dynamics.

Pentecostal Growth and the Charismatic Schism among Baptists in Brazil

Pentecostalism has been a global and multifaceted phenomenon from its inception. Scholars have debated for decades the way in which the movement appeared almost simultaneously in many places in the world.[7] The beginnings of Pentecostalism in the United States, however, are often traced to the

---

[6] For the issue of women pastors within the SBC, see Elizabeth Hill Flowers, *Into the Pulpit: Southern Baptist Women and Power since World War II* (Chapel Hill: University of North Carolina Press, 2012); Eileen Campbell-Reed, *Anatomy of a Schism: How Clergywomen's Narratives Reinterpret the Fracturing of the Southern Baptist Convention* (Knoxville: University of Tennessee Press, 2016).

[7] Allen Anderson, "Pentecostal and Charismatic Movements," in *The Cambridge History of Christianity*, ed. Hugh Mcleod (Cambridge: Cambridge University Press,

early 1900s. In 1906, under the leadership of African American pastor William Seymour, a group that met at Azusa Street in Los Angeles began a movement that would not only transcend geographical and denominational boundaries but also help reshape the global religious market.[8] The distinguishing theological markers of Pentecostalism would be the doctrines of divine healing, baptism in the Holy Spirit with the evidence of speaking in tongues, salvation, and the imminent second coming of Christ.[9]

The emergence of Brazilian Pentecostalism is directly connected to the Azusa Street group in general and to connections with the ministry of an early visitor to the Azusa mission, Baptist pastor William Durham, in particular.[10] In 1910 Luigi Francesconi, an Italian immigrant who was exposed to the Pentecostal message through Durham's ministry in Chicago, formed the first Pentecostal church in Brazil, namely, Christian Congregation in São Paulo. In the same year, two Swedish Baptist immigrants who had looser connections to Durham's ministry also arrived in Brazil. Gunner Vingren and Daniel Berg eventually formed what later became the largest non-Catholic denomination in Brazil, the Assemblies of God, but when they arrived in the country, they went to a church in the north, planted by the Swedish-born Southern Baptist missionary Erik Nelson.[11] Their Pentecostal teachings caused a local schism—an event that would be forever imprinted in Baptist denominational memory.

When Vingren and Berg arrived in Brazil, they did so as immigrants who were both Baptist and had known the Pentecostal experience in the United States, not as Pentecostal missionaries. Naturally, when they approached Nelson, the Southern Baptist missionary allowed his compatriots to lodge in the basement of the Belém Baptist Church, which he pastored. A few months after their arrival, Vingren led healing services and taught the Pentecostal doctrine

---

2014), 9:89–90; Douglas G. Jacobsen, *Thinking in the Spirit: Theologies of the Early Pentecostal Movement* (Bloomington: Indiana University Press, 2003), 9–11.

[8] For histories of the early Pentecostal movement, see Cecil M. Robeck Jr., *The Azusa Street Mission and Revival* (Nashville: Thomas Nelson, 2006); Grant Wacker, *Heaven Below: Early Pentecostals and American Culture* (Cambridge, Mass.: Harvard University Press, 2001); and Robert Mapes Anderson, *Vision of the Disinherited: The Making of American Pentecostalism* (Peabody, Mass.: Hendrickson, 1992).

[9] Donald Dayton, *Theological Roots of Pentecostalism* (Grand Rapids: Baker Academic, 1987), 19–23.

[10] The interaction between Baptists and Pentecostals, although historically neglected, has been treated extensively by C. Douglas Weaver. Weaver also mentions Durham as one of many Baptists who interacted with Pentecostalism. See *Baptists and the Holy Spirit: The Contested History with Holiness-Pentecostal-Charismatic Movements* (Waco, Tex.: Baylor University Press, 2019), 121–23.

[11] Allan Heaton Anderson, *To the Ends of the Earth: Pentecostalism and the Transformation of World Christianity* (New York: Oxford University Press, 2013), 49–50.

of baptism in the Holy Spirit, convincing many members of the Baptist church of the rightness of his teaching. After Vingren and Berg were excluded from the church, together with a few members, they began a ministry that eventually became the largest Pentecostal denomination in the largest Pentecostal country in the world: the Assemblies of God in Brazil.[12]

This historical relationship between Baptists and Pentecostals in Brazil is important because it shows their interconnected histories in the country as well as illustrates the reality that Baptists and Pentecostals became antagonist competitors in the religious market very early on. This reciprocal historical antagonism is, according to Brazilian sociologist Gedeon de Alencar, a result of their proximity and common historical roots. For Alencar, the Assemblies of God in Brazil is Baptist in both its historical and ecclesiological roots, but it also has in its DNA "an absolute necessity to deny this because its greatest enemy is precisely the Baptist church."[13] The historical animosity between the two communities is so significant that Baptist sources devoted much space to depicting the Pentecostals, in an attempt to discredit their fiercest competitors. As a result of this prominence of Pentecostals in Baptist polemics, Laura Premack, who studied early Pentecostalism in Brazil, has claimed that Baptist sources actually provide the most fruitful primary accounts of early Pentecostalism.[14]

The haunting memory of a Pentecostal infiltration within a Baptist church in 1910 never left the BBC. On the contrary, as time progressed and Pentecostalism expanded in the country, so did Baptist invective against Pentecostals. The Pentecostal movement grew faster than the Baptist denomination in Brazil from very early on, and Baptists, for most of their history, aggressively resisted explicit pentecostalization. Pentecostalism began to expand rapidly in Brazil during the 1950s due to demographic shifts, internal migration, urbanization, and postwar industrialization.[15] If in 1930 the number of Pentecostal and Baptist parishioners in Brazil was practically the same, by 1970 there were almost five times as many Pentecostals as Baptists.[16] The rapid growth of the Pentecostal movement, however, was not just a Brazilian phenomenon. Rather, it was a global development with unprecedented geopolitical effects.

[12] Laura Premack, "'The Holy Rollers Are Invading Our Territory': Southern Baptist Missionaries and the Early Years of Pentecostalism in Brazil," *Journal of Religious History* 35, no. 1 (2011): 3–4; Gedeon Alencar, *Matriz Pentecostal Brasileira: Assembleias de Deus, 1911–2011* (Rio de Janeiro: Novos Dialogos, 2013), 56–57.

[13] Alencar, *Matriz Pentecostal Brasileira*, 45.

[14] Premack, "'Holy Rollers Are Invading Our Territory," 5–6.

[15] Zwinglio Mota Dias and Rodrigo Portella, "Apresentação," in *Protestantes, Evangélicos e (Neo) Pentecostais: História, Teologias, Igrejas e Perspectivas*, ed. Zwinglio Mota Dias, Rodrigo Portella, and Elisa Rodrigues (São Paulo: Fonte Editorial, 2014), 19–20.

[16] Premack, "'Holy Rollers Are Invading Our Territory," 5.

In Africa, Christianity grew by 350 million adepts from 1900 to 2000. Today many of them are Pentecostal and charismatic.[17] Asian Christianity has also seen significant growth in numbers and Pentecostal strength.[18] In Latin America, however, Pentecostalism and charismatic tendencies have grown so significantly that already in 2010 over 50 percent of both Brazil's and Guatemala's Christian population self-identified as renewalists (Pentecostal or charismatic).[19] Worldwide, there were over six hundred million Pentecostal and charismatic Christians in 2010, and some project that by 2025 that number will grow to almost eight hundred million.[20]

This Pentecostal explosion has concerned Baptist leaders in Brazil, both local pastors and Southern Baptist missionaries, even before the Pentecostal and charismatic movements became a widely known phenomenon in academic circles. The *Jornal Batista* has published hundreds of anti-Pentecostal tracts since the 1910s. Local periodicals and books in Portuguese have also tried to discredit Pentecostals—as well as Methodists, Anglicans, and Presbyterians. At times, Baptist anti-Pentecostal anxieties in Brazil appeared in works whose audience was in the United States. Southern Baptist missionary Lester Bell, for example, wrote in his 1965 book entitled *Which Way in Brazil* that "Brazilian Baptists have a doctrinal problem. Pentecostalism is flourishing in most countries in South America, and especially in Chile and Brazil."[21] As Pentecostalism grew and became more socially acceptable, however, it also began influencing various aspects of Brazilian politics, culture, and public discourse. Some of this influence spilled over into all Protestant denominations and groups in Brazil. Explicit Baptist doctrinal support of Pentecostal belief and practice, however, never occurred in the BBC.

The expansion of Pentecostal-style belief and practice is, of course, nowhere more evident than in the growth of the charismatic movement within the Roman Catholic Church. If the majority of Brazilian Protestants practice a

---

[17] Philip Jenkins, *The Next Christendom: The Coming of Global Christianity* (Oxford: Oxford University Press, 2007), 4.

[18] For overviews of the expansion of Pentecostal and charismatic groups, see Donald E. Miller, Kimon H. Sargeant, and Richard Flory, eds., *Spirit and Power: The Growth and Global Impact of Pentecostalism* (New York: Oxford University Press, 2013); Jenkins, *Next Christendom*, 2007; Anderson, *To the Ends of the Earth*; Afeosemime U. Adogame and Shobana Shankar, eds., *Religion on the Move! New Dynamics of Religious Expansion in a Globalizing World* (Leiden: Brill, 2013); and Mark A. Noll, *The New Shape of World Christianity: How American Experience Reflects Global Faith* (Downers Grove, Ill.: IVP Academic, 2009).

[19] Miller, Sargeant, and Flory, *Spirit and Power*, 323.

[20] Anderson, *To the Ends of the Earth*, 5–6.

[21] Lester C. Bell, *Which Way in Brazil?* (Nashville: Convention, 1965), 112.

Spirit-centered form of Christianity, the same is true of Brazilian Catholics. Over 60 percent of Roman Catholics in Brazil, the majority of Catholics in the largest Catholic (as well as Pentecostal) country in the world, are charismatic.[22] In this context, traditional, non-Pentecostal Protestant denominations, such as the BBC, have for decades faced complex choices surrounding their relative numeric stagnation. Doctrinally, the official position of the BBC is still one of resistance toward Pentecostal and charismatic belief and practice, but there has been great pressure to adapt both formally and informally to Pentecostal forms and strategies.[23]

Scholars argue that Pentecostalism's adaptability to Brazilian culture is partially responsible for its success, together with its appeal to the lower socioeconomic demographics in the country.[24] The movement's expansion challenges traditional Protestants in Brazil (e.g., Methodists, Presbyterians, and Baptists) to adopt Pentecostal customs, especially as they pertain to liturgical forms and worship practices.[25] Baptists have responded in a variety of ways, and the liturgy of many Baptist churches in Brazil has been pentecostalized to varying extents. The official doctrinal stance of the BBC, however, went from being antagonistic to Pentecostal belief between 1910 and 1950 to aggressively anti-Pentecostal in the 1960s. The reason for this development was the attempt, by a group of influential Baptist ministers, to make room for Pentecostal doctrines in churches affiliated with the BBC.

[22] Andrew Chestnut, "The Spirit of Brazil: Charismatic Christianity among the World's Largest Catholic and Pentecostal Populations," in *Handbook of Contemporary Religions in Brazil*, ed. Bettina Schmidt and Steven Engler (Leiden: Brill, 2017), 77.

[23] Leonildo Silveira Campos, "Traditional Protestantism," in Schmidt and Engler, *Handbook of Contemporary Religions in Brazil*, 95–116.

[24] Gedeon Alencar, *Protestantismo Tupiniquim* (São Paulo: Aret Editorial, 2007), 83–100; Donizete Rodrigues and Manoel Ribeiro de Moraes, "A Pentecostalização de Povos Tradicionais na Amazônia: Aspectos Conceituais para uma Antropologia de Identidades Religiosas," *Horizonte* 16, no. 50 (2018): 915; Premack, "'Holy Rollers Are Invading Our Territory,'" 11–12.

[25] Henri Gooren, "The Pentecostalization of Religion and Society in Latin America," *Exchange* 39, no. 4 (2010): 355–76; Flávia Ferreira Pires and Rodrigo Otávio Serrão Santana de Jesus, "Do Brasil para o Mundo: Como Conceitos Clássicos Weberianos Podem Nos Ajudar a Entender o Sucesso Transnacional da Igreja Mundial do Poder de Deus?" *Ciências da Religião: História e Sociedade* 12, no. 1 (2014): 137–67; Carlos Souza, "O Protestantismo Histórico e a 'Pentecostalização': Novos Contornos da Identidade Evangélica," *Ciências da Religião: História e Sociedade* 12, no. 2 (2014): 61–90; Jesús Sánchez, "A Pentecostalização do Brasil x os 'Sem Religião'; Cura e Exorcismo: Entrevista a Pe. Jesús Hortal Sánchez, S.J," *Teocomunicação* 44, no. 2 (2014): 181–95.

There is a strong connection between the charismatic turn of Brazilian Baptist leaders who eventually left the BBC and foreign influences.[26] Under the influence of Southern Baptist missionary Rosalee Mills Appleby, pastors Enéas Tognini and José Rego do Nascimento pushed a movement of spiritual renewal within the BBC—which had been spearheaded by Appleby—toward a charismatic form. For almost a decade the dispute between traditional Baptists and the charismatic wing within the BBC was waged at annual meetings of the convention, in the pages of the *Jornal Batista*, in state conventions, and in specific churches. By 1965 it was clear that the anti-Pentecostal wing of the BBC had won, and the charismatic pastors and their churches felt forced to leave the denomination and form the NBC—which claimed to hold the same doctrines as the BBC, with the exception of the cessationism that claims that the gifts of the Spirit cannot be fully experienced today. This process sharpened the BBC's stance against Pentecostal doctrines and, despite the qualified changes BBC churches in Brazil have made in their liturgical practices and song choices, the convention continues to claim that it is not doctrinally Pentecostal and does not view favorably any of the three practices that are distinctively Pentecostal: speaking in tongues, prophecy, and divine healing. In the United States, however, Brazuca Baptist churches—forced to deal with migration dynamics that bring Pentecostal parishioners into their buildings—have had to be creative regarding the inclusion of quintessentially Pentecostal beliefs and practices that go beyond liturgical styles.

Pentecostalization in Brazuca Baptist Churches

The general picture, when it comes to Brazuca Baptist churches, is that these communities have more members who were introduced to Protestantism and indoctrinated in other denominations than members who are concerned with any definitive sense of Baptist distinctives and identity markers. The observations of a pioneering pastor whose career pastoring Brazilians in the United States has included working with several communities on the East and West Coasts illustrate this point:

> Yes, there is [more Pentecostalism in Baptist churches here than in Brazil]. And there is a reason. You cannot form a church of expatriates and decide "this church will be Baptist," because if you do this, you will have nobody. So the churches formed by expatriates will be churches that will adjust, or bring, or include all those who are believers no matter their denomination. We did

[26] João B. Chaves, "Exporting Holy Fire: Southern Baptist Missions, Pentecostalism, and Baptist Identities in Latin America," *Perspectives in Religious Studies* 47, no. 2 (2020): 202–14.

this in my church, and what we did really clearly was that we decided that we would accept everybody and our doctrine would be Baptist. And for this reason, many Pentecostals who went to Baptist churches because there was no Pentecostal church where they lived, they stayed because they could make the same style of services that they used to do in their Pentecostal churches in Brazil. When the Pentecostal churches began to grow in the United States, they were already used to their churches and did not want to leave. This was very common. In our city, we had Macedo [the Universal Church of the Kingdom of God]. Actually, the people who I considered to be the most faithful to the pastor were from Macedo's church [in Brazil]. Because they were used to being faithful to the pastor and they continued with the same system in the Baptist church. But in my church, we had Methodists, Presbyterians, Pentecostals, Baptists; we had it all.

A pastor who had recently arrived in the United States to pastor a church in Connecticut made a similar observation:

> Our church's situation is interesting because, when it was founded, over two decades ago, it was practically one of the only churches for Portuguese-speaking immigrants here in our city. And this created a situation in which Brazilians who were immigrating here from Brazil who belonged to different denominations were attracted to the church, because the church became, or was increasingly becoming, an option for community, fellowship, and social help. So much so that people from different denominations began to congregate together in the church. This brought some problems of a doctrinal nature because the church, even though Baptist, has a very different perspective, a perspective that one would not expect from a Baptist.

Another pastor, who led a number of communities in Florida and on the East Coast, also noticed this dynamic:

> The majority of members in churches here come from an evangelical origin in Brazil. And another great part who got closer to the church here because of a social need, and ended up finding the evangelical path and uniting the social with the religious, the so-called conversion happened. But most come from absolutely diverse denominational origins; they were not Baptists. The majority, actually, are people connected to Pentecostal and Neo-Pentecostal denominations. Being Baptist here in the United States is not even a question of identity. Few people look for a Baptist church out of a sense of identity or because of a previous connection with Baptist churches in Brazil. They go because they ask, "Which is the church that offers more benefits for the immigrant? More services? More comfort? More events? More things connected to our land?" People who came here

with a denominational connection with Baptists, they say, "I will go to the same place I had in Brazil." Others go to church, and the Baptist, Presbyterian, or Assemblies of God label matters little to them.

In terms of the makeup of the membership, Brazuca Baptist churches are quintessentially multidenominational.

Pentecostals and Neo-Pentecostals come to Brazuca Baptist churches in numbers greater than immigrants of any other denomination.[27] This does not mean that these parishioners saw anything particularly attractive in becoming Baptist, however. To be sure, the power of the Pentecostal-dominated Brazilian Gospel music industry informs Brazilian Protestant worship in general and churches that have adopted contemporary forms of worship—like most Brazuca Baptist churches—in particular. That in itself signals an approximation between Brazilian Protestant and Pentecostal forms of worship, which in turn may be perceived positively by members of Brazuca Baptist churches who come from a Pentecostal background. This feature, however, is rather ecumenical and does not distinguish Baptists from other traditionally non-charismatic denominations.

There are three factors that help explain the overwhelming presence of parishioners from Pentecostal backgrounds in Brazuca Baptist churches—none of them theological. These factors teach us more about Brazil-US migration dynamics than about distinctive characteristics of Brazuca Baptist churches. First, Brazuca Baptist churches have often been pioneers among Protestant Portuguese-speaking churches in large US cities and as such have attracted

---

[27] The term "Neo-Pentecostal" is used here to identify a form of Pentecostalism that is distinct from other, more classical forms of Pentecostalism. In this I follow a three-wave schema that has been applied to the history of the movement in Brazil. The schema differentiates three "waves" not only in relation to theological beliefs but also—and primarily—in relation to the level of Pentecostal interaction with wider society. The first wave was in the 1910s, with the creation of the Christian Congregation (1910) and the Assemblies of God (1914). The churches founded during this period emphasize holiness and practice tongues and healing. The second wave began in the 1950s and 1960s, when various indigenous and more dynamic groups emerged. The growth of some of these groups was facilitated by the fact that this period was characterized by the beginning of Brazilian mass urbanization. The theology of second-wave groups, however, did not differ radically from that of first-wave churches. The third wave began in the 1970s and was characterized by the creation of Neo-Pentecostal churches. At that stage, two-thirds of the country was already urban, and economic conditions had worsened for the lower classes. The period was also characterized by modernization under the military dictatorships. Mass media, something Neo-Pentecostals use widely, became a widespread reality. An emphasis on prosperity and exorcism—and the deemphasizing of holiness anxieties—characterized groups founded during this period. See Paul Freston, "Pentecostalism in Brazil: A Brief History," *Religion* 25, no. 2 (1995): 119–33.

people from a number of Christian, non-Catholic backgrounds. In addition, preliminary studies suggest that Brazilian Pentecostals migrate at a higher rate than people belonging to any other religious group, thus explaining their overwhelming numbers in Brazuca Baptist churches.[28] Finally, Brazuca pastors also agree that one of the most powerful tools for attracting Brazuca parishioners is a church's initiatives assisting immigrants—that is, programs that will benefit the parishioner's social well-being. Brazuca Baptist churches are aggressive in implementing such initiatives, and, as such, they position themselves well in the competition for immigrant members in the US religious market.

That said, the pentecostalizing forces within Brazuca Baptist communities are strong, affecting the way in which the identities of these communities develop. According to one pastor,

> What we have here is the predominance of a Neo-Pentecostal theology. But in the sense that the Pentecostal foundations are not the same in terms of the search of the so-called Pentecostals who live here. The question of the baptism with the Holy Spirit as a lived experience with the living God, the idea of being filled with the Spirit or spiritual overflowing, this is a language that is nonexistent. The language of today is of prosperity, success, overcoming, and so on. But the Brazilian Baptist churches here in the US have very little Baptist in them. Even because the great part of the members of Baptist churches here is formed by people who came from other, non-Baptist, Pentecostal matrixes and mostly Neo-Pentecostal. . . . So Brazilian Baptist churches in the United States are not Baptist in their DNA; they are hybrid. They are already genetically different.

One should notice that this pastor, despite his implicit criticism of the Prosperity Gospel, which he associates with Neo-Pentecostalism, actually has a positive view of classical forms of Pentecostalism when contrasting them with new forms of Pentecostal theologies of prosperity. In terms of expressions usually associated with Pentecostal beliefs and practices, however, despite the

---

[28] Ana Cristina Braga Martes, *New Immigrants, New Land: A Study of Brazilians in Massachusetts* (Gainesville: University Press of Florida, 2011), 73–76; Annie McNeil Gibson, *Post-Katrina Brazucas, Brazilian Immigrants in New Orleans* (New Orleans, La.: University of New Orleans Press, 2012), 227–29. While most studies of Brazilian immigrants in the United States do not differentiate between the categories of Protestant and Pentecostal, those that do note the strong presence of Pentecostalism among Brazilian immigrants. Martes, for instance, noted the overwhelming number of Pentecostals among Brazilian Baptists in Massachusetts. She theorized that the Pentecostal emphasis on individualism and the Prosperity Gospel encourages migration to the United States, while Roman Catholic emphasis on community, poverty, and social justice may hinder migrants from leaving Brazil. Gibson noted that in New Orleans the overwhelming majority of Brazuca Christians are Pentecostal.

diverse nature of these churches, Brazuca Baptist communities are generally more open than Baptist churches in Brazil and churches in their respective conventions in the United States.

For instance, a pastor in the south of the United States, who has several assistant pastors who were trained in Pentecostal seminaries and ordained in Pentecostal denominations, noted that "prophecy, cures, speaking in tongues, and miracles are welcomed practices in our church as long as [they are] not used as a form of changing the church's profile." In this pastor's imagination, pentecostalization does not require relinquishing his Baptist identity, nor is it a challenge to his SBC affiliation. A pastor from California said that

> we have people who are traditional Baptists, people who are Pentecostals, Methodists, charismatics, and from the new Pentecostal churches in Brazil. So we have people like this in the church. But they give me no trouble. I always say that our church must be a moderate church. I cannot please just the traditionalists or just the Pentecostals. They all have to meet in the middle. And then there is respect. In our services there is no speaking in tongues, usually, but if there is no one frowns upon that, as they would do in Brazil. Also it is a revivalistic service, modern, contemporary. A service in which people say "Glory" and "Hallelulah" but not to the extreme

The pastoral staff of this pastor's community has Pentecostal pastors who teach the theology courses offered by the church's Bible institute. One pastor who teaches in the institute calls himself a "Presbybapticostal," by which he means that he is simultaneously Presbyterian, Baptist, and Pentecostal. He was ordained through the Assemblies of God and has pastoral credentials recognized in his Baptist church. Another teacher was ordained in the Foursquare Church and said that he does not focus on the difference between Baptists and Pentecostals—which for him is only the idea that Pentecostals believe that one can lose one's salvation—but focuses rather on the commonalities.

Pioneer missionary Humberto Viegas Fernandes' talk to the Association of Hispanic Pastors of New York in 1986, delivered in Spanish and entitled "The Difference between Baptists and Pentecostals" (Diferencia entre los Bautistas e los Pentecostales), suggests that this pentecostalizing tendency has been a part of general Latinx practice for a long time. As he reported to the *Jornal Batista,*

> I affirmed, from the beginning, my somewhat vexing position, for not knowing properly what kind of Baptist I am today, although I am pastor of a church integrated into the Southern Baptist Convention. [It is] that the Baptists, just like the Pentecostals, are so divided and subdivided today in terms of their theology, doctrine, administration, and practices that [it] makes it harder for us to position ourselves. I limited myself to inform

them, in consequence, that I would concentrate on the traditional Baptists, the so-called orthodox Baptists, without allowing myself to get involved in the current terminological controversy in the southern camps between conservative, moderate, and liberals. . . . I told them immediately that today there are Baptists who are more Pentecostal than the Pentecostals themselves in terms of doctrine and content.[29]

Fernandes mentioned that there was a two-hour discussion session after his speech, yet another indicator of how Pentecostalism presses Latinx Baptists to go beyond traditional imaginings of Baptist identity. He did not attack Pentecostalism directly but did criticize what he saw as the movement's tendency to make the church a place for the entertainment of audiences rather than for the preaching of the gospel. Yet he remained rather positive about the movement at a time when the BBC showed very little flexibility in this regard.

The pentecostalization phenomenon, of course, is not an exclusive issue among Brazuca Baptists. On the one hand, it peculiarly affects Brazuca Baptists because, as already mentioned, most immigrants who go to Brazilian Baptist churches are part of the aggressive growth of Pentecostalism in Latin America. Yet it must be admitted that since the 1965 split between the BBC and the NBC over the issue of charismatic doctrine and practice, both conventions have grown closer to one another, as the BBC became generally more accepting of pentecostalized expressions of worship. Yet Brazuca Baptist churches are more pentecostalized than Baptists in Brazil, and most Brazuca Baptist leaders recognize this.

Women's Leadership: Economics, Imported Frameworks, and Cultural Climate

The issue of women's leadership in Brazuca Baptist churches, which I take here to include the ordination of women, is significant because most such churches are affiliated with the SBC, which does not accept women pastors. Yet Brazuca Baptist churches—through the OBBPNA—are having conversations about formalizing the favorable stance the majority of Brazuca pastors have on the issue of ordaining women to the ministry. On this topic, the peculiarity of Brazilian migration dynamics is once again a determining factor in the development of denominational identity. The three dominant factors here are the acceptance of women's ordination by the OBPB and the BBC, the economic independence of Brazilian women, which is greater in the United States than

---

[29] Humberto Viegas Fernandes, "Cartas de Nova Iorque: Igreja Palco," *Jornal Batista* LXXXVI, no. 38 (1986): 11–12.

in Brazil, and the appropriation of US family dynamics, which tend to be more egalitarian than those in Brazil.

As alluded to earlier, some state chapters of the OBPB decided to recognize the ordination of women Baptist ministers after a long and contested process.[30] The OBPB gave its local sessions the ability and freedom to vote for or against the recognition of women ministers, which, in practice, did not constitute a universal openness to women ministers but did open the door for them to enter the denominational fold in heretofore unprecedented ways. The OBBPNA, as a session of the OBPB, therefore also acquired official sanction to choose whether to recognize women ministers. The tendency of the OBBPNA today is to follow the path of other OBPB sessions in Brazil and bring women ministers into their denominational organization, but the connection of the majority of Brazuca Baptist churches to the SBC complicates matters.

At the 2016 annual meeting of the OBBPNA, the subject of recognizing women ministers was brought up when the name of a woman pastor was suggested for membership. The minutes of the meeting described the exchange:

> The president of the [ethics] commission also presented the name of pastor Lucileia Alves Faria, which was immediately succeeded by pastor Gessuy Freitas in order to explain that the subject of the acceptance of women pastors was already under study by the ethics commission itself. However, the members of this commission did not feel comfortable in making a definite decision and presenting it to the plenary, letting the plenary make the final decision about the acceptance of women pastors in the OBBPNA. Before the vote, many pastors lined up to deliberate about the subject. Pastor Ebenezer Carlos dos Santos proposed that a commission [be] created to study the subject and present their findings [at] the next assembly, next year. The proposal was unanimously accepted, and names were indicated for the commission.[31]

The tone of the discussions surrounding the issue, however, was conciliatory, and even the pastors who are against the recognition of women pastors acknowledge that they are a small minority among Brazuca Baptist pastors. A pastor who arrived from Brazil recently noted:

> I notice that, for instance, very few of my colleagues here in the United States have a posture, for example, against women's ordination. So I see the Baptist pastors here in the United States [as having] a much more liberal vision, and this vision is much more liberal not because they acquired this in their

---

[30] "Batistas Abrem Espaço para Que as Mulheres Sejam Pastoras," *Epoca*, accessed June 8, 2017, http://epoca.globo.com/ideias/noticia/2014/02/batistas-abrem-espaco -para-que-mulheres-sejam-bpastorasb.html.

[31] *Atas da (Minutes of) Ordem dos Pastores Batistas Brasileiros na América do Norte*, 2016, 1.

theological formation [in Brazil]. Surely their generation is one that was trained in Baptist theological seminaries in Brazil with a vision of traditional reformed theology. Now, what I see is an influence of pastors here, who are here more really because of a phenomenon of transformation and change that is happening in Brazil also. Why? Because of that rush. That concern with making their church here grow in numbers and then everything goes. I perceive this in my colleagues, a certain welcoming of that which before was not accepted.

Although the 2016 annual meeting of the OBBPNA gave the impression that women pastors would be officially approved at the 2017 annual meeting in San Francisco, the organization decided to postpone the matter because of the fragility of the reinstated AIBBAN and the connection of many churches with the SBC. The decision was to discuss the matter in the future and, at the same time, to honor and welcome women pastors who are either ordained in Brazuca churches or who are ordained in Brazil and move to the United States.

The tension here is, of course, that most Brazuca Baptist churches are technically Southern Baptist and as such are moving in a direction that once again shows that their primary ideological identification is with the BBC and that their sense of cooperation is most strongly imagined as ethnic cooperation with each other. The presence of women ministers in Brazuca Baptist churches, a reality that the OBBPNA recognizes and most of its members welcome, accentuates an unspoken and perhaps unnoticed difference between Brazuca Baptists and their Southern Baptist affiliation. The feeling of belonging to the BBC, although central, is but one of the main reasons for this tendency.

Another factor is the issue of acculturation to family arrangements in the United States. As Silvia Debiaggi has argued, there is a correlation between acculturation and gender roles among Brazilian immigrants. In other words, machismo diminishes as acculturation increases.[32] According to a study comparing Mexican and Brazilian immigrant Protestants in Florida, "women often take advantage of the American multicultural environment—with its new and different opportunities—to develop an increased awareness of gender and a capacity to resist systemic inequality."[33] In addition, Brazilian migrant

[32] Sylvia Duarte Dantas Debiaggi, *Changing Gender Roles: Brazilian Immigrant Families in the U.S.* (New York: LFB Scholarly Publishing, 2001), 27.

[33] Patricia Mola, Lucia Ribeiro, and Mirian Lizama, "Brazilian and Mexican Women Interacting with God in Florida," in *A Place to Be: Brazilian, Guatemalan, and Mexican Immigrants in Florida's New Destinations*, ed. Philip Williams, Timothy Steigenga, and Manuel A. Vásquez (New Brunswick, N.J.: Rutgers University Press, 2009), 191.

women should not be imagined as passive objects of male migration but rather as agents whose earning power increases after migration, creating space for autonomy inside and outside the home.[34]

The pastors of Brazuca Baptist churches recognize the increasing presence of women leading their communities. According to a pastor in Florida who has pastored a number of churches in the United States:

> I notice that, here in the United States, the women are more active in every-thing than in Brazil. First, because they work; in Brazil, fewer women work than here. Here, that is not the case; they all work. In addition, many women, because of the nature of their work, have an income higher than that of their husbands, so this gives them great autonomy. Women have their own cars, they have freedom to attend more meetings, they do not depend on their husbands. Women here depend on their husbands much less than in Brazil. So this means they are more active in church as well.

A Texas pastor said that, both in the home and in the church, "in general the women have the same level of decision-making as the husbands. When this does not happen, there is conflict." In addition, a small number of Brazuca churches already have women pastors, and many others de facto have women ministers. In one California church, the wives of the pastors are also called and considered to be pastors by those members who came from a Pentecostal background—a significant number of the church's constituency. This phenom-enon illustrates the heightened receptiveness to women's pastoral leadership in the community, because women pastors historically have been powerful leaders in Brazilian Pentecostalism. In the same church, the senior pastor actually encountered resistance from de facto women pastors he wanted to ordain. According to him, "I am in favor of ordaining women, of ordaining a woman who pastors in our church and does a better job than other pastors who work in the church. And I already told one, but because she has a Bap-tist background, she thinks it is unnecessary." The consensus among Brazuca Baptist pastors, even those not intentionally engaged in recruiting women for ordained ministry, is one that favors women's ordination. The concern for some leaders, however, as they pondered in 2016 making the decision official at the 2017 meeting of the OBBPNA, was how such a decision might affect their connection to the SBC. This connection can be illustrated by the minutes of the 2016 OBBPNA meeting itself:

---

[34] Gláucia de Oliveira Assis, "Gender and Migration from Invisibility to Agency: The Routes of Brazilian Women from Transnational Towns to the United States," *Wom-en's Studies International Forum* 46 (2014): 42.

It was asked that the financial contribution of the Western Connecticut Baptist Association, which made [it] possible for the New England pastors to come to this meeting, be registered. This proposition was joined by another proposal that a letter of thankfulness be written to them, and this proposal was unanimously accepted.

The peculiarity of the Brazuca Baptist churches in this case is that pastors who receive contributions from SBC denominational bodies to help them attend OBBPNA meetings are, by and large, in line with the OBBPNA's tendency to accept what the SBC has so adamantly rejected: the full inclusion of women. It is yet another tension that illustrates the ambiguous belonging of Brazuca Baptists who live in the SBC world but, in a number of important ways, are not of it.

Conclusion

The pentecostalization of Brazuca Baptists, even when unacknowledged by pastors who may not like to associate themselves openly with Pentecostalism because of the denominational stigma that still exists in Brazil, is another feature of the community that illustrates its unique identity in relation to Brazilian and Southern Baptists. Although the growth of Pentecostalism in Brazil does affect the official stance of the BBC, which is increasingly open to forms of worship generally associated with Pentecostalism, Brazuca Baptist churches are more pentecostalized than Brazilian Baptist churches—a result of the significant influx of migrants coming from a Pentecostal background. Taking that into consideration, it is clear that Brazuca Baptists are much more welcoming of Pentecostal beliefs and practices than are Southern Baptists.

Finally, Brazuca Baptist churches by and large take a positive stance on the ordination of women pastors. That is, they tend to be closer to recognizing what is already accepted in BBC circles: giving women pastors official denominational sanction. As of this writing, this stance has not been made official because of complex institutional dynamics. Ideological resistance to women's ordination, however, is the exception, not the rule, among Brazuca Baptist leaders. This fact presents a particular tension in most Brazuca Baptist churches because of their affiliation with the SBC. Yet the fact is that Brazuca churches have already ordained women, and a relevant OBBPNA position would only make public their private stance on the issue. That is, most Brazuca Baptist churches already deviate from the SBC norm either ideologically or in practice on this particular issue.

7
MAPPING

Migration Experiences and Incipient Immigrant Theologies

This August I celebrate 28 years of "self-exile." I arrived here on August 13th, 1981. It was the beginning of the Fall in Louisville. I thought that I would do my masters and doctorate in three or four years and then would go back to my Brazil, to continue to work on social justice issues and with the people of the slums of Recife. . . . However, here I am, for almost three decades. Delivering my lectures, writing my books, and living from the memory of other times. . . . (It is one of those things—those who understand me live there; those who do not understand me live here, and they really don't care) . . .

The problem of every exiled man is that he lives with two "ghosts"—the ghost of nostalgia and the ghost-of-the-other-destiny.

H. B. Cavalcanti[1]

During the most difficult waves of the COVID-19 pandemic, immigrant churches, much like churches composed mostly of US-born worshipers, helped shape the imagination of parishioners, gave guidelines regarding safety measures (sometimes in ways that revealed their evangélico convictions), and

[1] H. B. Cavalcanti, *Ensaios de um Nordestino Ausente* (Nashville: Westview, 2010), 9. Cavalcanti came from Brazil to study at Southern Baptist Theological Seminary. His journey north began with the help of US missionaries in Brazil. After graduating from the seminary with his master's degree and becoming disenchanted with the SBC, he went to Vanderbilt University for a graduate degree in sociology. He is now emeritus professor of sociology at James Madison University.

helped provide relief for struggling families.[2] A Brazuca Baptist church in Florida, for example, indiscriminately distributed food to families—immigrant or not—affected financially by the economic effects of the pandemic. In partnership with the Florida Baptist Convention, by November 2020 the church had distributed over thirty thousand boxes of food with the help of more than two thousand volunteers, predominantly Brazilian immigrants. Church leaders estimated that this initiative provided relief to over one hundred twenty thousand people affected by the crisis in Pompano Beach and surrounding communities. Not all churches in the United States have the infrastructure and personnel to replicate the impact of this Brazuca Baptist church. This example, however, illustrates further that immigrant churches are integral to US society and help—often through the work of undocumented parishioners—alleviate social issues that affect both the immigrant and native-born populations. The population of Pompano Beach—as well as many people living in other locations across the United States—would have fewer resources to endure the COVID-19 pandemic without the presence of immigrant churches that have worked to mitigate the damage of this crisis. People who insist on portraying immigrants—especially undocumented immigrants—as a monolithic block of "free riders" neglect their deep civic participation, carried out via voluntary labor and financial contributions often mediated by immigrant churches.

Beyond the many ways in which immigrant churches function similarly to churches ministering to native-born peoples, such as responding to national crises, the story of Brazuca Baptist churches shows that the experiences of migration undergone by foreign-born Christians, with their deep complexities, shape the role of immigrant churches and inform the theological imagination of faith community leaders. Brazuca Baptist leaders agree that the peculiar work of pastoring immigrant communities forces them to be creative regarding traditional theological dispositions, ecclesiological commitments, and pastoral strategies. Such creativity, in turn, develops in ways that often distance immigrant faith leaders and their communities from traditional religious life as it is lived both in the home country and in churches made by and for a native-born constituency. In the particular case of Brazuca Baptist churches, their difference manifests itself in their ambiguous belonging to both the BBC, which has trained their leaders, and to the SBC, to which they feel indebted.

Illustrating how migration dynamics affect immigrant churches, a longtime leader among Brazuca Baptist pastors described the nature of the immigrant church in the United States as a "Noah's ark," meaning it is incredibly diverse

---

[2] Rodrigo Serrão and João Chaves, "Immigrant Evangelicalism in the COVID-19 Crisis," *International Journal of Latin American Religions* 4, no. 2 (2020): 235–49.

and on the move geographically, existentially, legally, sociologically, linguistically, emotionally, denominationally, and spiritually. In so doing this leader emphasized how pastoring immigrants in the United States is wildly different from pastoring churches in his parishioners' home countries. In immigrant churches pastors often see themselves as called to help bring order to the chaos created by the traumas of migration.

In addition, the diversity with which these pastors have to deal transcends concerns often present in conversations about multiethnic and multicultural churches—especially when those conversations actually aim at diluting difference in favor of a whitened harmony. Immigrant churches are not only multiethnic and multiracial; they are also multilingual, multinational, have multilegal status, and are multidenominational and multigenerational. On the one hand, the radical diversity they embody reflects a clear manifestation of how the realities of a globalized world present themselves within faith communities of displaced peoples. On the other, it also shapes the contours of the immigrant churches' self-understanding.

The Complexities of the Transnational Brazuca Journey

The Brazuca Baptist journey, like that of immigrant churches in general, is rich, complex, transnational, and multifaceted. Their history reveals how Global South networks that have historical denominational ties with US-based religious bodies exploit those connections in order to thrive in their new country in surprising ways. Brazilian Baptists were born out of the complex history of Southern Baptist missions that, in Brazil, began its sustainable phase among Confederate exiles—immigrants from the United States who went to Brazil trying to reconstruct there a new form of the slaveholding South they so sorely missed.[3] These American immigrant missionaries and their local coreligionists created a Brazilian denominational machine that became a transnational success. By the time the BBC completed one hundred years of history, the convention had launched Baptist missions in Chile, Portugal, Bolivia, Paraguay, Mozambique, Angola, the Azores, Uruguay, Argentina, Rhodesia, Venezuela, France, Spain, Canada, South Africa, Peru, and Ecuador. It also had a mission in the United States, the land of its denominational founders.

Though the mission to the United States initially focused on Portuguese communities, it soon loosed itself from its official connections to the BBC in terms of missionary control. The mass migration of Brazilians to the United States in the 1980s transformed what had been an official mission of the BBC

---

[3] João B. Chaves, *The Global Mission of the Jim Crow South* (Macon, Ga.: Mercer University Press, forthcoming).

into a loose arrangement of churches whose leaders remembered the BBC fondly but were no longer under its auspices. The great majority of these communities became immigrant churches affiliated with the SBC, a connection that soon manifested its precariousness given the inability of the SBC to provide a welcoming environment in which these communities felt that the largest Protestant denomination in the United States was a fully appropriate partner.

Nevertheless, these communities have enjoyed some of the benefits of belonging to the SBC, such as networking and financial support. To be clear, some, but by no means all, Brazuca Baptist leaders are openly antagonistic toward their state or national conventions—they just don't think of them as highly as they lead these official bodies to believe. To deal with this tension and fulfill their need for deeper denominational connections, these churches created an association and an order of pastors with the intention of forming an ideal place for cooperation and partnership. This ethnic denominationalism illustrates the Brazuca Baptist conviction that they do not fully belong within the ministries of the SBC. Brazuca Baptist ethnic denominationalism has also given these immigrant communities more freedom to act together in ways that they feel the SBC would not welcome. Still, to date, the desire of some Brazuca Baptist leaders to create a separate denomination or to become a transnational arm of the BBC has not been fulfilled. Several issues have problematized Brazuca Baptists' attempts to establish a robust and institutionalized form of ethnic denominationalism in the form of a sustainable association, such as internal tensions, the role of future generations in Brazuca Baptist churches, and the transition of Brazuca churches from a focus on the Brazilian ethnic enclaves to broader audiences. However, the fact that Brazuca Baptist churches in general see a form of ethnic denominationalism as ideal remains—even if there are obstacles to achieving its viable shape.

The development of a Brazuca Baptist sense of mission and strategy has not been linear since the beginnings of the official Brazilian Baptist missionary presence in the United States. Brazilian Baptist work in the United States began as an effort to reach the Portuguese immigrant and morphed—in response to the surprising and unexpected flow of Brazilian migration—to a focus on Brazilian parishioners. As time progressed and the numbers of Brazilian immigrants fluctuated, Brazuca Baptist churches attempted to transition to a multicultural and multiethnic stance. That is not to say that there is not ethnic diversity in Brazuca Baptist churches. These communities have embraced Portuguese speakers from Latin America, Africa, and Europe and well as Spanish and English speakers who have gathered in Brazuca churches for different reasons. The language of Brazuca Baptist churches as well as their names—which transitioned from Portuguese to English—however, became more intentionally multiethnic as migration from Brazil diminished and the anxieties of maintaining the second generation of Brazilians grew.

Over time, these immigrant communities have engaged in a number of initiatives of social relief benefiting immigrants and US citizens alike. They have also given logistical and emotional support to a great many immigrants—many of them undocumented—whose success in adapting in the United States has been mediated partially by their ethnic religious communities. In addition, Brazuca Baptist churches have followed in the footsteps of the SBC—their founding denomination—by investing heavily in foreign missions both in Brazil and in other countries, an investment largely funded by undocumented parishioners to support social and economic relief beyond the US border. These transnational communities are an example of the multidirectional missionary impulse that has become so prominent in World Christianity. This narrative, however, has not been just about the progression of a transnational religious network, as important as that is for our limited knowledge of transnational religious bodies.

The Contextual Catalysts for Incipient Immigrant Theologies

The history of Brazuca Baptist churches also reveals how incipient immigrant theologies manifest themselves within faith communities that are pressured to adapt rapidly to new contexts and realities. The migrant experiences of Brazuca parishioners themselves are the most pressing catalyst for the theological unbelonging that characterizes these communities and opens space for incipient immigrant theologies. Leaders in immigrant communities in general seldom read theologies of migration produced by academic theologians who may have lived experiences in such communities but whose work—like this one—participates in academic dialogues in which the average immigrant Christian has little interest. Whenever the few leaders who have shown any interest in them whatsoever encountered contextual theologies, they have regarded them mostly as confirmations of convictions they already hold or discarded them as being too radical. The most pressing catalysts for theological creativity have sprung from the migration experiences of Brazuca Baptist leaders and their parishioners. In other words, for transnational religious networks, sociological realities guide theological and ecclesiological creativity in ways that do not fit neatly into formal theological systems. Leaders and parishioners in immigrant communities are not concerned with codifying their theological convictions into neat theological formulas. Rather, they seek to develop tools and a vocabulary that work practically as they try to navigate the struggles of immigrant living.

One of these experiences is the transient syndrome that characterizes Brazuca immigrants, that is, the fact that most Brazilian immigrants to the United States see themselves as target earners who will return to their home country and that, when in the United States, they tend to move freely from state to state in search of opportunities for better pay. This issue has kept most Brazuca churches from being able to develop solid projections of their future and challenges Brazuca Baptist leaders to develop pastoral practices addressing the fact that many of their parishioners never consider church membership to be a long-term possibility. This characteristic creates a sense of a "church on the move" that is peculiar to immigrant churches. These faith communities do not take for granted the assumption that they will survive beyond the first generation. Although there are plans for the maintenance of the community's mission for future generations—such as trying to be more appealing to non-Brazilians and using more English for younger people—these churches' commitment to caring for transient parishioners takes most of their energy and imagination. This is one of the reasons why measuring the impact made by particular immigrant churches is so complicated: sheer numbers don't account for the significant numbers of immigrants who benefit from the services provided by churches but who leave for a variety of reasons.

Another notable contextual challenge is the role that Brazuca Baptist churches play in facilitating immigrant adaptation to the United States. Unlike churches whose membership is composed primarily of Anglo-Americans, Brazuca Baptist churches occupy a central place in the lives of immigrants who see in them a mechanism of religious, social, and legal relief directly connected to their status as immigrants—especially those undocumented. One pastor, who has pastored churches in Brazil and in the United States, for example, related that the difference between pastoring Brazilian immigrants and pastoring Brazilians living in Brazil is "like water and wine. One [experience] has nothing to do with the other." He went on to say that the alienation of Brazilian migrants caused by being away from the homeland accounts for much of this difference. Another pastor said that the primary role of this church "is to integrate and to give emotional support. It is to integrate people into the culture, into the labor market, and to support them emotionally and spiritually." This sense of seeing the role of the church as an explicit mediating structure, taking into consideration the importance of helping undocumented immigrants in this process, is a central theme in Brazuca Baptist churches that try to balance this sensibility with the common perceived need to broaden their reach beyond their Brazilian parishioners.

In addition, Brazuca churches are churches that pay close attention to their context and try to navigate two primary worlds: the world of Brazilian evangelicalism and their immediate US context. Their existence takes place in a constant negotiation between these related but distinct realities. The most significant elements that comprise the role of migration dynamics in Brazuca Baptist theological change, however, include the overwhelming presence of undocumented parishioners, the rapid pentecostalization of Brazuca Baptists as a result of the influx of immigrants from a Pentecostal background, and the form of women's leadership in these communities.

The incipient immigrant theologies encouraged by the number of undocumented members in Brazuca Baptist churches, as well as by the influx of Pentecostal members and the correlated welcoming of the ordination of women, are a clear demonstration of how pastoral theological reflection is adaptable. Brazuca Baptists pastors, in a short period of time, went from a tendency toward legalism regarding immigration issues similar to that of many SBC-supported political candidates to expounding theologically legitimized advocacy for immigrant rights. The position of a few pastors during the 2016 presidential elections illustrates this point well.

When asked about their individual political proclivities as well as that of their communities, Brazuca leaders gave different responses, but all communicated differing levels of concern with what was then the potential election of Donald Trump. One pastor shared:

> It is, like, there is a fidelity with Southern Baptists in terms of principles and values. However, in practice, we don't agree with many things that happen there, especially in terms of immigration issues. For example, we are on the verge of a presidential election in which it is possible that the SBC will support Donald Trump, if he is the republican candidate. And our church will support Hillary Clinton, and I will say this publicly. Why? Because although we disagree [with Democrats] in many other issues, such as abortion, we have a lot to lose in terms of immigrant life if we support Donald Trump. At least in terms of his suggestion to deport twelve million [undocumented] immigrants.

When asked whether he was willing to risk his tax-exempt status for his explicit support of a political candidate, he shared, "Yes, yes. We are ready to risk anything. As long as our principles, values, and belief regarding the protection of immigrants are maintained."

One prominent pastor went further in his connection to the agenda of the Democratic Party, saying:

> Our church is basically Democrat in almost all segments. Human rights, state protection for those who need it, division of budgets that focuses on those who need the most, taxing the wealthy more and taxing less those who earn less. [And the Democrat support for same-sex marriage doesn't change

this] because, in my perspective, same-sex marriage is an individual issue even if the state may approve of it. The church works with individuals. The church's consciousness is not measured in relation to the state but in relation to the individual. The individual must be made conscious, the individual must be reached, the individual must be loved, and the individual must be accepted—which is another serious question.

Pastors who admitted being closer to the Republican Party did not show enthusiastic support for Donald Trump, instead tending to downplay his commitment to prosecute, arrest, and deport undocumented immigrants.

The political sensibilities of Brazuca church leaders, which are heavily informed by their roles pastoring undocumented immigrants as well as by their churches' dependence on the financial contributions of undocumented parishioners and their voluntary work, are important in at least two major interconnected ways. First, the distancing of immigrant church leaders from traditional evangelical support of the Republican Party reveals a rift between Southern Baptist ideological commitments and the well-being of many immigrant churches' constituents. Second, the ambiguity of immigrant evangelicals regarding their relationship to the traditional political leanings of US evangelicals problematizes a simplistic characterization of these communities that, on one hand, often have official relationships with religious bodies that are undeniably evangelical (such as the SBC) but that, upon closer inspection, do not fit the same theopolitical mold. My claim is that, in the case of Brazuca Baptists and other immigrant religious networks, this difference is not directly imported; rather, it is generated from within migrant dynamics experienced in the United States. That is, this study has argued that oftentimes it is the journey of immigrant churches in the United States that distances them from theopolitical leanings that would be easier to maintain in an immigrant's home country.

When it comes to issues of pentecostalization, Brazuca Baptist leaders have responded to the influx of members from Pentecostal backgrounds in a variety of ways. In general, however, Brazuca Baptist churches are more open to Pentecostal beliefs and practices than are churches of the BBC. The militant anti-Pentecostalism found in significant sectors of the BBC—although increasingly diminishing owing to the growing influence of Pentecostalism in Brazil—is virtually nonexistent in Brazuca Baptist churches. This difference is not accounted for in primarily disembodied theological reflections on the part of Brazuca Baptist pastors. Rather, it stands as a direct result of migration dynamics. As immigrants from different denominational backgrounds have flocked to Brazuca churches primarily out of a sense of ethnic solidarity, Brazuca Baptist churches have had to develop ways to avoid alienating their diverse membership, and, in the process, many communities have welcomed practices and beliefs associated with Pentecostalism. Practices such as speaking in tongues, prophecy, healing prayers, and others that would not be officially accepted by either the BBC or the SBC are commonplace in many Brazuca Baptist churches. Similarly, the broader acceptance of the ordination of women also sets Brazuca Baptists apart from the denominations with which they are associated. Although the BBC accepts the ordination of women—in that it recognizes the authority of state denominational bodies to decide on the confirmation of their women pastors—Brazuca Baptist pastors agree that women's leadership is more prominent in their churches than in Baptist churches in Brazil.

For pastors, the pentecostalization of Brazuca Baptists and other forms of ecumenical sensibilities are a result of their nature as communities of the displaced. Talking about the doctrinal creativity in his church, a pastor said, "All churches outside their country need to be flexible in all areas, including this doctrinal area. I see Pentecostal presence in all [Brazuca Baptist] churches. Every one of them." A second pastor, when asked what made his Baptist church Baptist, responded swiftly, "Our church is not concerned with being Baptist, from an ecclesiological point of view." Another pastor said that he was not "one of those Baptists who does not believe in the gifts of the Spirit." Yet another pastor described his church thus:

For strategic reasons we do not defend that we are a Baptist church. We are an evangelical church that teaches the Bible and has a Baptist theology because I was formed as a Baptist. And the people who are with us are not with us because we are Baptist; they are here because of the group's personality. So if you get a traditional Baptist and a traditional Pentecostal, one will not think that our church is Baptist and the other will not think it is Pentecostal.

The migration dynamics that affect immigrant communities—and force churches to pentecostalize—are the same that encourage immigrant churches to maintain a form of practical ecumenicity.

One of the most influential Brazuca Baptist pastors in the United States provided an explanation for his doctrinal inclusivity that shows well how this pentecostalization is also a form of practical ecumenism. Talking about how he managed the Sunday services of his church, he said:

We have people of all denominations in the church—Baptist, Presbyterian, Methodist, Assemblies of God. All denominations. The Brazilian church in America has the duty of being balanced in all its practices. A doctrinally and religiously balanced church, so that it is not tendentious toward [denominational] groups. I try to teach doctrine in a way that it is not offensive to Presbyterians. I try to say that baptism is by immersion, but I don't say that whoever is baptized by sprinkling is in sin. So, one is proactive in that in which one believes but one doesn't need to hit on that in which one does not believe. I would say we have a light, peaceful, inclusive liturgy. It is not a Pentecostal liturgy, not a traditional liturgy, but a contemporary liturgy. But is shocks many of the more traditional [Baptist] people.

Talking about a Wednesday service, however, this pastor was aware and fully welcoming of Pentecostal expressions of worship:

Now, we have a prayer group in our church, and this is interesting, that happens on Wednesdays from 7 p.m. to 8 p.m. in another service, in which there is a strong Pentecostal practice. We give people freedom, so that we don't put people in a box [by saying] "you have to believe this way"—they have the right to express themselves. So, there is a strong service they pray loudly and with intensity, they claim, and there is no problem with that.

This pastor emphasized the need to balance strategically different doctrinal tendencies within his church. Talking about how he used guest preachers to set the theological tone of the church, he shared:

For example, because we are a [denominationally] mixed church, when I begin to notice the Pentecostal side is taking over, I bring someone who balances that. So that we don't see a group totally immersed in a Pentecostal stream, because then you lose control [of the church]. It is an attempt to balance the pulpit as well, and the music.

The only group this pastor feared could end the ecumenical spirit of the church, however, was the Pentecostals, who represented the largest theological tendency within his church.

The role of Brazuca Baptist churches also transcends theological concerns and includes civic and social initiatives. Beyond bringing relief to disenfranchised communities of diverse backgrounds, Brazuca Baptist leaders engage in broader civic issues. As I write this chapter, for example, the US Census Bureau is using Brazuca Baptist pastors to engage the whole Brazilian immigrant community in order to urge Brazilians to identify their nationality in the census. In one government-sponsored video, a Brazuca Baptist pastor says, "I am here to tell you that the time has come for us to be counted as a Brazilian community in the United States. We cannot be left out of the census. We cannot be left out of the large governmental programs. If we are not counted, we will remain at the margins of society." Sending a message clearly directed to undocumented

Brazilians, the pastor says, "Why not participate? It is confidential and nothing will compromise you." The pastor also guides Brazilians in terms of their ethnic and national identification, saying, "Do not just say that you are Latino. Say that you are Brazilian with much pride." It is not surprising that Brazuca Baptist leaders were picked to address Brazilian immigrants in the United States. Some of these leaders have for over three decades provided a consistent presence in a highly volatile immigrant group. In immigrant churches, as in churches of other minoritized communities, pastors are more than purely religious agents. They are also social workers, civic thinkers, immigration advocates, and political agents with broad access within their respective groups.

Lessons from Incipient Immigrant Theologies

I find it valuable to repeat that theologies are maps of an always-changing land drawn by itinerant cartographers or inhabitants, perhaps immigrants. Changes in landscape, geopolitics, and in the cartographers themselves make old maps obsolete and require new ones to represent the new realities more accurately. Intellectual elites working to construct new maps and new cartographies in response to perceived inadequacies of old theological maps can often be tempted by their own specific agendas to construct maps more representative of themselves than of the groups they claim to chart. The varieties of Anglo-European theologies, Latin American Liberation theologies, Latinx theologies, Black theologies, and Feminist theologies, to name a few, are a testament to the fact that theological maps are tentative, limited, and temporary. Theologies are in constant dialogue with contexts. Contextual changes, such as the ones faced by migrants trying to adapt to a new land, are often pregnant with theological possibilities.

Immigrant churches open space for incipient theologies that are born out of the need for new theological maps, which emerge when old maps are deemed inadequate by particular groups of people. Yet these pastoral anxieties that spring from within the context of the Latinx diaspora are not articulated as academic, univocal, or even consistent formal theologies. The truth is that these immigrants, much like academic theologians, are still trying to figure out how to understand God and practice their religion in a complex, always-changing world. Unlike the world of academics who may feel safe within the confines of their departments and careers, however, the on-the-ground immigrant theologians of the Latinx diaspora are pastors and parishioners for whom theological systems have never been sufficient. That is not to say that those on the front lines of immigrant religious communities of the Latinx diaspora could not benefit from works produced in the towers of academia. They probably could! It is simply to say that they may be too busy practicing their own immigrant theologies to have the time to engage with formal theological constructions.

The responses some immigrant churches give to their contextual challenges are not, from the perspective of their leaders, necessarily uncontroversial or undertaken without pragmatic pressures. Oftentimes such changes come as the result of a painful process, as leaders who were theologically trained in denominationally connected institutions in their countries of origin begin to adapt to their new reality as migrants, pastoring immigrants and their US-born children. The struggles of undocumented immigrants, the need to negotiate the radical differences generated by migration patterns, and the conviction—informed by these migrant realities—that US-based denominations are not a place in which they fully belong, all challenge immigrant churches to engage in pastoral practices that are in tension with their official theological and ecclesiological commitments, represented by their institutional affiliations. The incipient theologies of immigrant churches are, in a deep sense, responses to the traumas of migration. They reveal themselves as cracks in the concrete illusions of predominantly white, US evangelical theopolitical commitments that still capture aspects of the imaginations of evangelicals throughout the hemisphere.

The directions in which these incipient immigrant theologies point are analogous to existing sensibilities present in the theological imagination of other minoritized groups. The roads taken to arrive at those sensibilities, however, pass through the particular experiences of migration. The pastoral commitment to direct time, resources, advocacy, and preaching toward the defense of undocumented parishioners not only resembles versions of the commitment to the preferential option for the poor—commonly associated with Latin American Liberation theology; such a pastoral commitment also relies on the important distinction between legality and morality. The practical ecumenism developed by pastors who betray official denominational loyalties in order to adapt to migration patterns points in a direction that transcends the usual stance of many denominational officials in the United States and in Latin America—for whom denominational "distinctives" remain central even in religious markets that continue to move toward postdenominationalism. The openness to women's ordination—which counters the stance of a number of evangelical denominations, including the SBC—reflects a shift toward a position in which the indispensable work of women in immigrant churches is paired with the expectation that women be treated entirely as equals. More foundationally, the fact that these dispositions represent responses to migration experiences and life in the United States demonstrates a rather expected claim: immigrant churches don't just change the US religious landscape but are also changed by the US context. Immigrant incipient theologies are a testament to how this process takes shape: as a response to the traumas of dislocation and to the complexities involved in adapting to a society with a deep history of brutalizing minoritized bodies. Latinx theological unbelonging, in this particular sense, is surely hardly surprising.

BIBLIOGRAPHY

Newspapers, Church Periodicals, and Reports

Batista Nacional

Boletim da Igreja Batista Brasileira em Washington

Brazilian Times

Folha da Primeira

Jornal Batista

Igreja Batista Brasileira de Washington D.C. *Atas da (Minutes of) Igreja Batista Brasileira de Washington D.C.*

Igreja Batista em Kearney. *Atas da (Minutes of) Igreja Batista em Kearney, N.J.*

Marques, Antônio. "Histórico da Primeira Igreja Batista da Grande Boston." Unpublished manuscript, n.d.

Missão Batista Brasileira em New Jersey. *Atas da (Minutes of) Missão Batista Brasileira em New Jersey.*

Ordem dos Pastores Batistas Brasileiros na América do Norte. *Atas da (Minutes of) Ordem dos Pastores Batistas Brasileiros na América do Norte.*

Primeira Igreja Batista Brasileira da Grande Boston. *Atas da (Minutes of) Primeira Igreja Batista Brasileira da Grande Boston.*

Primeira Igreja Batista de Língua Portuguesa de Danbury. *Atas da (Minutes of) Primeira Igreja Batista de Língua Portuguesa de Danbury.*

Primeira Igreja Batista de Língua Portuguesa de New Jersey. *Atas da (Minutes of) Primeira Igreja Batista de Língua Portuguesa de New Jersey.*

Primeira Igreja Batista de Língua Portuguesa de New York. *Estatuto da (Bylaws of) Primeira Igreja Batista de Língua Portuguesa de New York.*

———. *Atas da (Minutes of) Primeira Igreja Batista de Língua Portuguesa de New York.*

Walnut Street Baptist Church. *Atas da (Minutes of) Walnut Street Baptist Church.*

Interviews

Miguel Albanez, interview by author, Pompano Beach, Fla., December 12, 2016. Audio recording.

Silair Almeida, interview by author, Pompano Beach, March 2, 2016. Audio recording.

Ophir Barros, video interview with author, Danbury, Conn., October 26, 2015. Audio recording.

Josias Bezerra, video interview with author, Boca Raton, Fla., October 25, 2015. Audio recording.

Aloísio Campanha, phone interview with author, New York City, October 18, 2015. Audio recording.

Paulo Cappelozza, phone interview with author, Orlando, Fla., October 12, 2016. Audio recording.

Ledo Corral, phone interview with author, Austin, Tex., October 12, 2015. Audio recording.

Lecio Dornas, video interview with author, Orlando, Fla., October 15, 2015. Audio recording.

Gessuy Freitas, phone interview with author, Plymouth, Mass., November 3, 2016. Audio recording.

Sérgio Freitas, phone interview with author, Elizabeth, N.J., October 29, 2015. Audio recording.

Eddy Hallock, phone interview with author, Houston, Tex., June 21, 2016. Audio recording.

Francisco Izidoro, phone interview with author, New York City, January 5, 2017. Audio recording.

Ralph Manuel, phone interview with author, Annapolis, Md., December 12, 2016. Audio recording.

Antônio Marques, interview by author, Boston, March 20, 2017. Audio recording.

Hélio Martins, phone interview with author, New York City, December 7, 2015. Audio recording.

Carlos Mendes, phone interview with author, Washington, D.C., December 12, 2016. Audio recording.

Ribamar Monteiro, interview by author, San Francisco, January 6, 2016. Audio recording.

Geriel de Oliveira, phone interview with author, Vitória, ES, Brazil, February 13, 2017. Audio recording.

Daniel Paixão, phone interview with author, Orlando, July 13, 2016. Audio recording.

Levy Penido, phone interview with author, Mar de Espanha, MG, Brazil, October 29, 2015. Audio recording.

Alcione Silva, interview by author, Newark, N.J., January 5, 2017. Audio recording.

Edinete Silva, interview by author, San Francisco, March 18, 2016. Audio recording.

Girlan Silva, phone interview with author, Danbury, January 4, 2017. Audio recording.

Fausto Vasconcelos, phone interview with author, Washington, D.C., October 19, 2015. Audio recording.

Theses and Dissertations .

Azevedo, Israel Belo de. "A Palavra Marcada: Teologia Política dos Batistas Segundo o *Jornal Batista.*" Master's thesis, Seminário Teológico Batista do Norte do Brasil, 1983.

Cameron, David J. "Race and Religion in the Bayou City: Latino/a, African-American, and Anglo Baptists in Houston's Long Civil Rights Movement." Ph.D. diss., Texas A&M University, 2017.

Carrera, Richard. "Mexican American Baptists' Dependency on Anglo Baptist Institutions in South Texas: A Case Study in Bee County." Master's thesis, University of Texas–Pan American, 2000.

Chaves, João B. "Disrespecting Borders for Jesus, Power, and Cash: Southern Baptist Missions, the New Immigration, and the Churches of the Brazilian Diaspora." Ph.D. diss., Baylor University, 2017.

De Jesus, Rodrigo Serrão. "A Igreja Como Pedacinho do Brasil: Migrações e Religião na Capital do Texas." Master's thesis, Federa University of Paraíba, 2014.

———. "Winning 'Americans' for Jesus? Second-Generation, Racial Ideology, and the Future of the Brazilian Evangelical Church in the U.S." Ph.D. diss., University of South Florida, 2020.

Landers, John M. "Eric Alfred Nelson, the First Baptist Missionary on the Amazon, 1891–1939." Ph.D. diss., Texas Christian University, 1982.

Nascimento, Luiz C. "Religion and Immigration: Towards a Transformative Prophetic Spirit." Ph.D. diss., Princeton Theological Seminary, 2012.

Reis, Matt. "Brazilian Evangelicos in Diaspora in South Florida: Identity and Mission." Ph.D. diss., University of Edinburgh, 2021.

Rodriguez, Moises. "The Cultural Context of Southern Baptist Work among Mexican-Americans in Texas." Ph.D. diss., Baylor University, 1997.

Serrão, Rodrigo. "Winning America for Jesus? Second-Generation, Racial Ideology, and the Future of the Brazilian Evangelical Church in the U.S." Ph.D. diss., University of South Florida, 2020.

Silva, Célio Antônio Alcantara. "Capitalismo e Escravidão: A Imigração Confederada para o Brasil." Ph.D. diss., Universidade Estadual de Campinas, 2011.

Books, Articles, and Book Chapters

Adogame, Afeosemime U. *The African Christian Diaspora: New Currents and Emerging Trends in World Christianity.* London: Bloomsbury, 2013.

Adogame, Afeosemime, Raimundo Barreto, and Wanderley Rosa, eds. *Migration and Public Discourse in World Christianity.* Minneapolis: Fortress, 2019.

Adogame, Afeosemime U., and Shobana Shankar, eds. *Religion on the Move! New Dynamics of Religious Expansion in a Globalizing World.* Leiden: Brill, 2013.

Alencar, Gedeon. *Matriz Pentecostal Brasileira: Assembleias de Deus, 1911–2011.* Rio de Janeiro: Novos Dialogos, 2013.

———. *Protestantismo Tupiniquim.* São Paulo: Aret Editorial, 2007.

Alves, Rubem A. *Protestantism and Repression: A Brazilian Case Study.* Maryknoll, N.Y.: Orbis, 1985.

Anderson, Allan Heaton. *To the Ends of the Earth: Pentecostalism and the Transformation of World Christianity*. New York: Oxford University Press, 2013.

Anderson, Allen. "Pentecostal and Charismatic Movements." In *The Cambridge History of Christianity*, vol. 9, edited by Hugh Mcleod, 89–106. Cambridge: Cambridge University Press, 2014.

Anderson, Robert Mapes. *Vision of the Disinherited: The Making of American Pentecostalism*. Peabody, Mass.: Hendrickson, 1992.

Aponte, Edwin. *Santo: Varieties of Latina/o Spirituality*. Maryknoll, N.Y.: Orbis, 2012.

Araújo, João Pedro Gonçalves. *Batistas: Dominação e Dependência*. São Paulo: Fonte Editorial, 2015.

———. *Historias, Tradições e Pensamentos Batistas*. São Paulo: Fonte Editorial, 2015.

Bailey, Stanley R. "Group Dominance and the Myth of Racial Democracy: Antiracism Attitudes in Brazil." *American Sociological Review* 69, no. 5 (2004): 728–47.

Bailey, Stanley R., Mara Loveman, and Jeronimo O. Muniz. "Measures of 'Race' and the Analysis of Racial Inequality in Brazil." *Social Science Research* 42, no. 1 (2013): 106–19.

Barreto, Raimundo. "Beyond Contextualization: Gospel, Culture, and the Rise of Latin American Christianity." In *World Christianity as Public Religion*, edited by Raimundo Barreto, Ronaldo Cavalcanti, and Wanderley Rosa, 97–117. Minneapolis: Fortress, 2017.

Barton, Paul. *Hispanic Methodists, Presbyterians, and Baptists in Texas*. Austin: University of Texas Press, 2006.

Bell, Lester C. *Which Way in Brazil?* Nashville: Convention, 1965.

Bender, Courtney, Wendy Cadge, Peggy Levitt, and David Smilde, eds. *Religion on the Edge: De-centering and Re-centering the Sociology of Religion*. New York: Oxford University Press, 2012.

Bender, Thomas, ed. *Rethinking American History in a Global Age*. Berkeley: University of California Press, 2002.

Berryman, Phillip. *Religion in the Megacity: Catholic and Protestant Portraits from Latin America*. Eugene, Ore.: Wipf & Stock, 2006.

Beserra, Bernadete. *Brazilian Immigrants in the United States: Cultural Imperialism and Social Class*. New York: LFB Scholarly Publishing, 2006.

———. "Samba in Chicago: Escaping Hegemonic Multiculturalist Boundaries." *Latin American Perspectives* 39, no. 3 (2012): 106–19.

Bicalho, José Victor. *Yes, Eu Sou Brazuca ou a Vida do Imigrante Brasileiro nos Estados Unidos da América*. Governador Valadares: Fundação Serviços de Educação e Cultura, 1989.

Biney, Moses. "Transnationalism, Religious Participation, and Civic Responsibility among African Immigrants in North America," in Adogame, Barreto, and Rosa, *Migration and Public Discourse in World Christianity*, 51–65.

Bratcher, L. M. *Francisco Fulgencio Soren: Christ's Interpreter to Many Lands*. Nashville: Broadman, 1938.

Caldas, Carlos Ribeiro. "O Papel da Igreja Universal Brasileira do Reino de Deus na Globalização do Neopentecostalismo Atual." *Ciências da Religião* 8, no. 2 (2010): 107–21.

Calvillo, Jonathan. *The Saints of Santa Ana: Faith and Ethnicity in a Mexican Majority City*. New York: Oxford University Press, 2020.

Campbell-Reed, Eileen. *Anatomy of a Schism: How Clergywomen's Narratives Reinterpret the Fracturing of the Southern Baptist Convention*. Knoxville: University of Tennessee Press, 2016.

Campos, Leonildo Silveira. "Traditional Protestantism." In Schmidt and Engler, *Handbook of Contemporary Religions in Brazil*, 95–116.

Caputo, John D., ed. *Deconstruction in a Nutshell: A Conversation with Jacques Derrida*. New York: Fordham University Press, 1996.

Castro, Cristina Maria de, and Andrew Dawson, eds. *Religion, Migration, and Mobility: The Brazilian Experience*. New York: Routledge, 2017.

Cavalcanti, H. B. *Almost Home: A Brazilian American's Reflections on Faith, Culture, and Immigration*. Madison: University of Wisconsin Press, 2012.

———. *Ensaios de um Nordestino Ausente*. Nashville: Westview, 2010.

Cebulko, Kara B. *Documented, Undocumented, and Something Else: The Incorporation of Children of Brazilian Immigrants*. El Paso, Tex.: LFB Scholarly Publishing, 2013.

Chang, Derek. *Citizens of a Christian Nation: Evangelical Missions and the Problem of Race in the Nineteenth Century*. Philadelphia: University of Pennsylvania Press, 2010.

Chaves, João B. "Exporting Holy Fire: Southern Baptist Missions, Pentecostalism, and Baptist Identities in Latin America," *Perspectives in Religious Studies* 47, no. 2 (2020): 202–14.

———. *The Global Mission of the Jim Crow South*. Macon, Ga.: Mercer University Press, forthcoming.

———. "Migrating Theopolitics: The Effect of Undocumented Parishioners on the Pastoral Theology of Latin American Evangelicals in the United States." In Adogame, Barreto, and Rosa, *Migration and Public Discourse in World Christianity*, 69–82.

———. *O Racismo na História Batista Brasileira: Uma Memória Inconveniente do Legado Missionário*. Brasília: Novos Dialogos, 2020.

———. "Where Should We Go Next? A Call for the Critical Investigation of Possible Racial Encounters between Anglo-American and Mexican American Baptists in Texas during the Pioneer Period." *Baptist History and Heritage* 49, no. 3 (2004): 23–38.

Chaves, João, and C. Douglas Weaver. "Baptists and Their Polarizing Ways: Transnational Polarization between Southern Baptist Missionaries and Brazilian Baptists." *Review & Expositor* 116, no. 2 (2019): 160–74.

Chestnut, Andrew. "The Spirit of Brazil: Charismatic Christianity among the World's Largest Catholic and Pentecostal Populations." In Schmidt and Engler, *Handbook of Contemporary Religions in Brazil*, 76–94.

Chesnut, R. Andrew. *Born Again in Brazil: The Pentecostal Boom and the Pathogens of Poverty*. New Brunswick, N.J.: Rutgers University Press, 1997.

———. *Competitive Spirits: Latin America's New Religious Economy*. Oxford: Oxford University Press, 2007.

Connor, Phillip. *Immigrant Faith: Patterns of Immigrant Religion in the United States, Canada, and Western Europe*. New York: New York University Press, 2014.

Cook, David A. "The Variety of Transnational Religious Networks." In *Religion across Borders: Transnational Immigrant Networks*, edited by Helen Ebaugh and Janet Chafetz, 165–91. Walnut Creek, Calif.: AltaMira, 2002.

Corten, André. *Le Pentecôtisme au Brésil*. Paris: Karthala, 1995.

Corten, André, and Ruth R. Marshall-Fratani, eds. *Between Babel and Pentecost: Transnational Pentecostalism in Africa and Latin America*. Bloomington: Indiana University Press, 2001.

Dayton, Donald. *Theological Roots of Pentecostalism*. Grand Rapids: Baker Academic, 1987.

Debiaggi, Sylvia Duarte Dantas. *Changing Gender Roles: Brazilian Immigrant Families in the U.S.* New York: LFB Scholarly Publishing, 2001.

Dias, Zwinglio Mota, and Rodrigo Portella. "Apresentação." In *Protestantes, Evangélicos e (Neo) Pentecostais: História, Teologias, Igrejas e Perspectivas*, edited by Zwinglio Mota Dias, Rodrigo Portella, and Elisa Rodrigues, 19–26. São Paulo: Fonte Editorial, 2014.

Elliott, Becky. *Crossing at San Vicente: A History of First Baptist Church, Midland, Texas, and Their Commitment to the Mexican People across the Rio Grande River*. Austin: Nortex, 1998.

Espinosa, Gastón. *Latino Pentecostals in America: Faith and Politics in Action*. Cambridge, Mass.: Harvard University Press, 2014.

———. "Third Class Soldiers: A History of Hispanic Pentecostal Clergywomen in the Assemblies of God." In *Philip's Daughters: Women in Pentecostal-Charismatic Leadership*, edited by Estrelda Alexander and Amos Yong, 95–111. Eugene, Ore.: Pickwick, 2009.

Ferreira Pires, Flávia, and Rodrigo Otávio Serrão Santana de Jesus. "Do Brasil para o Mundo: Como Conceitos Clássicos Weberianos Podem Nos Ajudar a Entender o Sucesso Transnacional da Igreja Mundial do Poder de Deus?" *Ciências da Religião: História e Sociedade* 12, no. 1 (2014): 137–67.

Fleischer, Soraya. *Passando a América a Limpo: O Trabalho de Housecleaners Brasileiras em Boston*. São Paulo: Annablume Editora, 2002.

Flowers, Elizabeth Hill. *Into the Pulpit: Southern Baptist Women and Power since World War II*. Chapel Hill: University of North Carolina Press, 2012.

Freston, Paul, ed. *Evangelical Christianity and Democracy in Latin America*. Oxford: Oxford University Press, 2008

———. *Evangelicals and Politics in Asia, Africa and Latin America*. Cambridge: Cambridge University Press, 2001.

———. "Pentecostalism in Brazil: A Brief History." *Religion* 25, no. 2 (1995): 119–33.

———. *Religião e Política, Sim; Igreja e Estado, Não: Os Evangélicos e a Participação Política*. Vicosa: Ultimato, 2006.

———. "The Religious Field among Brazilians in the United States." In Jouët-Pastré and Braga, *Becoming Brazuca*, 255–68.

Freyre, Gilberto. *The Masters and the Slaves (Casa-Grande and Senzala): A Study in the Development of Brazilian Civilization*. Berkeley: University of California Press, 1987.

Fritz, Catarina. *Brazilian Immigration and the Quest for Identity*. El Paso, Tex.: LFB Scholarly Publishing, 2010.

———. "Redefining Racial Categories: The Dynamics of Identity among Brazilian-Americans." *Immigrants & Minorities* 33, no. 1 (2015): 45–65.

Gibson, Annie McNeil. *Post-Katrina Brazucas: Brazilian Immigrants in New Orleans.* New Orleans, La.: University of New Orleans Press, 2012.

Goldman, Frank. *Os Pioneiros Americanos no Brasil: Educadores, Sacerdotes, Covos e Reis.* São Paulo: Pioneira, 1972.

Gooren, Henri. "The Pentecostalization of Religion and Society in Latin America." *Exchange* 39, no. 4 (2010): 355–76.

Graziano, Manlio. *What Is a Border?* Stanford, Calif.: Stanford University Press, 2018.

Grijalva, Joshua. *A History of Mexican Baptists in Texas 1881–1981: Comprising an Account of the Genesis, the Progress, and the Accomplishments of the People Called "Los Bautistas de Texas."* Dallas: Baptist General Convention of Texas, 1982.

———. "The Story of Hispanic Southern Baptists." *Baptist History and Heritage* 18, no. 3 (1983): 40–47.

Hagan, Jacqueline Maria. *Migration Miracle: Faith, Hope, and Meaning on the Undocumented Journey.* Cambridge, Mass.: Harvard University Press, 2008.

Hartch, Todd. *The Rebirth of Latin American Christianity.* Oxford: Oxford University Press, 2014.

Harter, Eugene. *The Lost Colony of the Confederacy.* College Station: Texas A&M University Press, 2006.

Harvey, Paul. *Redeeming the South. Religious Cultures and Racial Identities among Southern Baptists, 1865–1925.* Chapel Hill: University of North Carolina Press, 1997.

Helgen, Erika. *Religious Conflict in Brazil: Protestants, Catholics, and the Rise of Religious Pluralism in the Early Twentieth Century.* New Haven, Conn.: Yale University Press, 2020.

Hinojosa, Felipe. *Latino Mennonites: Civil Rights, Faith, and Evangelical Culture.* Baltimore: Johns Hopkins University Press, 2014.

Horne, Gerald. *The Deepest South: The United States, Brazil, and the African Slave Trade.* New York: New York University Press, 2007.

Ireland, Rowan. *Kingdoms Come: Religion and Politics in Brazil.* Pittsburgh, Pa.: University of Pittsburgh Press, 1992.

Jacobsen, Douglas G. *Thinking in the Spirit: Theologies of the Early Pentecostal Movement.* Bloomington: Indiana University Press, 2003.

Jenkins, Philip. *God's Continent: Christianity, Islam, and Europe's Religious Crisis.* Oxford: Oxford University Press, 2010.

———. *The Next Christendom: The Coming of Global Christianity.* Oxford: Oxford University Press, 2007.

Jones, Judith Mac Knight. *Soldado Descansa! Uma Epopéia Norte-Americana sob os Céus do Brasil.* São Paulo: Jarde, 1967.

Jones, Robert P. *White Too Long: The Legacy of White Supremacy in American Christianity.* New York: Simon & Schuster, 2020.

Jouët-Pastré, Clémence, and Leticia J. Braga, eds. *Becoming Brazuca: Brazilian Immigration to the United States.* Cambridge, Mass.: David Rockefeller Center for Latin American Studies, 2008.

———. "Introduction: Interdisciplinary Perspectives on Becoming Brazucas." In Jouët-Pastré and Braga, *Becoming Brazuca*, 1–21.

Leal, João. "Migrant Cosmopolitanism: Ritual and Cultural Innovation among Azorean Immigrants in the USA." In *Cosmopolitanism in the Portuguese-Speaking World*, edited by Francisco Bethencourt, 233–49. Leiden: Brill, 2017.

Leon, Victor De. *The Silent Pentecostals: A Biographical History of the Pentecostal Movement among the Hispanics in the Twentieth Century*. La Habra: De Leon, 1979.

Léonard, Émile G. *O Protestantismo Brasileiro: Estudos de Eclesiologia e Historia Social*. São Paulo: ASTE, 1963.

Levitt, Peggy. *God Needs No Passport: Immigrants and the Changing American Religious Landscape*. New York: New Press, 2007.

———. "Religion on the Move: Mapping Global Cultural Production and Consumption." In Bender et al., *Religion on the Edge*, 159–76.

Lima, Álvaro Eduardo de Castro, and Alanni de Lacerda Barbosa Castro. *Brasileiros nos Estados Unidos: Meio Século (Re)Fazendo a América (1960–2010)*. Brasília: Fundação Alexandre de Gusmão, 2017.

Lin, Tony Tian-Ren. *Prosperity Gospel: Latinos and Their American Dream*. Chapel Hill: University of North Carolina Press, 2020.

Loveman, Mara, Jeronimo O. Muniz, and Stanley R. Bailey. "Brazil in Black and White? Race Categories, the Census, and the Study of Inequality." *Ethnic & Racial Studies* 35, no. 8 (2012): 1466–83.

Machado, Daisy L. *Of Borders and Margins: Hispanic Disciples in Texas, 1888–1945*. Oxford: Oxford University Press, 2003.

Madrazo, Tito. *Predicadores: Hispanic Preaching and Immigrant Identity*. Waco, Tex.: Baylor University Press, 2021.

Mafra, Clara Cristina Jost. *Os Evangélicos*. Rio de Janeiro: Jorge Zahar, 2001.

Maldonado, David. *Protestantes/Protestants: Hispanic Christianity within Mainline Traditions*. Nashville: Abingdon, 1999.

Margolis, Maxine. "Na Virada do Milênio: A Emigração Brasileira Para os Estados Unidos." In Martes and Fleischer, *Fronteiras Cruzadas*, 51–72.

Margolis, Maxine L. *Goodbye, Brazil: Émigrés from the Land of Soccer and Samba*. Madison: University of Wisconsin Press, 2013.

———. *An Invisible Minority: Brazilians in New York City*. Gainesville: University Press of Florida, 2009.

———. *Little Brazil: An Ethnography of Brazilian Immigrants in New York City*. Princeton, N.J.: Princeton University Press, 1993.

———. "Transnationalism and Popular Culture: The Case of Brazilian Immigrants in the United States." *Journal of Popular Culture* 29, no. 1 (Summer 1995): 29–41.

Martes, Ana Cristina Braga. *Brasileiros nos Estados Unidos: Um Estudo Sobre Imigrantes em Massachusetts*. São Paulo: Paz e Terra, 2000.

———. "Neither Hispanic, nor Black: We're Brazilian." In *The Other Latinos*, edited by José Luis Falconi and José Antônio Mazzotti, 231–56. Cambridge, Mass.: David Rockefeller Center for Latin American Studies, 2008.

———. *New Immigrants, New Land: A Study of Brazilians in Massachusetts.* Gainesville: University Press of Florida, 2011.

———. "Os Imigrantes Brasileiros e as Igrejas em Massachusetts." In *Cenas do Brasil Migrante*, edited by Rossana Rocha Reis and Teresa Sales, 87–122. São Paulo: Boitempo Editorial, 1999.

———. "Raça e Etnicidade: Opções e Constrangimentos." In Martes and Fleischer, *Fronteiras Cruzadas*, 73–98.

Martes, Ana Cristina Braga, and Soraya Fleischer, eds. *Fronteiras Cruzadas: Etnicidade, Gênero e Redes Sociais.* São Paulo: Paz e Terra, 2003.

Martínez, Juan Francisco. *Los Protestantes: An Introduction to Latino Protestantism in the United States.* Santa Barbara: Praeger, 2011.

———. *The Story of Latino Protestants in the United States.* Grand Rapids: Eerdmans, 2018.

Martínez-Vázquez, Hjamil A. *Made in the Margins: Latina/o Constructions of U.S. Religious History.* Waco, Tex.: Baylor University Press, 2013.

Matovina, Timothy. *Latino Catholicism: Transformation in America's Largest Church.* Princeton, N.J.: Princeton University Press, 2011.

McBeth, Leon. *The Baptist Heritage: Four Centuries of Baptist Witness.* Nashville: Broadman, 1987.

McDonnell, Judith, and Cileine de Lourenço. "Brazilian Immigrant Women: Race, Ethnicity, Gender, and Transnationalism." In Jouët-Pastré and Braga, *Becoming Brazuca*, 151–73.

Medina, Lara. *Las Hermanas: Chicana/Latina Religious-Political Activism in the U.S. Catholic Church.* Philadelphia: Temple University Press, 2005.

Mendonça, Antônio Gouvêa, and Prócoro Velasques Filho. *Introdução ao Protestantismo Brasileiro.* São Paulo: Loyola, 1990.

Menezes, Gustavo Hamilton. "Filhos da Imigração: A Segunda Geração de Brasileiros em Connecticut." In Martes and Fleischer, *Fronteiras Cruzadas*, 157–74.

Miller, Donald E., Kimon H. Sargeant, and Richard Flory, eds. *Spirit and Power: The Growth and Global Impact of Pentecostalism.* New York: Oxford University Press, 2013.

Mola, Patricia, Lucia Ribeiro, and Mirian Lizama. "Brazilian and Mexican Women Interacting with God in Florida." In *A Place to Be: Brazilian, Guatemalan, and Mexican Immigrants in Florida's New Destinations*, edited by Philip Williams, Timothy Steigenga, and Manuel A. Vásquez, 190–208. New Brunswick, N.J.: Rutgers University Press, 2009.

Mooney, Margarita. *Faith Makes Us Live: Surviving and Thriving in the Haitian Diaspora.* Berkeley: University of California Press, 2009.

Mulder, Mark T., Aida I. Ramos, and Gerardo Martí. *Latino Protestants in America: Growing and Diverse.* Lanham, Md.: Rowman & Littlefield, 2017.

Noll, Mark A. *The New Shape of World Christianity: How American Experience Reflects Global Faith.* Downers Grove, Ill.: IVP Academic, 2009.

Oliveira, Ana Maria Costa de. *O Destino (Não) Manifesto: Os Imigrantes Norte-Americanos no Brasil.* São Paulo: União Cultural Brasil-Estados Unidos, 1995.

Oliveira, Betty Antunes de. *Antônio Teixeira de Albuquerque: O Primeiro Pastor Batista Brasileiro.* Rio de Janeiro: Edição de Autora, 1982.

Oliveira, Zaqueu Moreira de. *Panorama Batista em Pernambuco*. Recife: Junta Evangelizadora Batista de Pernambuco, 1964.

———. *Perseguidos, Mas Não Desamparados: 90 Anos de Perseguição Religiosa Contra os Batistas Brasileiros (1880–1970)*. Rio de Janeiro: JUERP, 1999.

Oliveira Assis, Gláucia de. "Gender and Migration from Invisibility to Agency: The Routes of Brazilian Women from Transnational Towns to the United States." *Women's Studies International Forum* 46 (2014): 33–44.

Pereira, J. Reis. *História dos Batistas no Brasil (1882–1982)*. Rio de Janeiro: JUERP, 1982.

Pinheiro, Jorge, and Marcelo Santos, eds. *Os Batistas: Controvérsias e Vocação para a Intolerância*. São Paulo: Fonte Editorial, 2012.

Plainfield, Joseph Frank. *The Stranger within Our Gates*. Atlanta: Home Mission Board of the Southern Baptist Convention, 1938.

Portes, Alejandro, and Rubén G. Rumbaut. *Immigrant America: A Portrait*. Berkeley: University of California Press, 2014.

Premack, Laura. "'The Holy Rollers Are Invading Our Territory': Southern Baptist Missionaries and the Early Years of Pentecostalism in Brazil." *Journal of Religious History* 35, no. 1 (2011): 1–23.

Ramírez, Daniel. *Migrating Faith: Pentecostalism in the United States and Mexico in the Twentieth Century*. Chapel Hill: University of North Carolina Press, 2015.

Ramos-Zayas, Ana. "Between 'Cultural Excess' and 'Racial Invisibility': Brazilians and the Commercialization of Culture in Newark." In Jouët-Pastré and Braga, *Becoming Brazuca*, 271–86.

Reily, Duncan Alexander. *História Documental do Protestantismo no Brasil*. São Paulo: ASTE, 2003.

Robeck, Cecil M., Jr. *The Azusa Street Mission and Revival*. Nashville: Thomas Nelson, 2006.

Rodrigues, Donizete. *Jesus in Sacred Gotham: Brazilian Immigrants and Pentecostalism in New York City*. Amazon, 2014.

———. *O Evangélico Imigrante: O Pentecostalismo Brasileiro Salvando a América*. São Paulo: Fonte Editorial, 2016.

Rodrigues, Donizete, and Manoel Ribeiro de Moraes. "A Pentecostalização de Povos Tradicionais na Amazônia: Aspectos Conceituais para uma Antropologia de Identidades Religiosas." *Horizonte* 16, no. 50 (2018): 900–18.

Sales, Teresa. *Brasileiros Longe de Casa*. São Paulo: Cortez, 1999.

———. "Identidade Étnica Entre Imigrantes Brasileiros na Região de Boston, EUA." In *Cenas do Brasil Migrante*, edited by Rossana Rocha Reis and Teresa Sales, 17–44. São Paulo, Brazil: Boitempo Editorial, 1999.

Sánchez, Jesús. "A Pentecostalização do Brasil x Os 'Sem Religião'; Cura e Exorcismo: Entrevista a Pe. Jesús Hortal Sánchez, S.J." *Teocomunicação* 44, no. 2 (2014): 181–95.

Sanchez-Walsh, Arlene M. *Latino Pentecostal Identity: Evangelical Faith, Self, and Society*. New York: Columbia University Press, 2003.

Sandoval, Moises, ed. *Fronteras: A History of the Latin American Church in the USA since 1513*. San Antonio, Tex.: Mexican American Cultural Center, 1983.

Santos, Marcelo. *O Marco Inicial Batista*. São Paulo: Convicção, 2003.

Schmidt, Bettina, and Steven Engler, eds. *Handbook of Contemporary Religions in Brazil*. Leiden: Brill, 2017.

Seigel, Micol. *Uneven Encounters: Making Race and Nation in Brazil and the United States*. Durham, N.C.: Duke University Press, 2009.

Serrão, Rodrigo, and James Cavendish. "'The Social Functions and Dysfunctions of Brazilian Immigrant Congregations in '*Terra Incognita*.'" *Review of Religious Research* 60, no. 3 (2018): 367–88.

Serrão, Rodrigo, and João Chaves. "Immigrant Evangelicalism in the COVID-19 Crisis." *International Journal of Latin American Religions* 4, no. 2 (2020): 235–49.

Silva, Célio Antônio Alcantara. "Confederate and Yankees under the Southern Cross." *Bulletin of Latin American Research* 34, no. 3 (2015): 270–304.

Silva, Elizete da. *William Buck Bagby: Um Pioneiro Batista nas Terras do Cruzeiro do Sul*. Brasília: Editora Novos Diálogos, 2011.

Silva, Graziella Moraes, and Marcelo Paixão. "Mixed and Unequal: New Perspectives on Brazilian Ethnoracial Relations." In *Pigmentocracies: Ethnicity, Race, and Color in Latin America*, edited by Edward Telles, 172–217. Chapel Hill: University of North Carolina Press, 2014.

Souza, Carlos. "O Protestantismo Histórico e a 'Pentecostalização': Novos Contornos da Identidade Evangélica." *Ciências da Religião: História e Sociedade* 12, no. 2 (2014): 61–90.

Telles, Edward E. *Race in Another America: The Significance of Skin Color in Brazil*. Princeton, N.J.: Princeton University Press, 2014.

Tognini, Enéas. *História dos Batistas Nacionais: Documentário*. Brasília: Convenção Batista Nacional, 1993.

Tosta, A. "Latino, Eu? The Paradoxical Interplay of Identity in Brazuca Literature." *Hispania* 87, no. 3 (2004): 576–85.

Tyrrell, Ian. "Reflections on the Transnational Turn in United States History: Theory and Practice." *Journal of Global History* 4, no. 3 (2009): 453–74.

———. *Transnational Nation: United States History in Global Perspective since 1789*. 2nd ed. New York: Palgrave, 2015.

Vazquez, Manuel, and Cristina Rocha, eds. *The Diaspora of Brazilian Religions*. Boston: Brill, 2013.

———. "Introduction: Brazil in the New Global Cartography of Religion." In Vazquez and Rocha, *Diaspora of Brazilian Religions*, 1–42.

Vieira, Elsa R. P. "The Formative Years of the Brazilian Communities of New York and San Francisco through the Print Media: The Brazilians/The Brasilians and Brazil Today." In Jouët-Pastré and Braga, *Becoming Brazuca*, 81–102.

Villavicencio, Karla Cornejo. *The Undocumented Americans*. New York: One World, 2020.

Wacker, Grant. *Heaven Below: Early Pentecostals and American Culture*. Cambridge, Mass.: Harvard University Press, 2001.

Walsh, Arlene. "Jesus in the Hispanic Community: Images of Christ from Theology to Popular Religion." In *Jesus in the Hispanic Community: Images of Christ from*

Theology to Popular Religion, edited by Harold J. Recinos and Hugo Magallanes, 92–104. Louisville: Westminster John Knox, 2010.

Weaver, C. Douglas. *Baptists and the Holy Spirit: The Contested History with Holiness-Pentecostal-Charismatic Movements.* Waco, Tex.: Baylor University Press, 2019.

———. *In Search of the New Testament Church: The Baptist Story.* Macon, Ga.: Mercer University Press, 2008.

Williams, Philip, Timothy Steigenga, and Manuel A. Vásquez, eds. *A Place to Be: Brazilian, Guatemalan, and Mexican Immigrants in Florida's New Destinations.* New Brunswick, N.J.: Rutgers University Press, 2009.

Yamabuchi, Alberto Kenji. *O Debate Sobre a História das Origens do Trabalho Batista no Brasil: Uma Análise das Relações e dos Conflitos de Gênero e Poder na Convenção Batista Brasileira nos Anos 1960–1980.* São Paulo: Novas Edições Acadêmicas, 2015.

INDEX